- Go to **awmi.net/sg421** to download PDFs of the following resources for each lesson in this study guide:
    - o Outlines
    - o Discipleship Questions
    - o Scriptures
- Share as many copies as you'd like.
- These documents are not for resale.

A BETTER WAY TO PRAY

STUDY GUIDE

ANDREW WOMMACK

Unless otherwise indicated, all Scripture quotations are taken from the *King James Version* of the Bible.

A Better Way to Pray Study Guide
ISBN: 978-1-59548-277-8

Copyright © 2015 by Andrew Wommack Ministries Inc.
PO Box 3333
Colorado Springs CO 80934-3333

Published by Andrew Wommack Ministries Inc.

awmi.net

Table of Contents

How to Use Your Study Guide

Whether you are teaching a class, leading a small group, discipling an individual, or studying on your own, this study guide is designed for you! Here's how it works:

Each Lesson consists of the **Lesson** text, **Outline**, **Teacher's Guide**, **Discipleship Questions**, **Answer Key**, and **Scriptures**. Some studies also have additional information.

Outline for Group Study:

I.   If possible, briefly review the previous study by going over the **Answer Key/Teacher's Guide** answers for the **Discipleship Questions/Teacher's Guide** questions.

II. Read the current Lesson or Teacher's Guide aloud.
  A.   Be sure that each student has a copy of the Outline.
  B.   While the Lesson or Teacher's Guide is being read, students should use their Outlines to follow along.

III. Once the Lesson or Teacher's Guide is read, facilitate discussion and study using the Discipleship Questions/Teacher's Guide questions (all questions are the same).
  A.   Read one question at a time.
  B.   The group should use their Outlines to assist them answering the questions.
  C.   Have them read aloud each specifically mentioned scripture before answering the question.
  D.   Discuss the answer/point from the Lesson as desired.
  E.   As much as possible, keep the dicsussion centered on the scriptures and the Lesson or Teacher's Guide points at hand.
  F.   Remember, the goal is understanding (Matt. 13:19).
  G.   One individual should not dominate the discussion; instead, try to draw out the quieter ones for the group conversation.
  H.   Repeat the process until all of the questions are discussed/answered.

Materials Needed:

Study guide, Bible, and enough copies of the **Outline**, **Discipleship Questions**, and **Scriptures** for each student. (PDFs of the **Outlines**, **Discipleship Questions**, and **Scriptures** can be downloaded via the URL located on the first page of this study guide.)

Outline for Personal Study:

I.   Read the current **Lesson** text or **Teacher's Guide**.
    A.   Read additional information, if provided.
    B.   Meditate on the given scriptures, as desired.
II.   Answer the corresponding **Discipleship Questions/Teacher's Guide** questions.
III. Check your work with the **Answer Key/Teacher's Guide** answers.

Materials Needed:

Study guide, Bible, and a writing utensil.

Introduction

Are you ready for your prayer life to improve? Would you like to learn how to pray more accurately and receive God's answers more quickly? If so, you're reading the right book!

When the disciples asked Jesus how to pray, our Lord confronted the myths and misconceptions concerning prayer in His day. In fact, He spent quite some time countering false ideas and discussing what prayer is not, before He told them the proper way to pray. The religious system had become so hypocritical and phony that the Lord had to undo what they commonly thought prayer was, before He could effectively teach them what it is.

The contents of this book are neither *The Only Way to Pray* nor *You Won't Get Any Results If You Don't Pray This Way,* but rather **A Better Way to Pray**. I'll be sharing some things that will probably offend you—but rest assured that if I step on your toes, the Lord will heal them!

Everything I'm teaching against, I've done. God still loved me and I loved Him. We had a good relationship despite the fact that I was doing these things. However, I am now much more effective in seeing manifestations of my answered prayers than ever before in my life. I don't pray the way I used to fifteen, twenty, thirty years ago. I've matured quite a bit since then.

All across the body of Christ today, believers hold certain assumptions and exhibit totally wrong attitudes in prayer. Then they wonder why they aren't receiving their desired results. God wants this corrected!

I'm very aware that I will be countering a lot of common thinking about prayer. I may well offend some of the traditions you've held dear. But let me ask you this: If the way you are praying isn't getting good results, why would you resist change in this area?

I'm not the perfect example. I haven't arrived—but I've left. And I'm getting supernatural results to my prayers. I've even seen my own son raised up after being dead for five hours. Unless you are receiving better results than I am, you ought to at least consider the things I'm saying.

For many years now, I've meditated through every scripture in the Bible that uses any form of the word "pray." I believe what the Lord has revealed to me through His Word will really bless you. Even though it may be different from anything you've ever been taught before, I'm confident you'll find it—**A Better Way to Pray**!

Hypocrites Love to Pray

Prayer is the most abused part of the Christian life today. Misguided understandings about prayer mess up more people spiritually than anything else out there!

Jesus taught that there is right and wrong praying:

And when thou prayest, thou shalt not be as the hypocrites are: for they love to pray.
MATTHEW 6:5

Most believers don't associate hypocrites with prayer. They think, If you're praying, what could be wrong? Plenty—because hypocrites love to pray!

Just because it starts with the words "Our Father" and concludes with "in the name of Jesus, amen" doesn't mean it's prayer. A tremendous amount of what's being called "prayer" today offends God and opens the door to the devil. There are right and wrong ways to pray!

GOD'S MESSENGER BOY?

In 1969, I heard a wrong teaching that said Satan is "God's messenger boy." It said that the devil can only do what the Lord allows, and therefore God uses him to work good in our lives. That's totally wrong, but I didn't know it at the time. I took this teaching back to my girlfriend, and she bought into it completely.

On the tapes I gave her, there was an example of a boy who was too shy to witness to his classmates. He prayed and asked God to give him an incurable disease so he could show his faith in Christ by the way he responded to death. The next day, he developed leukemia. Four people were born again at his funeral.

Although this young man's faith brought some glory to God, this isn't correct praying. My girlfriend prayed the same prayer and was diagnosed with leukemia the next morning. Four people were born again at her funeral. However, God wasn't the one answering these two prayers by "blessing" them with leukemia. Satan took advantage of wrong praying and killed two young people before their time. Wrong praying gets wrong results!

PRAYING WRONG

Jesus had to reveal what prayer is *not* before He taught what it is (Matt. 6:5-13). The Lord Himself first had to counter the religious concepts concerning prayer in His day, or the people would never have been able to grasp what He was about to say.

It's just as bad today, if not worse! Like the Pharisees when Jesus confronted, prayer has become religious calisthenics. People use it to soothe their consciences, feeling like they've done something to manipulate and motivate God to move on their behalf—wrong motives!

The heart attitude behind your prayer interests God much more than the actual words you say. Just because you spend an hour or more in what you call "prayer" doesn't mean you're accomplishing anything. If your attitude is wrong, you're praying wrong!

> *And when thou prayest, thou shalt not be as the hypocrites are: for they love to pray standing in the synagogues and in the corners of the streets, that they may be seen of men. Verily I say unto you, They have their reward.*
>
> MATTHEW 6:5

"What holy people! Have you heard them storm the gates of heaven?" That little ego-stroking pat on the back is all they get because man's admiration is the only reward for such "praying." They won't receive anything from God!

Are you aware that you can exercise powerful spiritual gifts and make tremendous personal sacrifices but still not impress God? That's right! If you don't have the proper motive, it doesn't matter what you do. Praying in tongues, prophesying, having all faith, giving your possessions to the poor, or even laying down your life will all profit you nothing if done without God's kind of love (1 Cor. 13:1-3). In the kingdom, heart attitude makes all the difference!

If you aren't seeing the desired results from your prayer life, check your motives. Are your prayers truly motivated by love? I understand that this is hard to admit because you probably want to be positive and believe the best all the time. However, if you allowed yourself to take a critical and objective look at your own prayer life, would the honest evaluation be that it profits you nothing? Have you prayed for years and not seen the manifestation? Perhaps your body isn't healed or your finances still aren't really improving. Either way, it's just not working. Friend, it's not God who hasn't been answering; it's your prayers that have been wrong!

GOD ALREADY MOVED

Most Christians see prayer as an opportunity to "move God." They believe that He can do anything but that He has yet to do what they've prayed for. In this mentality, prayer is how to make God do something. If this is what you believe, your prayer life rests on an extremely faulty foundation.

God has already done everything He's ever going to do. He moved once and for all in the death, burial, and resurrection of Jesus Christ. Through the Atonement, God has already forgiven and healed every person who will ever be forgiven or healed. Now He doesn't even have to lift His little finger to cause a healing or salvation!

As far as God's concerned, the sins of the entire world have already been forgiven. The Lamb's perfect sacrifice dealt decisively with the past, present, and future sins of every believer and unbeliever alike. This doesn't mean everyone is just automatically saved (or healed). All individuals must receive for themselves by faith what Jesus Christ has already provided in order to actually benefit from it. A gift given isn't fully yours until it's received.

As Christians, we are to instruct people to believe and receive what God has already done for them through the Atonement. That's why the popular evangelistic method of "asking Jesus to come into your heart" is biblically inaccurate. Technically speaking, we don't have to "ask" God to "save" us. This implies that the Lord hasn't done anything yet—and won't until after we make our request. Then, depending on how He feels about us, He'll either respond positively or negatively. This is completely incorrect because Jesus did everything for all of us 2,000 years ago.

The Philippian jailer approached Paul and Silas, asking, *"Sirs, what must I do to be saved?"* They answered, *"Believe on the Lord Jesus Christ, and thou shalt be saved"* (Acts 16:30-31). Believe what? Believe that Jesus fully dealt with sin at Calvary. Payment has already been made. Now it's just a matter of believing and receiving.

"I DON'T KNOW"

After a meeting once, a lady informed me that she had asked the Lord into her heart a hundred times but still didn't have any assurance of salvation. I told her, "Tonight we'll pray and you'll get assurance!" After praying with her to receive salvation, I asked, "Are you saved?"

She responded, "Well, I don't know."

"What do you mean you don't know?" Pointing to my open Bible, I shared with her, "The Word says right here in Romans 10:9, *'That if thou shalt confess with thy mouth the Lord Jesus, and shalt believe in thine heart that God hath raised him from the dead, thou shalt be saved.'* Did you confess with your mouth?"

"Yes."

"Do you believe God raised Jesus from the dead?"

"Yes."

"Are you saved?"

"I don't know."

"Look with me at verse 13. *'For whosoever shall call upon the name of the Lord shall be saved.'* Are you a whosoever?"

"Well, I guess I am."

"Did you call on the name of the Lord?"

"Yes."

"Are you saved?"

"I don't know."

She simply could not believe that she was saved!

RECEIVE WHAT HE'S DONE

In a situation like that, what would you think if I said to you, "I'm not sure why God hasn't saved her. Would you please join with me in prayer, fasting, and agreement for her salvation? We shouldn't let go of God until He saves her!"

You'd probably disagree with me, answering, "No, Andrew, that's not the way it works. God has already done it. If she hasn't received, then her receiver is the problem, not God's giver!"

What if someone in a wheelchair came forward for healing during a service? If I prayed and didn't see that person rise out of the wheelchair immediately, I could ask the audience, "How many of you will stand in faith together with me? Let's fast and pray in agreement, not letting go of God until He heals this person." I bet I could persuade 90 percent of the people to go along with that!

Yet God's Word clearly proclaims, *"As ye have therefore received Christ Jesus the Lord, so walk ye in him"* (Col. 2:6). In the same way you appropriate and walk in forgiveness of sin, you receive healing, deliverance, prosperity, and everything else. If begging God to save the lady in the first scenario is inappropriate, then doing so for healing or anything else in the Christian life is absolutely wrong too! Christ already made full provision for the abundant life through His atonement. It's now not up to Him to do, but it's up to you to receive what He's done.

HEAL THE SICK!

Sometimes Christians approach God, praying, "I know You can heal me, but You haven't done it yet. Therefore, I want to learn how to make You heal me." This is rank unbelief! They don't believe that He's already done it, and they think they can *make* Him do it. Wrong! Such unbelief explains why more people aren't experiencing healing.

In our Bible schools and teaching seminars, we confidently instruct people not to "pray" for the sick, but to heal them. Jesus commanded us in Matthew 10:8 to *"heal the sick, cleanse the lepers, raise the dead,* [and] *cast out devils"* (brackets mine). There's a huge difference between healing the sick and just praying for them.

John G. Lake understood this difference. As a world-renowned missionary preacher, Lake had a powerful healing ministry based in Spokane, Washington. Instead of doing all the work himself, he trained associates called "healing practitioners." Whenever people requested prayer, Lake sent his practitioners out with little bottles of oil and told them, "Don't come back until they're healed!" These believers didn't just go pray for sick people; they healed them!

The longest it took for a practitioner to come back was three-and-a-half weeks. It might have taken a while, but the practitioner saw that person healed. Lake stated that not a single associate ever returned without seeing an individual healed. The associates stayed and diligently worked with the sick until the healing manifested.

Although this might sound foreign to you, these are just normal results when you understand and believe that God has already done His part. Jesus Christ completed everything necessary to save and heal every person. You believed and received salvation. Healing comes the exact same way. It shouldn't be any harder to receive your healing, since He provided it at the same time as forgiveness for your sin. Neither does it take any more faith to raise people from the dead than to see them born again!

IT'S JACKHAMMER TIME!

The greatest manifestation of God's power came when you were born again. By nature, you were a child of the devil. He had legal rights and claims to you. As a citizen of the kingdom of darkness, the Enemy legitimately dominated your life. At the time of your salvation, you hadn't been fasting, praying, studying the Word, attending church, paying tithes, or living a holy life. Yet without any such effort, you received the greatest miracle of all! It happened because you believed it was already done. How could you doubt that God would do what He had already done?

The Gospel is "good news" (what He's done), not "good prophecy" (what He's going to do). News in a newspaper has taken place in the past. The good news of the Gospel is that God has already forgiven you. Why would you choose to go to hell with your sins forgiven? Why not take advantage of the Lord's generous provision? You just need to understand that He's already done His part. The question isn't "Will God save you?" but "Will you accept His salvation?" The gift has been given, but will you receive it?

It's the same with everything else in the Christian life. God has already healed, prospered, and delivered us. Yet most people beg and plead, attempting to manipulate and control God through prayer. Their underlying attitude is *How do I make God do something He's unwilling to do?* That's totally wrong! Prayer is not something we use to try to twist God's arm to make Him do something. Prayer is receiving by faith what He has already done.

Should the Lord tarry, believers one hundred years from now will look back on most of the concepts being peddled as "intercession" today and think, *How ignorant and barbaric can you get?* Nobody in their right mind should believe the majority of current teaching being passed off as "intercession" in the body of Christ. It's one of the biggest areas of deception and bondage in the church today!

Before Jesus taught what prayer is, He revealed what it's not. Let's take a jackhammer to our faulty foundations and throw them out; they're only hindering us!

Outline

I. Jesus taught that there is right and wrong praying.

> *And when thou prayest, thou shalt not be as the hypocrites are: for they love to pray standing in the synagogues and in the corners of the streets, that they may be seen of men. Verily I say unto you, They have their reward.*
>
> MATTHEW 6:5

   A. A tremendous amount of what's being called "prayer" today offends God and opens the door for the devil.

   B. Jesus had to reveal what prayer is *not* before He taught what it is (Matt. 6:5-13).

   C. The Lord Himself first had to counter the religious concepts concerning prayer in His day, or the people would never have been able to grasp what He was about to say.

II. The heart attitude behind our prayer interests God much more than the actual words we say (Matt. 6:5)—if our attitude is wrong, we're praying wrong!

   A. Praying in tongues, prophesying, having all faith, giving our possessions to the poor, or even laying down our lives will all profit us nothing if done without God's kind of love (1 Cor. 13:1-3).

   B. In the kingdom, heart attitude makes all the difference!

   C. If we aren't seeing the desired results from our prayer lives, we need to check our motives.

   D. It's not God who hasn't been answering; it's our prayers that have been wrong.

III. God has already done everything He's ever going to do.

   A. He moved once and for all in the death, burial, and resurrection of Jesus Christ.

   B. All of us must receive for ourselves by faith what Jesus Christ has already provided in order to actually benefit from it.

      i. A gift given isn't fully ours until it's received!

C. As Christians, we are to instruct people to believe and receive what God has already done for them through the Atonement (Acts 16:30-31).

IV. Payment has already been made—now it's just a matter of believing and receiving (see Romans 10:9 and 13).

A. God's Word clearly proclaims, *"As ye have therefore received Christ Jesus the Lord, so walk ye in him"* (Col. 2:6).

B. In the same way we appropriate and walk in forgiveness of sin, we receive healing, deliverance, prosperity, and everything else!

C. Christ already made full provision for the abundant life through His atonement.

D. It's now not up to Him to do but us to receive what He's done.

V. Jesus commanded us in Matthew 10:8 to *"heal the sick, cleanse the lepers, raise the dead, [and] cast out devils"* (brackets mine).

A. There's a huge difference between healing the sick and just praying for them.

B. Jesus Christ completed everything necessary to save and heal every person—it shouldn't be any harder to receive our healing, since He provided it at the same time as forgiveness for our sin.

C. It doesn't take any more faith to raise people from the dead than to see them born again!

VI. The Gospel is "good news" (what He's done), not "good prophecy" (what He's going to do)!

A. God has already forgiven, healed, prospered, and delivered us.

B. Prayer is receiving by faith what He has already done.

Teacher's Guide

1. Jesus taught that there is right and wrong praying.

   And when thou prayest, thou shalt not be as the hypocrites are: for they love to pray standing in the synagogues and in the corners of the streets, that they may be seen of men. Verily I say unto you, They have their reward.

   MATTHEW 6:5

   A tremendous amount of what's being called "prayer" today offends God and opens the door for the devil. Jesus had to reveal what prayer is not before He taught what it is (Matt. 6:5-13). The Lord Himself first had to counter the religious concepts concerning prayer in His day, or the people would never have been able to grasp what He was about to say.

1a. A tremendous amount of what's being called "prayer" today does what?
   Offends God and opens the door to the devil

1b. What did the Lord Himself first have to counter, or the people would never have been able to grasp what He was about to say?
   The religious concepts concerning prayer in His day

2. The heart attitude behind our prayer interests God much more than the actual words we say (Matt. 6:5)—if our attitude is wrong, we're praying wrong! Praying in tongues, prophesying, having all faith, giving our possessions to the poor, or even laying down our lives will all profit us nothing if done without God's kind of love (1 Cor. 13:1-3). In the kingdom, heart attitude makes all the difference! If we aren't seeing the desired results from our prayer lives, we need to check our motives. It's not God who hasn't been answering; it's our prayers that have been wrong.

2a. Read 1 Corinthians 13:1-3. What should be your motivation when you pray?
   Love

2b. If God hasn't been answering your prayers, what's the problem?
   Your prayers have been wrong

3. God has already done everything He's ever going to do. He moved once and for all in the death, burial, and resurrection of Jesus Christ. All of us must receive for ourselves by faith what Jesus Christ has already provided in order to actually benefit from it. A gift given isn't fully ours until it's received! As Christians, we are to instruct people to believe and receive what God has already done for them through the Atonement (Acts 16:30-31).

3a.   Read Acts 16:30-31. God moved once and for all in what?
The death, burial, and resurrection of Jesus Christ

3b.   As a Christian, what are you to instruct people to believe and receive?
What God has already done for them through the Atonement

4.   Payment has already been made—now it's just a matter of believing and receiving (see Romans 10:9 and 13). God's Word clearly proclaims, "As ye have therefore received Christ Jesus the Lord, so walk ye in him" (Col. 2:6). In the same way we appropriate and walk in forgiveness of sin, we receive healing, deliverance, prosperity, and everything else! Christ already made full provision for the abundant life through His atonement. It's now not up to Him to do but us to receive what He's done.

4a.   Read Romans 10:9, 13; and Colossians 2:6. Since the payment has already been made, now it's just a matter of what?
Believing and receiving

4b.   How do you receive healing, deliverance, prosperity, and everything else?
In the same way you appropriate and walk in forgiveness of sin

5.   Jesus commanded us in Matthew 10:8 to *"heal the sick, cleanse the lepers, raise the dead,* [and] *cast out devils"* (brackets mine). There's a huge difference between healing the sick and just praying for them. Jesus Christ completed everything necessary to save and heal every person—it shouldn't be any harder to receive our healing, since He provided it at the same time as forgiveness for our sin. It doesn't take any more faith to raise people from the dead than to see them born again!

5a.   Is there a difference between praying for the sick and healing them?
Yes

5b.   Why shouldn't it be any harder to receive your healing than forgiveness for your sin?
Because Jesus provided both at the same time and in the same way

6.   The Gospel is "good news" (what He's done), not "good prophecy" (what He's going to do)! God has already forgiven, healed, prospered, and delivered us. Prayer is receiving by faith what He has already done.

6a.   What is good news?
The Gospel—what He's done

6b. If God has already done everything for you, how should that affect how you pray?
You no longer have to wait on God to do something; you only have to receive by faith what He has already done

Discipleship Questions

1. A tremendous amount of what's being called "prayer" today does what?

2. What did the Lord Himself first have to counter, or the people would never have been able to grasp what He was about to say?

3. Read 1 Corinthians 13:1-3. What should be your motivation when you pray?

4. If God hasn't been answering your prayers, what's the problem?

5. Read Acts 16:30-31. God moved once and for all in what?

6. As a Christian, what are you to instruct people to believe and receive?

7. Read Romans 10:9, 13; and Colossians 2:6. Since the payment has already been made, now it's just a matter of what?

8. How do you receive healing, deliverance, prosperity, and everything else?

9. Is there a difference between praying for the sick and healing them?

10. Why shouldn't it be any harder to receive your healing than forgiveness for your sin?

11. What is good news?

12. If God has already done everything for you, how should that affect how you pray?

Answer Key

1. Offends God and opens the door to the devil

2. The religious concepts concerning prayer in His day

3. Love

4. Your prayers have been wrong

5. The death, burial, and resurrection of Jesus Christ

6. What God has already done for them through the Atonement

7. Believing and receiving

8. In the same way you appropriate and walk in forgiveness of sin

9. Yes

10. Because Jesus provided both at the same time and in the same way

11. The Gospel—what He's done

12. You no longer have to wait on God to do something; you only have to receive by faith what He has already done

Scriptures

MATTHEW 6:5-13

And when thou prayest, thou shalt not be as the hypocrites are: for they love to pray standing in the synagogues and in the corners of the streets, that they may be seen of men. Verily I say unto you, They have their reward. [6] But thou, when thou prayest, enter into thy closet, and when thou hast shut thy door, pray to thy Father which is in secret; and thy Father which seeth in secret shall reward thee openly. [7] But when ye pray, use not vain repetitions, as the heathen do: for they think that they shall be heard for their much speaking. [8] Be not ye therefore like unto them: for your Father knoweth what things ye have need of, before ye ask him. [9] After this manner therefore pray ye: Our Father which art in heaven, Hallowed be thy name. [10] Thy kingdom come. Thy will be done in earth, as it is in heaven. [11] Give us this day our daily bread. [12] And forgive us our debts, as we forgive our debtors. [13] And lead us not into temptation, but deliver us from evil: For thine is the kingdom, and the power, and the glory, for ever. Amen.

1 CORINTHIANS 13:1-3

Though I speak with the tongues of men and of angels, and have not charity, I am become as sounding brass, or a tinkling cymbal. [2] And though I have the gift of prophecy, and understand all mysteries, and all knowledge; and though I have all faith, so that I could remove mountains, and have not charity, I am nothing. [3] And though I bestow all my goods to feed the poor, and though I give my body to be burned, and have not charity, it profiteth me nothing.

ACTS 16:30-31

And brought them out, and said, Sirs, what must I do to be saved? [31] And they said, Believe on the Lord Jesus Christ, and thou shalt be saved, and thy house.

ROMANS 10:9

That if thou shalt confess with thy mouth the Lord Jesus, and shalt believe in thine heart that God hath raised him from the dead, thou shalt be saved.

ROMANS 10:13

For whosoever shall call upon the name of the Lord shall be saved.

COLOSSIANS 2:6

As ye have therefore received Christ Jesus the Lord, so walk ye in him.

MATTHEW 10:8

Heal the sick, cleanse the lepers, raise the dead, cast out devils: freely ye have received, freely give.

How Long Do You Pray?

Even though much of today's so-called "prayer" offends God, He's big enough to handle it. Our heavenly Father is great enough to put up with some immaturity in His beloved children.

Everything I'm teaching against, I once did. God tolerated and even blessed me while I still prayed these ways. He wasn't mad at me, but many of my so-called "prayers" went unanswered.

If I confront one of the ways you pray, please don't think I'm saying God is mad at you. He's not! God's a good God. But if you are like I was, you're snared by the words of your mouth.

I discovered that there are right and wrong ways to pray. Through His Word, the Lord radically changed my view and practice of prayer over the years. I'm so glad He did, because my mindset needed to be changed.

KEEP AN OPEN HEART

As you progress through this study, keep an open heart and an ear tuned in to the Holy Spirit. He's your Teacher and Guide who leads you into all truth. Don't let an occasional offense stop you from participating in this study all the way through to the end. By continuing to hold on to unproductive prayer patterns, you have much more to lose than gain! In fact, your humility and willingness to consider before the Lord what I am sharing with you could mean the difference between life and death for you or someone you love. Trust me—it's not worth the risk!

I don't claim to have "arrived" concerning prayer, but I've definitely left! In my life and ministry, I regularly see miracles happen of every kind. My own son was raised up after being dead for five hours. I've seen many blind eyes and deaf ears opened, not to mention many cancers healed, people coming out of wheelchairs, and demons cast out. Also, our ministry experiences a constant flow of abundant provision to do what God has called us to do. I don't mention these things to condemn you or exalt me, because all of the glory belongs to our Lord Jesus Christ!

However, I do want to challenge you to consider these results compared to what you're getting. If you aren't seeing these kinds of things on a regular basis, why would you want to keep holding on to a less productive form? Honestly evaluate your prayer life as I confront different attitudes and popular understandings. This is your chance to recognize and root out unwanted hindrances that have been choking your effectiveness in prayer. Remember, growing pains just mean you're being stretched as you mature!

PUBLIC RELIGIOSITY

But thou, when thou prayest, enter into thy closet, and when thou hast shut thy door, pray to thy Father which is in secret; and thy Father which seeth in secret shall reward thee openly.

MATTHEW 6:6

People have actually challenged me, contending, "You should never pray in public!" Jesus prayed in public. The parallel of this passage begins in Luke 11:1 when Christ's public praying caused the disciples to ask Him to teach them to pray. If the Lord literally meant to always pray in secret so that nobody ever heard you, then He broke His own instructions. In Matthew 6:5-6, Jesus basically declared, "Don't be like the hypocrites who pray for the attention and recognition of people."

Having been to many churches, I've heard all kinds of public "prayer." People often speak loudly in a form of King James English, thinking it's more spiritual. I'm not against the *King James Version* of the Bible (it's actually my favorite), but I don't feel like I have to talk that way to God in order to truly pray. I've met individuals who never talk *King James* style except when they "pray." They become all religious sounding and speak in a different tone of voice, "Thou musteth doeth this for me!" That's hypocritical!

A REAL DRAG

It may shock you, but God doesn't enjoy many of our prayers! I found this out the hard way. When I first became really excited about the Lord, people told me I needed to pray an hour a day. I thought, *If an hour a day is good, then two or three would be even better!* So, I disciplined myself to pray for one to three hours daily. For months, perhaps even years, I began this regimented prayer time at 7:00 sharp!

Trying to spend a certain segment of time praying each day greatly frustrated me. In fact, it never really seemed to produce any good results. Many believers have started and stopped this not only once but multiple times. For me, it just never seemed to flow.

Many people who truly love God with all of their hearts find it difficult to pray in such a prescribed manner. Their once-vibrant relationship with the Lord becomes stifled, mechanical, and lifeless instead. Despite what's been taught, this rigid model of praying for a certain period of time each day is not consistent with the whole of God's Word. If you're attempting to pray this way, perhaps the reason it's not flowing is because the Holy Spirit is trying to talk you out of it!

This practice did help me learn to discipline myself. I wasn't spending my time watching television or doing something else harmful to my faith, but overall, this prayer time was a real drag!

WHY AM I DOING THIS?

I remember first starting out. I closed my eyes and prayed for what seemed to me to be an extended period of time. After a while, I wondered, *How long have I prayed?* Looking up at my clock, I saw that five minutes had passed—five minutes! I thought it had been at least thirty minutes, perhaps even an hour. Disappointment set in as I continued praying. I thought, *God, this hour is never going to pass!*

I'd be enjoying the Lord's presence and great things would be happening each day while studying the Word and worshiping. Then it would be time for me to go "pray." Finally, around 6:45 one day, I confided, "God, I don't mean this to be bad. Really, I love You. It's not a problem with You at all, but this prayer time stinks. I hate it! This time seems like the slowest hour of my whole day! I don't mean to be critical, but I'm just telling You the way it is. Beginning at 6:30, I start dreading it!"

Promptly, the Lord spoke to my heart, "I start dreading it at 6:00! Personally, I can hardly stand that hour!"

Immediately, my lightning-fast mind reasoned, *If God isn't enjoying it and I'm not enjoying it, then why am I doing this?* So, I quit praying like that, and my spiritual life greatly improved!

Jesus addressed this very thing in Matthew 6:7:

> *But when ye pray, use not vain repetitions, as the heathen do: for they think that they shall be heard for their much speaking.*

From God's perspective, praying an hour a day has no value in and of itself.

NO VIRTUE

Most people basically believe that the longer they pray, the better it is and the more likely that God will answer. Therefore, praying longer is the solution to everything. Brothers and sisters, there is absolutely no virtue in long praying!

Jesus normally kept His prayers short. Only twice in the whole New Testament did He pray all night. Since both are recorded in all four Gospels, you might think it was eight. Really, it was just two different occasions. The Lord didn't usually pray for extended amounts of time.

The shorter the prayer, the greater the faith! *"Peace, be still"* calmed a raging storm (Mark 4:39). That was prayer! *"Lazarus, come forth"* raised the dead with just three words (John 11:43). As you understand prayer more correctly, yours will shorten too. In fact, a friend of mine teaches that "Help!" is a great prayer!

A BETTER WAY TO PRAY

When I pray for longer periods of time, a significant portion is usually spent praying in tongues. I'm not so much petitioning God as I am promoting my own spiritual growth. I'm praying for and receiving wisdom and revelation from the Lord. Self-edification is an important New Testament purpose of prayer (1 Cor. 14:4 and Jude 20-21).

However, the majority of the body of Christ views prayer primarily as an opportunity to petition God. They see it very narrowly as their time to plead with Him to meet their needs. Of course, there are scriptures that reveal that asking and receiving are a valid use of prayer, but you ought to confine it to 5 percent or less of your prayer life. Based on my relationship with the Lord, I believe this is best.

DON'T FOOL YOURSELF

What would be left of most Christians' prayer lives if all the repenting for sin, asking for things, and intercession were subtracted? Hardly anything! Most people's prayers consist of "O God, I'm so sorry that I've failed again. Help me overcome this problem. God, heal this and provide that." And if they're really spiritual, they'll add, "Do this for these other people!" That's about what it amounts to.

Adam and Eve prayed for none of those things! They had nobody to intercede for, no demons to cast out, and no kingdoms to tear down. They had no clothes, food, houses, or even jobs to believe for—no petitions at all—but yet they met with God every evening in the cool of the day and communed with Him. Their conversations with God had nothing in them concerning sin, lack, need, problems, repenting, begging, or pleading. Yet they prayed—communed with Him— every single day!

Prayer becomes religious when you try to use it for something God never intended. That's why it doesn't flow. You can promise Him "I'm going to pray an hour a day if it kills me!" and then do it for a week, a month, or two months. But it never lasts, because that's not the way He's leading you. Don't fool yourself into thinking you'll be heard by praying for long periods of time or using certain words to petition Him again and again and again. The Lord made it very clear that this isn't what prayer is (Matt. 6:7).

ALL DAY LONG!

Many years ago, a fellow from a church in another state came to Colorado Springs to preach. His whole message and ministry centered on exhorting people to pray an hour a day using the Lord's Prayer. I attended his meetings and received some benefit from what he shared.

Then he came over to see me in my office. Right away, he asked, "How much do you pray each day?"

His question took me entirely off guard! I'd never really sat down and figured that up before. As I thought about it, I wondered, *Why does this guy want to know how long I pray each day?* I could only think of two possible reasons: 1) He wanted to compare himself to me in the hope that he'd come out looking better (build up his ego and feel good about himself). 2) He wanted to condemn me and use his apparent "spiritual leverage" to somehow start manipulating and controlling me to respond favorably to him. Those were the only two benefits I could see to his question.

While pondering how to answer him, the Lord asked me, "How much time did you spend with your wife yesterday?" I told Him we'd spent the whole day together doing different things. "If you were with Jamie all day long, how could you reduce your relationship down to spending just one hour with her and call it an improvement?" He continued, "I'm available to you all the time. I'll never leave you nor forsake you. If you reduced our relationship down to just one hour of prayer a day, that would be a sorry relationship compared to what we already enjoy!"

So, in like manner, I boldly responded to this brother, "Do you know what? I spend all day with God in prayer!"

A look of shock came over his face as he stammered, "N-n-no…you just don't understand what I mean…."

"No, you don't understand what I mean. I spend all day in communion with God. That's prayer!"

CONSTANT COMMUNION

Prayer is communion with God! If He's with you all of the time, you ought to be praying all of the time. The expression of this communion isn't limited to a particular set of body positions. In the Bible, people knelt, raised their hands, and even looked up into heaven at times, but don't make a religious form out of these things and require their presence in order to consider something "prayer." You can pray with your eyes open or closed, hands raised or down, standing, kneeling, or prostrate. Since meditation is prayer (Ps. 5:1), you don't even have to talk out loud! Your communion with God should be constant.

There are "special times" when you have an intimate relationship with someone. My wife and I don't have a schedule that allows us to have a "date night" every single week, but we go out and do things together regularly. The face-to-face time alone that we share helps build intimacy into our marriage relationship. Without setting aside these times, it'd be easy to get so busy with life that we'd never have time for each other.

Likewise, it's appropriate to isolate yourself alone with God for special times of intimacy—but not all of the time! You must learn to relate to Him in the midst of your daily responsibilities and weekly routines because they occupy the majority of your life. It's totally unrealistic for spouses to limit their relationship only to their "special times" together. Jesus, your eternal Husband, is the same! Don't limit your relationship with Him to just "dates." Walk and talk with Him all day, every day!

Some people try to make their relationship with God be this constantly spectacular thing. They think they must be screaming at the top of their lungs, kneeling, hands held high, tears rolling down their cheeks, lightning bolts flashing, and thunder crashing all around in order to really be "in communion with God." If that's what you consider "prayer," you're never going to prosper!

One of the things that made me certain that Jamie was the girl I was supposed to marry was the fact that we just enjoyed being with each other. Unlike other girls, I didn't have to entertain or impress her. We could spend hours without saying a word and have a great time together. There's a place for this kind of attitude in prayer.

God wants each of us to mature to the point where we can enjoy just hanging out with Him. He desires our fellowship when there's nothing being said and nothing specific happening other than being together and loving each other.

Personally, I like to build my relationship with God through studying Scripture. Reading the Bible is prayer to me because I do it with my heart, not just my head. When I'm fellowshipping with God, one scripture can occupy me for hours! As I meditate, ask questions, and let Him speak, revelation comes. This is prayer!

Outline

I.   There are right and wrong ways to pray.

    A. Because of this, it's important for us to keep open hearts and ears tuned in to the Holy Spirit throughout this study.

    B. Holding on to unproductive prayer patterns could mean the difference between life and death for us or our loved ones.

    C. We should honestly evaluate our prayer lives as different attitudes and popular understandings are confronted.

    D. This is a great chance to recognize and root out unwanted hindrances that choke our effectiveness in prayer.

    E. Growing pains mean we're being stretched as we mature!

II.   Certain religious misconceptions exist about prayer.

    A. One is that we aren't supposed to pray in public.

    B. But Jesus never said not to pray in public; in fact, He did it Himself (see Luke 11:1)—He just didn't want us praying strictly to be seen by others.

    C. Another misconception is that we should pray an hour a day.

    D. God never instructed us to pray for a certain period of time each day, and this is not consistent with the whole of God's Word.

    E. In fact, from God's perspective, praying an hour a day has no value in and of itself.

III. Some people believe that longer prayers are better prayers.

    A. Jesus normally kept His prayers short (see Mark 4:39 and John 11:43) and seldom prayed for extended periods of time.

B. The shorter the prayer, the greater the faith!

C. When Andrew prays for longer periods of time, a significant portion is usually spent praying in tongues.

D. Self-edification is an important New Testament purpose of prayer (1 Cor. 14:4 and Jude 20-21).

IV. The majority of the body of Christ views prayer primarily as an opportunity to petition God.

A. They see it very narrowly as their time to plead with Him to meet their needs.

B. Most Christians' prayer time is spent repenting of sin, asking for things, and in intercession.

C. Prayer becomes religious when people try to use it for something God never intended.

V. Prayer is simply communion with God.

A. Our communion with God should be constant.

B. It's appropriate to isolate ourselves alone with God for special times of intimacy—but not all of the time!

C. We must learn to relate to Him in the midst of our daily responsibilities and weekly routines, because they occupy the majority of our lives.

D. We should walk and talk with Him all day, every day.

VI. Some people try to make their relationship with God be a constantly spectacular thing.

A. God wants each of us to mature to the point where we can enjoy just hanging out with Him.

B. He desires our fellowship when there's nothing being said and nothing specific happening other than being together and loving each other.

C. Even reading the Bible is a form of prayer when we do it with our hearts, not just our heads, and learn to meditate, ask questions, and allow God to speak to us.

Teacher's Guide

1.   There are right and wrong ways to pray. Because of this, it's important for us to keep open hearts and ears tuned in to the Holy Spirit throughout this study. Holding on to unproductive prayer patterns could mean the difference between life and death for us or our loved ones. We should honestly evaluate our prayer lives as different attitudes and popular understandings are confronted. This is a great chance to recognize and root out unwanted hindrances that choke our effectiveness in prayer. Growing pains mean we're being stretched as we mature!

1a.   What can holding on to unproductive prayers patterns do?
It can mean the difference between life and death for you or your loved ones

1b.   As you progress through this study, this is your chance to recognize and root out unwanted hindrances that have been doing what?
Choking your effectiveness in prayer

2.   Certain religious misconceptions exist about prayer. One is that we aren't supposed to pray in public. But Jesus never said not to pray in public; in fact, He did it Himself (see Luke 11:1)—He just didn't want us praying strictly to be seen by others. Another misconception is that we should pray an hour a day. God never instructed us to pray for a certain period of time each day, and this is not consistent with the whole of God's Word. In fact, from God's perspective, praying an hour a day has no value in and of itself.

2a.   What doesn't Jesus want you doing when you pray?
Praying strictly to be seen by others

2b.   From God's perspective, does praying an hour a day have any value in and of itself?
No

3.   Some people believe that longer prayers are better prayers. Jesus normally kept His prayers short (see Mark 4:39 and John 11:43) and seldom prayed for extended periods of time. The shorter the prayer, the greater the faith! When Andrew prays for longer periods of time, a significant portion is usually spent praying in tongues. Self-edification is an important New Testament purpose of prayer (1 Cor. 14:4 and Jude 20-21).

3a.   Read Mark 4:39 and John 11:43. How do these verses show how Jesus normally prayed?
He kept His prayers short

3b.   Read 1 Corinthians 14:4 and Jude 20-21. What is an important New Testament purpose of prayer?
Self-edification

4.   The majority of the body of Christ views prayer primarily as an opportunity to petition God. They see it very narrowly as their time to plead with Him to meet their needs. Most Christians' prayer time is spent repenting of sin, asking for things, and in intercession. Prayer becomes religious when people try to use it for something God never intended.

4a.   How does the majority of the body of Christ primarily and narrowly view prayer?
As an opportunity to petition God and plead with Him to meet their needs

4b.   What does prayer become when people try to use it for something God never intended?
Religious

5.   Prayer is simply communion with God. Our communion with God should be constant. It's appropriate to isolate ourselves alone with God for special times of intimacy—but not all of the time! We must learn to relate to Him in the midst of our daily responsibilities and weekly routines, because they occupy the majority of our lives. We should walk and talk with Him all day, every day.

5a.   What is prayer?
Communion with God

5b.   Why must you learn to relate to Him in the midst of your daily responsibilities and weekly routines?
Because they occupy the majority of your life

6.   Some people try to make their relationship with God be a constantly spectacular thing. God wants each of us to mature to the point where we can enjoy just hanging out with Him. He desires our fellowship when there's nothing being said and nothing specific happening other than being together and loving each other. Even reading the Bible is a form of prayer when we do it with our hearts, not just our heads, and learn to meditate, ask questions, and allow God to speak to us.

6a.   God wants you to mature to what point?
Where you can enjoy just hanging out with Him

6b.   When is reading the Bible prayer?
When you do it with your heart, not just your head—meditating, asking questions, and allowing God to speak to you

Discipleship Questions

1. What can holding on to unproductive prayers patterns do?

2. As you progress through this study, this is your chance to recognize and root out unwanted hindrances that have been doing what?

3. What doesn't Jesus want you doing when you pray?

4. From God's perspective, does praying an hour a day have any value in and of itself?

5. Read Mark 4:39 and John 11:43. How do these verses show how Jesus normally prayed?

6. Read 1 Corinthians 14:4 and Jude 20-21. What is an important New Testament purpose of prayer?

7. How does the majority of the body of Christ primarily and narrowly view prayer?

8. What does prayer become when people try to use it for something God never intended?

9. What is prayer?

10. Why must you learn to relate to Him in the midst of your daily responsibilities and weekly routines?

11. God wants you to mature to what point?

12. When is reading the Bible prayer?

Answer Key

1. It can mean the difference between life and death for you or your loved ones

2. Choking your effectiveness in prayer

3. Praying strictly to be seen by others

4. No

5. He kept His prayers short

6. Self-edification

7. As an opportunity to petition God and plead with Him to meet their needs

8. Religious

9. Communion with God

10. Because they occupy the majority of your life

11. Where you can enjoy just hanging out with Him

12. When you do it with your heart, not just your head—meditating, asking questions, and allowing God to speak to you

Scriptures

MATTHEW 6:5-7

And when thou prayest, thou shalt not be as the hypocrites are: for they love to pray standing in the synagogues and in the corners of the streets, that they may be seen of men. Verily I say unto you, They have their reward. [6] But thou, when thou prayest, enter into thy closet, and when thou hast shut thy door, pray to thy Father which is in secret; and thy Father which seeth in secret shall reward thee openly. [7] But when ye pray, use not vain repetitions, as the heathen do: for they think that they shall be heard for their much speaking.

LUKE 11:1

And it came to pass, that, as he was praying in a certain place, when he ceased, one of his disciples said unto him, Lord, teach us to pray, as John also taught his disciples.

MARK 4:39

And he arose, and rebuked the wind, and said unto the sea, Peace, be still. And the wind ceased, and there was a great calm.

JOHN 11:43

And when he thus had spoken, he cried with a loud voice, Lazarus, come forth.

1 CORINTHIANS 14:4

He that speaketh in an unknown tongue edifieth himself; but he that prophesieth edifieth the church.

JUDE 20-21

But ye, beloved, building up yourselves on your most holy faith, praying in the Holy Ghost, [21] Keep yourselves in the love of God, looking for the mercy of our Lord Jesus Christ unto eternal life.

PSALM 5:1

Give ear to my words, O LORD, consider my meditation.

Serious Misconceptions

Don't let Satan beat you up because you don't spend thirty minutes to an hour a day locked up in some closet, tearing down strongholds, rebuking demons, screaming and hollering, and such. There's no need to feel condemned. God's already as pleased with you as He can be! Much of the traditional teaching on prayer is impossible to implement in daily life.

Are you the mother of small children? You'd be missing God if you locked yourself in a closet to pray for an hour or two each day! His will isn't for you to separate yourself for prolonged periods of time while your children go unsupervised. Letting your kids destroy the house and kill each other while you're in there "talking to God" is not spiritual. In the times when you can't be alone with Him, you can pray without ceasing all day, every day, in the midst of everything else. You can be in constant communion with God, and He's pleased with that!

Prayer ought to be something you can fit into your normal day. If you can have some special time alone, on your knees, eyes closed, with nothing distracting you, take advantage of it. Just remember that prayer doesn't have to be that way to please God. You should be able to pray while you're driving down the street (eyes open, of course!), working, maintaining your house, doing laundry, etc. Be creative and find ways to commune with Him all day long.

GO TO BED!

You simply cannot live life in the real world the way many people teach prayer. They talk about waking up two or three hours before anyone else in order to pray. Then they pump you up and send you out full of inspiring stories. If you can do it—great! But if you have kids that keep you up until 10 and awaken you two or three times during the night, and then you have to rush off to work by 5 a.m., you won't be able to get up that early to pray. And God doesn't want you to, either! *"It is vain for you to rise up early, to sit up late…for so he giveth his beloved sleep"* (Ps. 127:2).

When I first started seeking the Lord, I had a strong desire to serve Him. They told me I had to either stay up at night or get up early in the morning to pray. I remember staying up late, trying to pray. I'd fall asleep and then feel so condemned over it!

One time after waking up late at night on my knees, I prayed, "God, I'm so sorry! What can I do to keep from falling asleep when I pray?"

He answered, "Go to bed and get a good night's rest. Then you can pray without falling asleep!"

Nowadays, if I fall asleep while studying the Word or praying, I just take a nap! After getting some rest, I return to whatever I was doing before and everything's just fine.

What I'm communicating is destroying some popular attitudes and models of prayer. We might as well face it: God is not pleased with all of our religious calisthenics. Really, that's all they are. Many Christians are just like these hypocrites Jesus spoke of. They pray for the recognition they receive from others. They pray to soothe their consciences, thinking that doing their religious duty forces God to "move" and give them what they want. God doesn't work that way, and He's not impressed with how long we spend in prayer.

GOD ALREADY KNOWS

Be not ye therefore like unto them [the heathen using vain repetitions and long prayers, verse 7]: *for your Father knoweth what things ye have need of, before ye ask him.*

MATTHEW 6:8, BRACKETS MINE

Prayer is not to inform God of how bad your situation is. He already knows what you need—even before you ask!

Have you ever prayed "O God, the doctor said…" and then followed with a detailed rehash of your medical professional's negative report? God understands the situation better than you do! He doesn't need to know what your boss, spouse, banker, or anyone else has said about it. It's simply not necessary or beneficial to give God a detailed description of your problem.

Many Christians picture in their minds a huge desk in heaven piled high with millions of prayers for God to process. They assume He's swamped, and it might take Him months to get to their request. Therefore, they take it upon themselves to inform Him of their urgency, praying "You need to get to this one quickly!" They hope He'll then move their request up to the top of the pile and stamp "approved" on it. This mental image and its related attitudes are completely wrong. God is not bogged down, months behind, or unaware of your urgency. Prayer is not to inform "poor, misinformed" God of how bad your situation is.

Because most people are ignorant of this, problems, needs, and urgency occupy a large percentage of prayer. If telling God about problems and how bad they are were removed from people's prayers, not much would be left. That's why I advise most women to quit praying for their husbands.

"O God, my husband beats me, abuses the kids, and even kicks our dog. He spends our money out drinking, gambling, and buying dirty magazines. He's a complete reprobate!" She will tell God how bad her husband is for forty-five minutes before closing the prayer with, "But I believe You're going to save him, in Jesus' name." She spends forty-five minutes in unbelief, rehearsing the problem, and five seconds in faith. Then she'll ask me, "Why am I not encouraged?" That's not an encouraging prayer!

DEATH & LIFE

Death and life are in the power of the tongue.

PROVERBS 18:21A

Even in "prayer," your words produce either death or life. Praying God's solution, from the Word, releases life, but praying negatively and focusing on your problems only energizes and strengthens those problems—whether you realize it or not.

The Lord interrupted Charles Capps one time while he was praying. "Charles, what are you doing?"

"I'm praying!"

"No, you're not. That's complaining!"

Many people who think they're praying are really just griping, murmuring, and complaining. They are releasing the power of death into their lives through their negativity in prayer. God's not pleased with that!

Prayer has become so religious. We need to recognize these hypocritical forms and attitudes for what they are. After we clear out everything that prayer isn't, we'll be able to lay a proper foundation of what it is. Again, I am speaking first and foremost from my own life. I'm not going to criticize anything that I haven't already done.

MOODY

I used to organize all-night prayer meetings. After rounding the people up, we'd intercede our hearts out as the sun went down. However, I ended up staying awake and praying all night long by myself because everyone else always left by 10 or 11 p.m.

I've prayed all night many times. As a soldier on bunker guard in Vietnam, I prayed four hours every night for thirteen months. Four hours! This was before I spoke in tongues. You can pray for the whole world in thirty minutes if you don't speak in tongues! Four hours wasn't easy, but I forced myself to do it.

At one time or another in my life, I've done all of these things that I'm now teaching against. I'm not doing any of them now and am receiving better results than ever before. I love God more and He loves me. We have a great relationship! He's not upset at all that I'm not doing any of those

---

A BETTER WAY TO PRAY

things anymore. You might be tempted in your heart to condemn me, but until you start getting better results, maybe you should consider making these changes.

Dwight L. Moody began as a poor shoe salesman teaching Sunday school to youngsters. He didn't even have a sixth-grade education. Over time, Moody's legendary zeal and success in leading others to the Lord opened the door for him to preach on every continent and in front of such royalty as the Queen of England. Hundreds of thousands of people were born again under his ministry. This man was powerful in God!

Moody led a disciplined life that enabled him to do much of what he did. He devoted forty-five minutes to both prayer and Bible study from 12 noon to 12:45 each day because the rest of his time, he was out ministering and traveling in various ways. According to current models of prayer being taught in the body of Christ, it would be considered impossible for Moody to be so effective—yet he was. One hundred years later, he still impacts the world through the Moody Bible Institute in Chicago and branch schools in Spokane, Washington, and Plymouth, Michigan. The man did more than most of us have ever dreamed of.

We have some serious misconceptions regarding what prayer is all about!

Outline

I.   We shouldn't allow Satan to condemn us concerning prayer.

    A. Much of the traditional teaching on prayer is impossible to implement in daily life.

        i. For instance, if we have small children, we wouldn't be able to lock ourselves away from them to pray.

    B. In the times when we can't be alone with Him, we can pray without ceasing all day, every day, in the midst of everything else.

    C. We can be in constant communion with God, and He's pleased with that!

    D. Prayer should be something we fit into our normal daily routine.

II. God is not pleased with all of our religious calisthenics.

    A. Many teach that we have to get up early in the morning to pray, but that's not often realistic (Ps. 127:2).

    B. Many Christians are just like the hypocrites Jesus spoke of.

        i. They pray for the recognition they receive from others and to soothe their consciences.

    C. God's not impressed with how long we spend in prayer.

III. Prayer is not to inform God how bad our situations are.

    A. He already knows what we need—even before we ask (Matt. 6:8).

    B. It's simply not necessary or beneficial to give God a detailed description of our problems.

    C. For most people, their problems, needs, and urgency occupy a large percentage of their prayers.

D. If these things were removed from their prayers, not much would be left.

IV. Even in "prayer," our words produce either death or life.

Death and life are in the power of the tongue.

PROVERBS 18:21A

A. Praying God's solution from the Word releases life, but praying negatively and focusing on our problems only energizes and strengthens those problems.

B. Many people who think they're praying are really just griping, murmuring, and complaining.

C. Complaining is not the same as praying.

D. We can release the power of death into our lives through our negativity in prayer—and God's not pleased with that!

V. Dwight L. Moody led a disciplined life that enabled him to do much of what he did, including leading hundreds of thousands of people to the Lord and founding Moody Bible Institute.

A. He only devoted forty-five minutes to prayer and Bible study from 12 noon to 12:45 each day because the rest of his time, he was out ministering and traveling.

B. According to current models of prayer being taught in the body of Christ, it would be considered impossible for Moody to be so effective—yet he was.

C. He did more than most of us have ever dreamed of.

Teacher's Guide

1.   We shouldn't allow Satan to condemn us concerning prayer. Much of the traditional teaching on prayer is impossible to implement in daily life. For instance, if we have small children, we wouldn't be able to lock ourselves away from them to pray. In the times when we can't be alone with Him, we can pray without ceasing all day, every day, in the midst of everything else. We can be in constant communion with God, and He's pleased with that! Prayer should be something we fit into our normal daily routine.

1a.   Why is much of the traditional teaching on prayer impossible to implement in daily life?
       Because family, schedules, etc., don't usually allow for spending hours a day in prayer

1b.   What is God pleased with?
       When you're in constant communion with Him

2.   God is not pleased with all of our religious calisthenics. Many teach that we have to get up early in the morning to pray, but that's not often realistic (Ps. 127:2). Many Christians are just like the hypocrites Jesus spoke of. They pray for the recognition they receive from others and to soothe their consciences. God's not impressed with how long we spend in prayer.

2a.   What is God not pleased with?
       All of your religious calisthenics

2b.   Is God impressed with you when you get up early to pray or spend a long time in prayer?
       No

3.   Prayer is not to inform God how bad our situations are. He already knows what we need—even before we ask (Matt. 6:8). It's simply not necessary or beneficial to give God a detailed description of our problems. For most people, their problems, needs, and urgency occupy a large percentage of their prayers. If these things were removed from their prayers, not much would be left.

3a.   Prayer should not be used to inform God of what?
       How bad your situation is

3b.   It's simply not necessary or beneficial to give God a detailed description of what?
       Your problems

4.   Even in "prayer," our words produce either death or life.

Death and life are in the power of the tongue.

PROVERBS 18:21A

Praying God's solution from the Word releases life, but praying negatively and focusing on our problems only energizes and strengthens those problems. Many people who think they're praying are really just griping, murmuring, and complaining. Complaining is not the same as praying. We can release the power of death into our lives through our negativity in prayer—and God's not pleased with that!

4a.   Read Proverbs 18:21a. What does praying God's solution from the Word release?
       Life
4b.   What is the result of complaining in prayer?
       You release the power of death into your life, and you do not please God

5.   Dwight L. Moody led a disciplined life that enabled him to do much of what he did, including leading hundreds of thousands of people to the Lord and founding Moody Bible Institute. He only devoted forty-five minutes to prayer and Bible study from 12 noon to 12:45 each day because the rest of his time, he was out ministering and traveling. According to current models of prayer being taught in the body of Christ, it would be considered impossible for Moody to be so effective—yet he was. He did more than most of us have ever dreamed of.

5a.   Why would current models of prayer indicate that Dwight L. Moody should not have been effective?
       Because he only spent forty-five minutes a day in both prayer and Bible study
5b.   Why was he so effective?
       He led a disciplined life

Discipleship Questions

1. Why is much of the traditional teaching on prayer impossible to implement in daily life?

2. What is God pleased with?

3. What is God not pleased with?

4. Is God impressed with you when you get up early to pray or spend a long time in prayer?

5. Prayer should not be used to inform God of what?

6. It's simply not necessary or beneficial to give God a detailed description of what?

7. Read Proverbs 18:21a. What does praying God's solution from the Word release?

8. What is the result of complaining in prayer?

9. Why would current models of prayer indicate that Dwight L. Moody should not have been effective?

10. Why was he so effective?

Answer Key

1. Because family, schedules, etc., don't usually allow for spending hours a day in prayer

2. When you're in constant communion with Him

3. All of your religious calisthenics

4. No

5. How bad your situation is

6. Your problems

7. Life

8. You release the power of death into your life, and you do not please God

9. Because he only spent forty-five minutes a day in both prayer and Bible study

10. He led a disciplined life

Scriptures

PSALM 127:2

It is vain for you to rise up early, to sit up late, to eat the bread of sorrows: for so he giveth his beloved sleep.

MATTHEW 6:7-8

But when ye pray, use not vain repetitions, as the heathen do: for they think that they shall be heard for their much speaking. [8] Be not ye therefore like unto them: for your Father knoweth what things ye have need of, before ye ask him.

PROVERBS 18:21

Death and life are in the power of the tongue: and they that love it shall eat the fruit thereof.

"Our Father"

After this manner therefore pray ye.

MATTHEW 6:9

Jesus didn't intend for what is traditionally called "The Lord's Prayer" (Matt. 6:9-13) to be recited word for word the way it's been done in church. Technically speaking, this isn't even a true New Testament prayer. You might be surprised to hear that, but notice that it's not prayed in the name of Jesus. Right before He died, the Lord said,

> *And in that day you will ask Me nothing. Most assuredly, I say to you, whatever you ask the Father in My name He will give you. [24] Until now you have asked nothing in My name. Ask, and you will receive, that your joy may be full.*

JOHN 16:23-24, *NEW KING JAMES VERSION*

A New Covenant prayer must be prayed in the name of Jesus.

The Lord was giving us a model for prayer, not something to repeat. If you are reciting the words *"Our Father which art in heaven"* (Matt. 6:9) and saying "The Lord's Prayer," you're just soothing your conscience. Your feeling of *I'm really observing my religious duty!* is all you're getting out of it, because merely speaking these words doesn't earn you anything from God. This is nothing more than the vain repetition Jesus taught against in Matthew 6:7.

Jesus was communicating scriptural principles through this model prayer.

ENTER WITH PRAISE

> *Enter into his gates with thanksgiving, and into his courts with praise: be thankful unto him, and bless his name.*

PSALM 100:4

This is how you're supposed to begin prayer—by entering into His presence thanking, praising, and blessing Him. It's exactly what Jesus told us to do in Matthew 6:9: *"Our Father which art in heaven, Hallowed be thy name."*

Begin prayer by acknowledging your special relationship to God your Father. Don't just approach Him as "God," "Judge," or "Creator"; that's impersonal and distant. Every New Testament believer has a close, personal relationship with God that supersedes even the very best of what Old Testament saints had. Isn't that awesome?

Come into God's presence praising and worshiping Him. Ascribe the glory due His name—He's your loving heavenly Father! Thank Him for this special relationship. Remind yourself of His goodness and mercy, that He's not mad at you. Even if you've blown it again, He's not condemning you. God is pleased with you and loves you dearly. As you enter into His presence, remember: He's your Father!

What would you think if you saw children come into their father's presence and begin to say "We know that we haven't talked to you all day long. Of course, you must be very displeased with us. Forgive us again…" and then continue by begging and pleading for mercy and cleansing? You'd think, *That's not a very good father! He's made his children afraid to come near him if they haven't done everything just right. They think that if they haven't talked to him all day, he's going to be mad at them. Come on!*

Every one of us has been guilty of entering into our Father's presence with a sense of unworthiness, saying, "God, I haven't prayed. I'm not loving the way I should. I didn't do this or that." We come in concerned about, dominated by, and focused on our own failure instead of His goodness. Our Father doesn't like His children approaching Him that way. If you feel like you're so sorry, then praise Him for the fact that He loves such a sorry person as you! Instead of focusing on your unworthiness, thank Him for His goodness!

"JUST ACT LIKE I LOVE YOU!"

Honey was the large watchdog I left with my mother when I went to Vietnam. She was three-fourths German Shepherd and one-fourth Chow Chow. Her name came from her beautiful, honey-colored fur coat. Honey would bark, run, and jump on the fence (which bowed out in one spot from her constantly doing this) whenever someone walked by. Looking mean, she scared the daylights out of many people.

However, Honey's toughness melted in a heartbeat if you opened up the back gate. She'd immediately scramble to move herself out of your way. You see, Honey had been beaten with a trace chain before I got her. Even though she looked mean, in reality she was quite timid. Every time this dog came up to me, she'd run until about ten feet away. At that point, she'd stop, roll over, start whimpering pitifully, and continue scooting up to me on her side. Honey wanted me to pet her but was constantly afraid I might hit her instead.

One day I was meditating on these exact verses from Matthew 6 and Psalm 100. I remember walking out and sitting down on my back porch. Here came Honey running across the yard to me. When she arrived within a few feet of where I sat, she rolled over on her side and started whimpering. By this time, I'd had enough of her antics, so I stood up and let her have it: "Honey, one time I wish you would just come up, jump on me, and treat me like a normal dog would. Everybody who sees you thinks I beat you! They believe I'm a mean master. I just get so embarrassed when people observe how you act toward me!"

Then the Lord spoke to my heart, "Son, that's exactly the way I feel about you. Just one time I wish you would approach Me, saying, 'Daddy! Father!' and not talk about how sorry you are or how you know you don't deserve My goodness and mercy. Just one time I'd like you to come into My presence and act like I love you!"

NOT AFRAID OF FATHER

This is what Jesus was talking about in Matthew 6:9. Enter His gates with thanksgiving. Praise Him, praying, "Father! Thank You for being my Father!" You wouldn't expect an earthly dad to treat his child as badly as you might expect your heavenly Father to treat you. If children approached their parents the way religion conditions people to approach God, those parents would be accused of child abuse!

People outside the church hear the way we talk about the Lord: "God sent the September 11 attacks. He's judging America and we need to pray for His clemency. The Lord will completely destroy our ungodly nation if we don't get down on our knees and beg for forgiveness now." It's no wonder people aren't turning to God. That's not an accurate representation of who He is!

God's not mad at you. It doesn't matter how sorry you are. He took all of His anger out on His own Son 2,000 years ago at the cross. Jesus proclaimed, *"It is finished"* (John 19:30). Now you can approach Him without fear, based on what Christ has done. God's just glad to hear from you. He's not going to upbraid you. He isn't like that!

Go ahead and enter His gates with thanksgiving and praise Him. Thank Him for the fact that He is holy and kind, pure and good. Praise Him for being your Father and not your Judge! He'll be the Judge of unbelievers, but He isn't going to judge you. Your judgment was placed upon Jesus. When you stand before Him on that day as a believer in Christ, it'll be for the presentation of your eternal reward, not condemnation. There's simply no need to be afraid of your loving heavenly Father!

MANIFESTING HEAVEN ON EARTH

Thy kingdom come. Thy will be done in earth, as it is in heaven.

MATTHEW 6:10

Jesus continued to praise God, declaring, "Father, I know it's Your will for things to be done on earth the way they are in heaven." In heaven, there's no sickness. Therefore, it's not God's will for you to be sick. There's no poverty in heaven. So, it's not God's will for you to be poor here on earth. In the presence of the Lord, there is abundant joy, shouting, singing, praising, and worshiping. That's what heaven is like, and it's how He expects us to be here on earth.

Religion has sold us a bill of goods. It's taught us to always expect God to be half ticked off. It's convinced us that we must constantly try to appease an angry God. Wrong, wrong, wrong! That's not the way Father wants it to be. If we Christians really understood this part of the model prayer, we'd quit believing that God is the one who brings bad things into our lives to teach us something. God doesn't make us sick. He doesn't put poverty in our lives. He doesn't cause our marriages to fail because we weren't serving Him at the time. God doesn't kill our children because we weren't reading the Bible. Religion teaches that garbage. It's no wonder we aren't getting better results in prayer!

God wants His will to be done on earth as it is in heaven. This should serve as a guideline for what we expect from Him. We should pray that what's already waiting for us in heaven would begin to manifest here in our lives on earth. Eternal life has already begun!

TAKE IT!

Give us this day our daily bread.

MATTHEW 6:11

Notice that this verse isn't a question, because there's no question mark at the end. It's not saying, "O God, I know I don't deserve it, but would You please give me a crumb so I won't starve and perish today?" No! This is a demand: "Give us this day our daily bread!" It's not an arrogant demand in the vein of "God, I'm forcing You!" but more like a little kid who comes into the kitchen at lunchtime, declaring, "I want something to eat!" Does the parent slap them and require, "Beg me!"? No! Providing meals is just part of the family relationship. Children expect Mom and Dad to meet their needs. It's familiarity with their parents' love that makes them bold in their approach.

God wants us to be this way with Him. He desires all believers to be so familiar with His love that our approach toward Him is bold (Heb. 4:16). He yearns for His children to believe that all of the provision they need has already been made and that they just have to reach out in faith and take it. "Father, thank You! I receive my healing. I take my prosperity. I love You, Father!" You aren't making God do something. You just know in your heart that He's already supplied, so you reach out and take it.

Not many Christians approach God this way. They come before Him more like beggars than children. They should pray, "Father, I thank You that You have already provided everything I need. You never deny me anything good!" Instead, they enter His presence feeling like God doesn't really want to move in their lives. Therefore, they beg and plead with Him to make Him move on their behalf. That attitude stinks! It's religious bondage, not true prayer. God is offended, and it doesn't bless them. Tear that stuff up and start over!

"Give us this day our daily bread!" Just take advantage of what He's already done. Appropriate it!

FORGIVEN & DELIVERED

*And forgive us our debts, as we forgive our debtors. [13] And lead us not
into temptation.*

MATTHEW 6:12-13A

It's obvious this isn't a New Covenant prayer. Your sins have been forgiven. You don't need to keep confessing them and praying, "Forgive me my sins, forgive me my sins." Once you've believed and received the Lord, your sins are forgiven—past, present, and future.

We don't have to pray, "God, don't lead us into temptation." Of course He won't! What loving Father would? Jesus spoke these things in Matthew 6 *before* the cross and His resurrection. He was led into temptation on our behalf and overcame the devil (Matt. 4:1-11). If we are being led into temptation, we can be sure that it isn't God (James 1:13-14). In light of this truth, we can pray, "Father, we know it's not Your will for us to be tempted." That's fine.

*But deliver us from evil: For thine is the kingdom, and the power, and the glory, for
ever. Amen.*

MATTHEW 6:13B

Through faith in Christ, we've transferred kingdoms. Jesus has already delivered us out of the kingdom of darkness and set us in the kingdom of light. The evil one lost his legal hold on us completely, and we now belong to our loving heavenly Father. For this, we praise Him. Hallelujah!

Outline

I.   Jesus didn't intend for what is traditionally called "The Lord's Prayer" (Matt. 6:9-13) to be recited word for word the way it's been done in church.

   A. Technically speaking, this isn't even a true New Testament prayer—a New Covenant prayer must be prayed in the name of Jesus (John 16:23-24).

   B. The Lord was giving us a model for prayer, not something to repeat.

   C. Jesus was communicating scriptural principles through this model prayer.

II. We should begin prayer by acknowledging our special relationship to God our Father.

   A. He is no longer only our Judge, our Creator, or God, but He is our Father.

   B. We should come into His presence praising and worshiping Him (Ps. 100:4).

   C. As we enter into His presence, instead of focusing on our unworthiness and failures, we should thank Him for His goodness.

   D. God does not want us to approach Him with a sense of unworthiness, because Jesus has made us worthy.

      i.   If we feel sorry for ourselves, then we should praise Him for loving such sorry people!

III. God also expects us to come into His presence unafraid.

   A. If children approached their parents the way religion conditions us to approach God, those parents would be accused of child abuse!

   B. When Jesus proclaimed *"It is finished"* (John 19:30), He made a way for us to approach our heavenly Father without fear.

   C. God is not mad at us!

IV.   God expects for earth to be just like heaven for the believer.

   Thy kingdom come. Thy will be done in earth, as it is in heaven.

                                                                    MATTHEW 6:10

   A. If we Christians really understood this part of the model prayer, we'd quit believing that
       God is the one who brings bad things into our lives to teach us something.

   B. Because it's God's will that earth is like heaven, we should pray that what's already
       waiting for us in heaven would begin to manifest here in our lives on earth.

V.   Matthew 6:11 teaches that it's okay for us to expect God to meet our needs, just like children
     expect their parents to meet their needs.

   A. It's familiarity with their parents' love that makes them bold in their approach.

   B. God desires all of us to be so familiar with His love that our approach toward Him is
       bold (Heb. 4:16).

   C. He yearns for us to believe that all of the provision we need has already been made—we
       just have to reach out in faith and take it.

   D. Yet most of us approach God more like beggars than children.

VI.   Once we've believed and received the Lord, our sins are forgiven—past, present, and future.

   And forgive us our debts, as we forgive our debtors. [13] And lead us not into
   temptation, but deliver us from evil: For thine is the kingdom, and the power, and
   the glory, for ever. Amen.
                                                                    MATTHEW 6:12-13

   A. Jesus spoke these things in Matthew 6 *before* the cross and resurrection.

   B. We no longer have to ask for our sins to be forgiven, and we certainly don't have to ask
       God not to lead us into temptation.

      i.   If we are being tempted, we can be sure that it isn't God tempting us
            (James 1:13-14).

C. Jesus has already delivered us out of the kingdom of darkness and set us in the kingdom of light—instead of asking Him to do all of these things in Matthew 6:12-13, we can simply praise Him that they are already done.

Teacher's Guide

1.   Jesus didn't intend for what is traditionally called "The Lord's Prayer" (Matt. 6:9-13) to be recited word for word the way it's been done in church. Technically speaking, this isn't even a true New Testament prayer—a New Covenant prayer must be prayed in the name of Jesus (John 16:23-24). The Lord was giving us a model for prayer, not something to repeat. Jesus was communicating scriptural principles through this model prayer.

1a.   Read Matthew 6:9-13 and John 16:23-24. Why is "The Lord's Prayer" not meant to be recited word for word?
        If you were to use this prayer today, it would need to be prayed in the name of Jesus; the prayer tells you to ask God for things He has already provided for you through the death of Jesus, such as forgiveness and daily provision

1b.   What was Jesus communicating through this model prayer?
        Scriptural principles

2.   We should begin prayer by acknowledging our special relationship to God our Father. He is no longer only our Judge, our Creator, or God, but He is our Father. We should come into His presence praising and worshiping Him (Ps. 100:4). As we enter into His presence, instead of focusing on our unworthiness and failures, we should thank Him for His goodness. God does not want us to approach Him with a sense of unworthiness, because Jesus has made us worthy. If we feel sorry for ourselves, then we should praise Him for loving such sorry people!

2a.   Read Psalm 100:4. Why is it important to begin prayer by acknowledging your special relationship to God?
        Because He is no longer only your Judge, your God, and your Creator; He is your Father

2b.   How should you come into His presence?
        Praising and worshiping Him and focusing on His goodness

3.   God also expects us to come into His presence unafraid. If children approached their parents the way religion conditions us to approach God, those parents would be accused of child abuse! When Jesus proclaimed *"It is finished"* (John 19:30), He made a way for us to approach our heavenly Father without fear. God is not mad at us!

3a.   How does God expect you to enter His presence?
        Unafraid

3b.   How can you do this?
Because Jesus made a way for you to approach your Father when He declared, *"It is finished"* (John 19:30)

4.   God expects for earth to be just like heaven for the believer.

Thy kingdom come. Thy will be done in earth, as it is in heaven.

MATTHEW 6:10

If we Christians really understood this part of the model prayer, we'd quit believing that God is the one who brings bad things into our lives to teach us something. Because it's God's will that earth is like heaven, we should pray that what's already waiting for us in heaven would begin to manifest here in our lives on earth.

4a.   Why would you possibly think that God brings bad things into your life to teach you something?
Because you don't know or believe that God expects earth to be like heaven for the believer

4b.   Once you know God's will in this area, what should you do?
You should pray that what's already waiting for you in heaven would begin to manifest here in your life on earth

5.   Matthew 6:11 teaches that it's okay for us to expect God to meet our needs, just like children expect their parents to meet their needs. It's familiarity with their parents' love that makes them bold in their approach. God desires all of us to be so familiar with His love that our approach toward Him is bold (Heb. 4:16). He yearns for us to believe that all of the provision we need has already been made—we just have to reach out in faith and take it. Yet most of us approach God more like beggars than children.

5a.   Read Matthew 6:11 and Hebrews 4:16. What will help you learn to approach God boldly?
Becoming familiar with His love

5b.   What does God yearn for you to believe?
That all of the provision you need has already been made—you just have to reach out in faith and take it

6.   Once we've believed and received the Lord, our sins are forgiven—past, present, and future.

> *And forgive us our debts, as we forgive our debtors. [13] And lead us not into temptation, but deliver us from evil: For thine is the kingdom, and the power, and the glory, for ever. Amen.*
>
> MATTHEW 6:12-13

Jesus spoke these things in Matthew 6 before the cross and resurrection. We no longer have to ask for our sins to be forgiven, and we certainly don't have to ask God not to lead us into temptation. If we are being tempted, we can be sure that it isn't God tempting us (James 1:13-14). Jesus has already delivered us out of the kingdom of darkness and set us in the kingdom of light—instead of asking Him to do all of these things in Matthew 6:12-13, we can simply praise Him that they are already done.

6a.   Read Matthew 6:12-13. Why is this not a New Testament way to pray?
       Because once you've believed and received the Lord, your sins—including those in the future—are already forgiven, you don't have to ask God not to lead you into temptation, and Jesus has already delivered you from evil

6b.   What is a proper response to what God has done for us in Matthew 6:12-13?
       To praise Him

Discipleship Questions

1. Read Matthew 6:9-13 and John 16:23-24. Why is "The Lord's Prayer" not meant to be recited word for word?

2. What was Jesus communicating through this model prayer?

3. Read Psalm 100:4. Why is it important to begin prayer by acknowledging your special relationship to God?

4. How should you come into His presence?

5. How does God expect you to enter His presence?

6. How can you do this?

7. Why would you possibly think that God brings bad things into your life to teach you something?

8. Once you know God's will in this area, what should you do?

9. Read Matthew 6:11 and Hebrews 4:16. What will help you learn to approach God boldly?

10. What does God yearn for you to believe?

11. Read Matthew 6:12-13. Why is this not a New Testament way to pray?

12. What is a proper response to what God has done for us in Matthew 6:12-13?

Answer Key

1. If you were to use this prayer today, it would need to be prayed in the name of Jesus; the prayer tells you to ask God for things He has already provided for you through the death of Jesus, such as forgiveness and daily provision

2. Scriptural principles

3. Because He is no longer only your Judge, your God, and your Creator; He is your Father

4. Praising and worshiping Him and focusing on His goodness

5. Unafraid

6. Because Jesus made a way for you to approach your Father when He declared, *"It is finished"* (John 19:30)

7. Because you don't know or believe that God expects earth to be like heaven for the believer

8. You should pray that what's already waiting for you in heaven would begin to manifest here in your life on earth

9. Becoming familiar with His love

10. That all of the provision you need has already been made—you just have to reach out in faith and take it

11. Because once you've believed and received the Lord, your sins—including those in the future—are already forgiven, you don't have to ask God not to lead you into temptation, and Jesus has already delivered you from evil

12. To praise Him

Scriptures

MATTHEW 6:9-13
After this manner therefore pray ye: Our Father which art in heaven, Hallowed be thy name. [10] Thy kingdom come. Thy will be done in earth, as it is in heaven. [11] Give us this day our daily bread. [12] And forgive us our debts, as we forgive our debtors. [13] And lead us not into temptation, but deliver us from evil: For thine is the kingdom, and the power, and the glory, for ever. Amen.

JOHN 16:23-24, *NEW KING JAMES VERSION*
And in that day you will ask Me nothing. Most assuredly, I say to you, whatever you ask the Father in My name He will give you. [24] Until now you have asked nothing in My name. Ask, and you will receive, that your joy may be full.

MATTHEW 6:7
But when ye pray, use not vain repetitions, as the heathen do: for they think that they shall be heard for their much speaking.

PSALM 100:4
Enter into his gates with thanksgiving, and into his courts with praise: be thankful unto him, and bless his name.

JOHN 19:30
When Jesus therefore had received the vinegar, he said, It is finished: and he bowed his head, and gave up the ghost.

HEBREWS 4:16
Let us therefore come boldly unto the throne of grace, that we may obtain mercy, and find grace to help in time of need.

MATTHEW 4:1-11
Then was Jesus led up of the Spirit into the wilderness to be tempted of the devil. [2] And when he had fasted forty days and forty nights, he was afterward an hungred. [3] And when the tempter came to him, he said, If thou be the Son of God, command that these stones be made bread. [4] But he answered and said, It is written, Man shall not live by bread alone, but by every word that proceedeth out of the mouth of God. [5] Then the devil taketh him up into the holy city, and setteth him on a pinnacle of the temple, [6] And saith unto him, If thou be the Son of God, cast thyself down: for it is written, He shall give his angels charge concerning thee: and in their hands they shall bear thee up, lest at any time thou dash thy foot against a stone. [7] Jesus said unto him, It is written again, Thou shalt not tempt the Lord thy God. [8] Again, the devil taketh him up into an exceeding high mountain, and sheweth him all the kingdoms of the world, and the glory of them; [9] And saith unto him, All these things will I give thee, if thou wilt fall down and worship me. [10] Then saith Jesus unto him, Get thee hence, Satan: for it is written, Thou shalt worship the Lord thy God, and him only shalt thou serve. [11] Then the devil leaveth him, and, behold, angels came and ministered unto him.

JAMES 1:13-14

Let no man say when he is tempted, I am tempted of God: for God cannot be tempted with evil, neither tempteth he any man: [**14**] But every man is tempted, when he is drawn away of his own lust, and enticed.

"OUR FATHER"

Make a Prayer Sandwich!

Christ's model prayer started with praise: *"Our Father which art in heaven, Hallowed be thy name"* and ended with praise: *"For thine is the kingdom, and the power, and the glory, for ever. Amen"* (Matt. 6:9 and 13). This is what I like to call the "sandwich technique." Start your prayer thanking Him, praising Him, and declaring how big He is. Then, slide in your petition and end by praising Him some more. When you approach God with your request by slipping it in between two healthy slices of praise and thanksgiving, you'll find that you don't really have that much to ask Him for.

"O God, the doctor told me I'm going to die! I remember this same condition killed Aunt Suzie. It's so bad!" That kind of "praying" just discourages you. It builds up fear and depression. What if you prayed more like this: "Father, thank You that Your name is above every name. Cancer has a name. AIDS has a name. These things the doctor told me are in my body have names. You are above them all! Thank You that You are greater, stronger, and more powerful than all of this!" Spend another five or ten minutes just praising Him for His greatness. Then by the time you're ready to put your request in, it'd be more like "Father, this is so small in comparison to what You're able to do. I shouldn't even have to ask, but the doctor did say that I'm going to die. So, since Jesus has already provided my healing, I'll just receive it!" Then go back to praising and worshiping Him. In light of who God is, nothing is really that big of a problem.

Many people pray "Our Judge, which art in heaven. You are so very far away. O God, I'm going to die" and then spend forty minutes talking about what the doctor said before ending with "Heal me in the name of Jesus, if it be Thy will" and wonder why they're depressed. That's a depressing, ineffective prayer! The only one going to answer that type of prayer is the devil.

PRAISE

Whatever you focus on will magnify in your eyes. Focus on the problem and it'll grow. Focus on God (who is your solution), and your vision of Him will increase. This is why the direction of your prayer is so important. Will you choose to magnify God or your problem? The one you magnify will grow stronger in your life and the other, weaker.

A huge amount of prayer ought to be praise. Praise is important because it blesses God and strengthens you. The Lord inhabits the praises of His people (Ps. 22:3). That's the main reason church services usually start with praise and worship!

One of the words in the original language for *prayer* literally means worship. Another means to kiss the face. Prayer is worship, and worship is prayer. Prayer is kissing our Father's face. Prayer is loving and communing with God.

Brothers and sisters, most of what we're doing is not prayer; it's griping and complaining. It's doing things to make us feel better, like we've earned something from God: "God will hear us now because we prayed for an hour!" Wrong! "Stretching" our prayer provides zero benefit. It's just religion.

If you begin approaching God with a new attitude, it'll make a big difference in your life. God wants you set free from the religious bondages that have been imposed upon you. He didn't lead you under them; other people put them on you, or perhaps they were self-imposed. Either way, God wants you free because He's not like that!

GOD IS A PERSON

Do you want to destroy your family? Here's an effective way to do it. Have a "special time" of fellowship from 7 to 8 p.m. every night. Just make it a law that *nothing* can supersede. For that hour every evening, you "fellowship." The kids might be on the phone or playing in the backyard. Mom might be finishing up the dishes. Dad might be checking email. But when that grandfather clock finishes chiming 7 o'clock high, every family member must be present and accounted for in the living room! Then it's "1, 2, 3, FELLOWSHIP!" You'll ruin your family doing that!

It's a good concept to set aside time to do things together as a family, but when you're rigid and legalistic with a set daily time, it just kills the enjoyment after a while. People like variation and spontaneity. Of course, you must spend time with someone to have a healthy relationship, but you need to be a little subtler than that. You ought to do things together because you *want* to, not because you *have* to. The moment you start dictating "You have to do this!" something rises up on the inside of others that answers, "I don't want to!"

God is a Person. He doesn't enjoy your coming to Him because you have to. The Lord would say, "Go back to watching television. I'd prefer you do that than spend an hour griping and complaining at Me!" Just like anyone else, God would rather you spend time with Him because you want to.

It takes time to build a strong relationship with God. I meet people wherever I go who have benefited from my ministry in some way. They appreciate what the Lord has done through me, so they try to become my best friend in ten minutes. They want me to spill my guts and tell them what my "needs" are so they can "pray" for me. It seems spiritual, but usually they're just prying into my personal business. You can't become intimate with me and be my best "pal" in just ten minutes! True friendship doesn't work that way. It can't be dictated or demanded. An intimate relationship must be developed over time, whether it's with God or anyone else.

GOD IS SUBTLE

Don't try to build your relationship with God too intensely either. Some of you think you need a lightning bolt from heaven to come curl your hair in the morning! If you asked God for that today, what would you need in order to "feel" His love tomorrow? If God didn't perform something bigger and better, you'd wonder, *What happened, Lord? Yesterday You zapped me, but today I don't feel a thing! Why don't You love me anymore?* He'd have to jump through a new hoop each day just to keep you satisfied. This is the worst thing that could ever happen to you. Instead of maturing in intimacy with Him, you'd become addicted to spectacular experiences. God's not going to do that!

The Lord delights in using subtle ways to reveal Himself. Jesus could have manifested in a much more "glorious" manner when He came to the earth. He could've ridden in on a comet and landed on top of the temple at midnight. An earthquake could have shaken everyone in Jerusalem out of bed to see the spectacular arrival of the Light of the World. Instead, the King of kings arrived in a lowly stable. The animals' feed trough served as His first bed. The angels didn't sing their heavenly birth announcement to the royal family in the palace; they serenaded a few humble shepherds in the fields outside of town. Jesus even described Himself as *"meek and lowly in heart"* (Matt. 11:29).

If I'd been the one who was resurrected, I wouldn't have appeared first to Mary Magdalene and that ragtag group of disciples. No way! I would've gone straight to Pilate's house and shaken the foot of his bed, asking, "Are your hands clean yet?" I'd have visited those soldiers who had blindfolded, spat on, beaten, and mocked me, demanding, "Prophesy, if you are the Christ!" Walking through the walls of their barracks, I'd have asked them, "Hey, guys, would you like me to tell you something now?" To top it all off, I would've hovered over Jerusalem so everyone who had seen me crucified could see me resurrected from the dead. There were hundreds of thousands of people in town for the Passover. They would have all fallen down and worshiped—but Jesus didn't do that. In fact, the Scriptures clearly record that after His resurrection, He never appeared bodily to anyone who didn't already believe in Him. That's just the way God is!

God loves faith! He wants you to respond to Him by faith. Of course, God can talk to you in an audible voice. He just chooses not to very often because it brings Him more pleasure when you listen and respond to His still, small voice. God could have a bird sit on your shoulder and tell you everything you need to know. He could easily order every dog that walks by to bark "God loves you!" He could even spell out directions for your day using the clouds, but that's not His nature!

RELATIONSHIP BEYOND THE BEDCHAMBERS

You don't have to be in a heightened emotional state in order to "pray." If you feel you must cry and wail, weep and travail, every time you talk with God, then you're like the spouses who want to live their lives at the intimacy level of making love to their mates every moment of every day. It's an unrealistic expectation! Life doesn't happen that way. That's not how relationships last. It's an *important* part, but it's only a *small* part of the whole.

I once heard a psychologist speak on the subject of healthy relationships. What she shared really blessed me. At the time, I'd been invited as one of the speakers for a statewide conference for crisis pregnancy centers. Even though I no longer serve on the board, for a period of time I helped organize, start, and establish the Colorado Springs Pregnancy Center. It's really grown and has made a positive impact on the community.

The speaker shared why people today have such a hard time sustaining marriage relationships. She described ten different stages of bonding between a husband and wife, each one serving a purpose. They included learning to talk on different levels, holding hands, listening, hugging, etc. Each stage builds the relationship deeper in intimacy toward the "peak": the culmination of the marital physical relationship. Because sex has been so heavily promoted in today's society, people tend to just skip over these other important stages, thinking that intimacy is all about intercourse. They don't realize that they can't just have sex all day, every day! Thus, marriages break down over time because the couples hadn't established these other stages of bonding for intimacy in their relationships. A marriage can't last if sex is the only thing holding it together!

It's the same in our relationship with God. As the bride of Christ, there are times of special intimacy (and praise God for them), but we can't limit our entire relationship to the royal bedchambers!

I've had incredible supernatural experiences with God, but I don't talk about them publicly very much. I've been caught up in the spirit and gone somewhere for long periods of time. God has done some really awesome things in my life. However, if I shared about these more, people would try to make a doctrine out of them. These things happened years apart. In fact, it's probably been over a decade since I've had one of those overwhelming supernatural experiences.

"Well now, Andrew, it's a shame your relationship with God has cooled off so much." Cooled off? Not on your life! My relationship with God is deeper and more intimate than ever before. I'm still green and growing! You just have to learn how to enjoy God.

DON'T MISS OUT!

Recently I spent an entire weekend at home, which is a rare treat for me. The whole time, I wandered around our property, praising God for every type of flower He's blessed us all with. They're beautiful and I told Him so! God is pleased with that. I also thanked Him for the recent good weather. And it was the greenest it had ever been!

The reason that's such a blessing to me is because forest fires forced us from our mountainside home a while ago. Although we spent two and a half weeks evacuated from our house, the Lord saw to it that the fire stopped one mile away. Because our house is over a ridge, my view isn't even affected. Praise God!

You just need to learn how to fellowship with God in the midst of everyday life. Do you know how to appreciate Him in the small things? Are you always trying to do something earthshaking or monumental to build your intimacy with Him? You can't sustain your relationship that way. Adam and Eve walked in the cool of the Garden with God. I'm sure their conversations consisted of "Father, I saw a flower today that I've never seen before. You did a great job!" That's prayer. It's communion with God. Don't miss out on who the Lord is by making your relationship with Him too intense!

Outline

I. We can use Jesus' model prayer to learn the "sandwich technique" of praying.

    A. Christ's model prayer started with praise: *"Our Father which art in heaven, Hallowed be thy name"* and ended with praise: *"For thine is the kingdom, and the power, and the glory, for ever. Amen"* (Matt. 6:9 and 13).

    B. We should start our prayers thanking God, praising Him, and declaring how big He is.

    C. Then, we can slide in our petitions and end by praising Him some more.

    D. When we pray this way, we'll discover that we don't really have that much to ask Him for.

II. Whatever we focus on in prayer will magnify in our eyes.

    A. So, instead of focusing on our problems, we should focus on God (our solution), and then our vision of Him will increase.

    B. Most of our prayer time should be spent praising God, not telling Him about our problems.

    C. Praise is important because it blesses God, because it strengthens us, and because the Lord inhabits the praises of His people (Ps. 22:3).

III. God is a Person, and we should treat our relationship with Him as we do other relationships we want to develop.

    A. God wants us to spend time with Him because we want to, not because we have to.

    B. Just like with our other relationships, it takes time to build a strong relationship with God.

    C. Intimate relationships must be developed over time, whether with God or anyone else.

IV. We must be careful not to become addicted to God's spectacular experiences.

  A. The Lord delights in using subtle ways to reveal Himself, and He won't always come to us in a spectacular manner.

  B. Jesus described Himself as *"meek and lowly in heart"* (Matt. 11:29).

  C. God wants us to respond to Him by faith, not by always having to see the spectacular.

V. We don't always have to be in a heightened emotional state to pray.

  A. There will be times of special intimacy with God, but we shouldn't limit our experiences with Him to these times.

  B. These occasions make up an important part of our relationship with God, but only a small part of the whole.

  C. It's most important that we learn how to fellowship with God in the midst of everyday life.

  D. We should work on learning to appreciate Him in the small things and not always try to do something earthshaking or monumental to build our intimacy with Him.

Teacher's Guide

1.   We can use Jesus' model prayer to learn the "sandwich technique" of praying. Christ's model prayer started with praise: *"Our Father which art in heaven, Hallowed be thy name"* and ended with praise: *"For thine is the kingdom, and the power, and the glory, for ever. Amen"* (Matt. 6:9 and 13). We should start our prayers thanking God, praising Him, and declaring how big He is. Then, we can slide in our petitions and end by praising Him some more. When we pray this way, we'll discover that we don't really have that much to ask Him for.

1a.   What is the "sandwich technique" of praying?
Start and end your prayers with praise and put your requests in the middle
1b.   What will you find when you approach God with this type of prayer?
That you don't really have that much to ask Him for

2.   Whatever we focus on in prayer will magnify in our eyes. So, instead of focusing on our problems, we should focus on God (our solution), and then our vision of Him will increase. Most of our prayer time should be spent praising God, not telling Him about our problems. Praise is important because it blesses God, because it strengthens us, and because the Lord inhabits the praises of His people (Ps. 22:3).

2a.   What will magnify in your eyes?
Whatever you focus on
2b.   What should and shouldn't you focus on in prayer?
You should focus on God, not on your problems

3.   God is a Person, and we should treat our relationship with Him as we do other relationships we want to develop. God wants us to spend time with Him because we want to, not because we have to. Just like with our other relationships, it takes time to build a strong relationship with God. Intimate relationships must be developed over time, whether with God or anyone else.

3a.   How should you treat your relationship with God?
As you do other relationships you want to develop
3b.   How must an intimate relationship be developed, whether it's with God or anyone else?
Over time

4.   We must be careful not to become addicted to God's spectacular experiences. The Lord delights in using subtle ways to reveal Himself, and He won't always come to us in a spectacular manner. Jesus described Himself as "meek and lowly in heart" (Matt. 11:29). God wants us to respond to Him by faith, not by always having to see the spectacular.

4a.   Read Matthew 11:29. How does Jesus' description of Himself express how He wants to reveal Himself to you?
       In subtle, not always spectacular, ways

4b.   How does God want you to respond to Him?
       By faith

5.   We don't always have to be in a heightened emotional state to pray. There will be times of special intimacy with God, but we shouldn't limit our experiences with Him to these times. These occasions make up an important part of our relationship with God, but only a small part of the whole. It's most important that we learn how to fellowship with God in the midst of everyday life. We should work on learning to appreciate Him in the small things and not always try to do something earthshaking or monumental to build our intimacy with Him.

5a.   What part of your relationship with God do special times of intimacy play?
       An important but small part

5b.   In learning to appreciate God, what things should you work on?
       The small things

Discipleship Questions

1.   What is the "sandwich technique" of praying?

2.   What will you find when you approach God with this type of prayer?

3.   What will magnify in your eyes?

4.   What should and shouldn't you focus on in prayer?

5.   How should you treat your relationship with God?

6.   How must an intimate relationship be developed, whether it's with God or anyone else?

7.   Read Matthew 11:29. How does Jesus' description of Himself express how He wants to reveal Himself to you?

8.   How does God want you to respond to Him?

9.   What part of your relationship with God do special times of intimacy play?

10. In learning to appreciate God, what things should you work on?

Answer Key

1. Start and end your prayers with praise and put your requests in the middle

2. That you don't really have that much to ask Him for

3. Whatever you focus on

4. You should focus on God, not on your problems

5. As you do other relationships you want to develop

6. Over time

7. In subtle, not always spectacular, ways

8. By faith

9. An important but small part

10. The small things

Scriptures

MATTHEW 6:9

After this manner therefore pray ye: Our Father which art in heaven, Hallowed be thy name.

MATTHEW 6:13

And lead us not into temptation, but deliver us from evil: For thine is the kingdom, and the power, and the glory, for ever. Amen.

PSALM 22:3

But thou art holy, O thou that inhabitest the praises of Israel.

MATTHEW 11:29

Take my yoke upon you, and learn of me; for I am meek and lowly in heart: and ye shall find rest unto your souls.

MAKE A PRAYER SANDWICH!

Begging from God

And it came to pass, that, as he was praying in a certain place, when he ceased, one of his disciples said unto him, Lord, teach us to pray, as John also taught his disciples.

While Matthew 6:9-13 is commonly called "The Lord's Prayer," Luke 11:2-4 offers it again in abbreviated form:

And he said unto them, When ye pray, say, Our Father which art in heaven, Hallowed be thy name. Thy kingdom come. Thy will be done, as in heaven, so in earth. [3] Give us day by day our daily bread. [4] And forgive us our sins; for we also forgive every one that is indebted to us. And lead us not into temptation; but deliver us from evil.

Then, in verses 5-8, Jesus shared a parable that's commonly used to teach prayer. However, what's most often taught is exactly opposite of what the Lord meant!

And he said unto them, Which of you shall have a friend, and shall go unto him at midnight, and say unto him, Friend, lend me three loaves; [6] For a friend of mine in his journey is come to me, and I have nothing to set before him? [7] And he from within shall answer and say, Trouble me not: the door is now shut, and my children are with me in bed; I cannot rise and give thee.[8] I say unto you, Though he will not rise and give him, because he is his friend, yet because of his importunity he will rise and give him as many as he needeth.

This passage is commonly taught that God is like this "friend": You must go to Him when you have a need, but when you first ask for it to be met, He may answer "No" or "I'm not ready." Therefore, you must stay after God, badgering Him and persistently praying your request over and over again until you make Him give you what you need. Sometimes this is called "importunity in prayer." Basically, you must bombard the gates of heaven until they open.

Another twist on this same idea teaches that "God won't answer your prayer by yourself; you need to involve other people. By bombarding heaven with a hundred million others, God will finally be forced to let go and give us revival!" Even though many Christians actually believe this, it's not what this parable is saying.

CONTRAST, NOT COMPARISON

Jesus was making a contrast, not a comparison. Do you have a "friend" like that? If you went to his or her house at midnight seeking help for an urgent need, would that friend deny you simply because it's inconvenient? Would he or she answer you from the window, "I'm in bed. My spouse and kids are sleeping. Go away and leave me alone!" That's no friend! Friends don't treat each other that callously. An acquaintance might, but not a friend.

The Lord used this physical example to show that if a friend would treat you better than this, why would you think God must be badgered, begged, and pled with to meet your need? Why would your heavenly Father, who sent His Son to bear your sin and who loves you infinitely more than anyone else ever could, treat you worse than a selfish human being?

You probably wouldn't expect a friend to treat you this badly! And if you think God would, you have more faith that people will treat you better than God. The whole point of the parable is that God won't treat you this badly (Luke 11:9-13). It's a contrast!

I use this logic all the time. My friend Don Krow and I ministered to a man on his deathbed nearly every day for several months. This guy had trouble believing that God would heal him. His compassionate wife kept praying and crying over him. Finally, one day I just asked, "Do you think that if your wife had the ability to heal you, she'd withhold it just because you didn't read your Bible or you weren't the man that you should've been? Do you think there's anything in your life that you haven't done right that would cause her to just let you die?"

Offended, he answered, "No way! She'd do anything, even die for me if she could!"

"And you think God Almighty loves you less than your wife!"

This fellow had more faith in his spouse's love for him than in God's. That's the very attitude Jesus was challenging through this parable.

INSULTING GOD

God is not like this "friend" who must be badgered. "You need to grab hold of God and not let go until He gives you what you're asking for!" No! That's against God's character. It's an insult to Him. Yet this very attitude has been widely taught and practiced as "prayer." "You just have to stay after God and make Him do it." You aren't going to make God do anything!

If the Lord hasn't already supplied your need by grace, your faith can't make Him do it. Contrary to popular belief, faith does not move God. He's not the one who's stuck! Neither does He need to "move." God has already done everything! The Lord is never taken by surprise, because He established the supply long before you ever had the need. It's not like He has to go out and do something to provide your answer. Since He's already done His part, you don't have to beg and plead.

God has already done it! He's not up there in heaven with His arms folded, demanding, "Beg a little harder; you're not serious yet. Once you've suffered enough, then I'll answer…maybe!" That may be the perception you have, but God's not like that. He's trying to get His blessings to you!

If the Lord didn't need our cooperation to see His power manifest, there'd be zero sickness on earth today. Nobody would wear eyeglasses, suffer allergies, or even endure a cold. God is so willing to meet all of our needs that He's already done it. He's trying to get His healing to us. He's trying to bless every last one of us!

God wants revival more than we do! We don't have to plead with Him to pour out His power. The way we've been taught to beg in "prayer" is absolutely wrong.

"Let's pray for revival. We need to ask God to pour out His Spirit!" Do you realize what that's saying? It implies that God is responsible for the dead condition of the church. If He wanted to, He could just pour out His Spirit, and miracles would start happening, people would be revived, churches would fill up, the government would improve, and cycles of destruction would reverse. "All God needs to do is lift His little finger!" Wrong!

NOT TICKED OFF!

God's not holding anything back! He isn't saying, "I'm not going to bless America, because you haven't done what I wanted. You removed prayer from schools and the Ten Commandments from public buildings—see if I'll move!" God's not like that. He's doing everything He can to bless our country. It's not a matter of begging Him to become motivated; He already is. "But we must pray and beseech God to pour out His Spirit!" That's slander. He already did (Acts 2:1-4)! "God's not moving because He's ticked off at us due to sin. We need to plead for His mercy!" Wrong! Jesus loves us and He's not ticked off!

I used to preach, "If God doesn't judge America, He'll have to apologize to Sodom and Gomorrah!" Now I boldly declare, "If God judges America, He'll have to apologize to Jesus!" The destruction of Sodom and Gomorrah happened before the cross, but since then, Christ has atoned for sin. There's a big difference between then and now. God is not ready to judge this nation.

Since God isn't going to judge us, does that mean we're safe, secure, and problem free? No, we ruin ourselves by giving place to the devil. If America doesn't turn around from going in this wrong direction, there's far worse ahead. But it's not God who's causing the tragedy, forsaking us, or withholding His Spirit. We've turned our backs on Him. Yes, we must repent and turn from our self-destructive ways, but we don't need to plead with God to pour out His Spirit all over again. Can you see the difference?

Outline

I.   Matthew 6:9-13 is commonly called "The Lord's Prayer," and Luke 11:2-4 offers it again in abbreviated form.

   A.   Immediately afterward, Jesus shared a parable often used to teach about prayer (Luke 11:5-8).

   B.   However, what's most often taught is exactly opposite of what the Lord meant!

   C.   It's taught that God is like the "friend" in the parable, and we have to beg Him to answer our prayers.

   D.   But Jesus was making a contrast, trying to show that God would never treat us as badly as the "friend" in the parable (Luke 11:9-13).

II.   It's an insult to God to think we have to badger Him to do something.

   A.   If the Lord hasn't already supplied our need by grace, our faith can't make Him do it.

   B.   Contrary to popular belief, faith does not move God.

   C.   God has already done everything and met all of our needs.

      i.   Since He's already done His part, we don't have to beg and plead.

   D.   He's trying to get His blessings to us, but we have to cooperate with Him to see His power manifest.

III.   We are taught that we must pray and beseech God to pour out His Spirit—that's slander because He already did (Acts 2:1-4).

   A.   God's not holding anything back!

   B.   God's not mad at us because of our sin, and we don't have to plead for His mercy.

C. He's doing everything He can to bless our country.

D. But, although God isn't going to judge us, we're not safe and secure.

E. We ruin ourselves by giving place to the devil.

F. We must repent and turn from our self-destructive ways, but we don't need to plead with God to pour out His Spirit all over again.

Teacher's Guide

1.   Matthew 6:9-13 is commonly called "The Lord's Prayer," and Luke 11:2-4 offers it again in abbreviated form. Immediately afterward, Jesus shared a parable often used to teach about prayer (Luke 11:5-8). However, what's most often taught is exactly opposite of what the Lord meant! It's taught that God is like the "friend" in the parable, and we have to beg Him to answer our prayers. But Jesus was making a contrast, trying to show that God would never treat us as badly as the "friend" in the parable (Luke 11:9-13).

1a.   Read Matthew 6:9-13 and Luke 11:1-13. What was Jesus trying to do by teaching these two passages?
Make a contrast

1b.   What is the whole point of the parable in Luke 11:5-8?
That God won't treat you as badly as the "friend" in the parable

2.   It's an insult to God to think we have to badger Him to do something. If the Lord hasn't already supplied our need by grace, our faith can't make Him do it. Contrary to popular belief, faith does not move God. God has already done everything and met all of our needs. Since He's already done His part, we don't have to beg and plead. He's trying to get His blessings to us, but we have to cooperate with Him to see His power manifest.

2a.   Thinking that you have to badger God to make Him do something does what to Him?
Insults Him

2b.   Why don't you ever have to beg and plead with God to get Him to answer your prayers?
Because He's already done His part

3.   We are taught that we must pray and beseech God to pour out His Spirit—that's slander because He already did (Acts 2:1-4). God's not holding anything back! God's not mad at us because of our sin, and we don't have to plead for His mercy. He's doing everything He can to bless our country. But, although God isn't going to judge us, we're not safe and secure. We ruin ourselves by giving place to the devil. We must repent and turn from our self-destructive ways, but we don't need to plead with God to pour out His Spirit all over again.

3a.   Is there ever a time when you have to pray for God's mercy because of your sin or your country's sins?
No

3b.   How are you ruining yourself?
By giving place to the devil

Discipleship Questions

1. Read Matthew 6:9-13 and Luke 11:1-13. What was Jesus trying to do by teaching these two passages?

2. What is the whole point of the parable in Luke 11:5-8?

3. Thinking that you have to badger God to make Him do something does what to Him?

4. Why don't you ever have to beg and plead with God to get Him to answer your prayers?

5. Is there ever a time when you have to pray for God's mercy because of your sin or your country's sins?

6. How are you ruining yourself?

Answer Key

1.   Make a contrast

2.   That God won't treat you as badly as the "friend" in the parable

3.   Insults Him

4.   Because He's already done His part

5.   No

6.   By giving place to the devil

Scriptures

LUKE 11:1-13

And it came to pass, that, as he was praying in a certain place, when he ceased, one of his disciples said unto him, Lord, teach us to pray, as John also taught his disciples. [2] And he said unto them, When ye pray, say, Our Father which art in heaven, Hallowed be thy name. Thy kingdom come. Thy will be done, as in heaven, so in earth. [3] Give us day by day our daily bread. [4] And forgive us our sins; for we also forgive every one that is indebted to us. And lead us not into temptation; but deliver us from evil. [5] And he said unto them, Which of you shall have a friend, and shall go unto him at midnight, and say unto him, Friend, lend me three loaves; [6] For a friend of mine in his journey is come to me, and I have nothing to set before him? [7] And he from within shall answer and say, Trouble me not: the door is now shut, and my children are with me in bed; I cannot rise and give thee. [8] I say unto you, Though he will not rise and give him, because he is his friend, yet because of his importunity he will rise and give him as many as he needeth. [9] And I say unto you, Ask, and it shall be given you; seek, and ye shall find; knock, and it shall be opened unto you. [10] For every one that asketh receiveth; and he that seeketh findeth; and to him that knocketh it shall be opened. [11] If a son shall ask bread of any of you that is a father, will he give him a stone? or if he ask a fish, will he for a fish give him a serpent? [12] Or if he shall ask an egg, will he offer him a scorpion? [13] If ye then, being evil, know how to give good gifts unto your children: how much more shall your heavenly Father give the Holy Spirit to them that ask him?

MATTHEW 6:9-13

After this manner therefore pray ye: Our Father which art in heaven, Hallowed be thy name. [10] Thy kingdom come. Thy will be done in earth, as it is in heaven. [11] Give us this day our daily bread. [12] And forgive us our debts, as we forgive our debtors. [13] And lead us not into temptation, but deliver us from evil: For thine is the kingdom, and the power, and the glory, for ever. Amen.

ACTS 2:1-4

And when the day of Pentecost was fully come, they were all with one accord in one place. [2] And suddenly there came a sound from heaven as of a rushing mighty wind, and it filled all the house where they were sitting. [3] And there appeared unto them cloven tongues like as of fire, and it sat upon each of them. [4] And they were all filled with the Holy Ghost, and began to speak with other tongues, as the Spirit gave them utterance.

BEGGING FROM GOD

"Repent, God, Repent!"

M ost Christians believe that the only difference between the Old Testament and the New is one blank page in the Bible. They don't understand that the establishment of the New Covenant made a huge difference in the way everything works, including prayer!

In Genesis 18, God visited Abraham and promised him some tremendous blessings. Then He told him that He was planning to destroy Sodom and Gomorrah. God sent His two accompanying angels there to scout things out. Sodom and Gomorrah were on the verge of judgment.

Standing before the Lord,

> *Abraham drew near, and said, Wilt thou also destroy the righteous with the wicked?*
> *[24] Peradventure there be fifty righteous within the city: wilt thou also destroy and*
> *not spare the place for the fifty righteous that are therein? [25] That be far from thee*
> *to do after this manner, to slay the righteous with the wicked: and that the righteous*
> *should be as the wicked, that be far from thee: Shall not the Judge of all the earth*
> *do right?*
>
> GENESIS 18:23-25

Abraham was pretty bold to talk to God this way! "Aren't You better than this? Don't You have more integrity? Would You really do something that bad? It just wouldn't be right!" This is definitely not a good way for us to pray.

A DIFFERENT COVENANT

Abraham got by with this because it was a different covenant; Jesus hadn't yet atoned for man. However, it's wrong for a New Testament believer to plead with God this way. The Lord was angry at sin in the Old Covenant, so it was okay for Abraham to do this. But to apply this Old Testament example to us today, saying "God's mad! If our nation doesn't repent, He's going to judge us!" is simply not true. Yes, He judged Sodom and Gomorrah, but no, God's not going to do the same thing today.

Many voices called the terrorist attacks on September 11, 2001, God's judgment on America for our many national sins. "God has given us a warning. If we don't repent, then He's going to do widespread terrible things!" No, He's not.

At the time of Sodom and Gomorrah, the Lord's wrath toward sin hadn't yet been satisfied. Therefore, He judged them and did other similar things in the Old Testament. However, Jesus Christ made a huge difference! Now we're in the New Covenant, and God's anger toward sin has been appeased.

"TURN FROM YOUR FIERCE WRATH, O LORD!"

Abraham was acting as a mediator. Mediators stand in between and seek to peacefully reconcile two opposing parties who are angry and have a dispute with each other. God was holy, but man was unholy. Due to this, God's justice needed to be satisfied. Under the Old Covenant, it was right for Him to release His wrath. In order to show mercy, God had to have "intercessors" like Abraham pray, "Turn from Your fierce wrath, O Lord!"

It's amazing that Almighty God would even consider such a request, but the Lord loved this man Abraham and had a covenant with him. God didn't honor and bless him because he deserved it. On two occasions, Abraham willingly let a man take his wife and almost commit adultery with her just to spare his own hide. If he would've done something like that today, we'd consider him a scoundrel. Even though Abraham made serious mistakes, God had given him His word, and He honored it!

Abraham asked, "Lord, if You find fifty righteous in Sodom and Gomorrah, would You still destroy the entire city?"

God answered, "Nope! If there are fifty righteous there, I won't do it."

"How about forty? Thirty? Twenty?"

"If there are twenty righteous there, I won't do it."

"How about ten?" Abraham finally negotiated God down to ten and stopped there. However, it turned out that Lot was the only righteous person living in all of Sodom and Gomorrah, so God went ahead and destroyed them all except Lot's immediate family. But in the process, He had supernaturally responded to Abraham's intercession!

"GET OUT OF MY WAY"

Moses did the same thing (Ex. 32:9-14). Furious, God declared, *"Now therefore let me alone, that my wrath may wax hot against them, and that I may consume them: and I will make of thee a great nation"* (Ex. 32:10). Basically, the Lord said, "Moses, get out of My way! Leave Me alone so I can destroy all of these people. I'll start over and use you to make a brand-new nation!"

"REPENT, GOD, REPENT!"

There are some powerful things here. God told Moses to leave Him alone so He could do what He wanted. Subtly, the Lord was acknowledging that Moses had power with Him. If Moses pled for mercy, he would keep God from executing His wrath.

And Moses besought the LORD his God, and said, LORD, why doth thy wrath wax hot against thy people, which thou hast brought forth out of the land of Egypt with great power, and with a mighty hand? [12] Wherefore should the Egyptians speak, and say, For mischief did he bring them out, to slay them in the mountains, and to consume them from the face of the earth? Turn from thy fierce wrath, and repent of this evil against thy people.

EXODUS 32:11-12

THE LORD REPENTED!

Moses told God, "Repent!" What nerve! Do you know what's even more amazing? *"And the LORD repented of the evil which he thought to do unto his people"* (Ex. 32:14). A mere man said, "God, repent! Don't You realize that the Egyptians will hear what happened and say that You were able to deliver Your people out of Egypt, but You couldn't take them into the Promised Land, that You're just too weak? This isn't going to look good on Your resumé. God, repent!" And He did!

"Intercessors" today contend, "That's what we're doing. We're praying, 'O God, repent from Your fierce wrath. Don't pour out Your judgment on our country!'" They teach that God's ticked off because of the sin in people's lives, and He's ready to judge the nation. They believe the Lord won't heal people until they grovel in the dirt or repent, or an "intercessor" pleads for mercy. Basically, they say they have to approach God like He's the grumpy, inconvenienced, sleeping "friend" in Luke 11:5-8 who's reluctant to lend them three loaves of bread for their guest at midnight: "Don't bother Me. I'm ticked off at you. You haven't been seeking Me, so you deserve whatever you get!" Therefore, since God isn't prone to answer, they believe they must beg, plead, and badger Him until He pours out His Spirit. That's absolutely the wrong attitude in prayer!

To one degree or another, everyone has been influenced by this erroneous view. Praying with an adversarial, demanding, self-righteous attitude toward the Lord is totally offensive to Him. Why? Because that's not trust in Christ or believing what He's already done.

REBELLION JUDGED

Korah, Dathan, and Abiram openly challenged Moses' authority. Finally, he shouted out in anger, "If these people die a natural death, then you will know that God did not send me. But if a brand-new thing happens so that the earth opens up and swallows them alive, them and everything that belongs to them, then you'll know that I am a true man of God" (Num. 16:28-30). That's quite a test!

A BETTER WAY TO PRAY

Immediately, the earth opened up and swallowed Korah, Dathan, Abiram, all who followed them, their families, and their possessions, and then closed in again upon them. The rest of the people present took off running in sheer terror!

However, the very next day, all of the Israelites assembled. Mad at Moses, they accused him, saying, "You killed the people of God!" As they criticized Moses, God's glory appeared in a cloud over the tabernacle. Moses saw it and informed Aaron, "God's upset!" Again, the Lord instructed Moses, "Get out of My way so that I can destroy these people" (Num. 16:41-45).

Moses told Aaron to get a censer and put some coals from the fire in it (incense represents the sweet-smelling aroma of prayer rising up before the Lord). "Run into the people and stand between the living and the dead. Then the plague will stop!" As Aaron ran into the crowd and past the dead, he finally stood in front of the plague. When it came up to the censer Aaron was holding, the plague was stayed, God's wrath was appeased, and the rest of the Israelites were spared (Num. 16:46-50).

I've actually heard people use this very scripture to preach, "God's wrath is poured out and destruction has begun. If we as intercessors, like Abraham and Moses, will stand and pray 'Turn from Your fierce wrath,' we can stop God from pouring out His judgment and preserve this nation!" Basically, that's what is being taught and called "prayer." It's absolutely wrong!

ANDREW'S RECOMMENDATIONS FOR FURTHER STUDY

For an in-depth study of the truth that Christ's atonement has completely satisfied the wrath of God toward sin, please refer to my teaching entitled *The War Is Over*.

Outline

I. Most of us as Christians don't understand that the establishment of the New Covenant made a huge difference in the way everything works, including prayer!

    A. Abraham was able to beg and plead with God (Gen. 18:23-25) because it was a different covenant then; Jesus hadn't yet atoned for our sins.

    B. The Lord was angry at sin in the Old Covenant, so it was okay for Abraham to pray the way he did.

    C. At the time of Sodom and Gomorrah, the Lord's wrath toward sin hadn't yet been satisfied.

    D. Now we're in the New Covenant, and God's anger toward sin has been appeased.

II. Abraham and Moses (Ex. 32:9-14) both acted as mediators.

    A. Mediators seek to peacefully reconcile two opposing parties who have a dispute with each other.

    B. Abraham and Moses each negotiated with God not to destroy the people.

    C. Moses went so far as to tell God to repent—and He did!

III. Many of us as Christians today believe we still must beg, plead, and badger God until He answers our prayers.

    A. Praying with an adversarial, demanding, self-righteous attitude toward the Lord today (like Moses did in Num. 16:28-50) is totally offensive to Him because it means we aren't trusting in what Jesus has already done.

    B. Much of what is taught about prayer and intercession today is a totally wrong way for New Testament believers to pray.

    C. We no longer have to beg God to turn from His wrath.

ANDREW'S RECOMMENDATIONS FOR FURTHER STUDY

For an in-depth study of the truth that Christ's atonement has completely satisfied the wrath of God toward sin, please refer to my teaching entitled *The War Is Over.*

Teacher's Guide

1.   Most of us as Christians don't understand that the establishment of the New Covenant made a huge difference in the way everything works, including prayer! Abraham was able to beg and plead with God (Gen. 18:23-25) because it was a different covenant then; Jesus hadn't yet atoned for our sins. The Lord was angry at sin in the Old Covenant, so it was okay for Abraham to pray the way he did. At the time of Sodom and Gomorrah, the Lord's wrath toward sin hadn't yet been satisfied. Now we're in the New Covenant, and God's anger toward sin has been appeased.

1a.   Read Genesis 18:23-25. Why was it okay for Abraham to pray the way he did?
He was under a different covenant, and Jesus hadn't yet atoned for sin; the Lord was angry at sin in the Old Covenant

1b.   In the New Covenant, what has been appeased?
God's anger toward sin

2.   Abraham and Moses (Ex. 32:9-14) both acted as mediators. Mediators seek to peacefully reconcile two opposing parties who have a dispute with each other. Abraham and Moses each negotiated with God not to destroy the people. Moses went so far as to tell God to repent— and He did!

2a.   How were Abraham and Moses acting as mediators?
They stood between God and the people to keep God from destroying them

2b.   What happened when Moses told God to repent?
He did

3.   Many of us as Christians today believe we still must beg, plead, and badger God until He answers our prayers. Praying with an adversarial, demanding, self-righteous attitude toward the Lord today (like Moses did in Num. 16:28-50) is totally offensive to Him because it means we aren't trusting in what Jesus has already done. Much of what is taught about prayer and intercession today is a totally wrong way for New Testament believers to pray. We no longer have to beg God to turn from His wrath.

3a.   Read Numbers 16:28-50. What is totally offensive to the Lord?
Praying with an adversarial, demanding, and self-righteous attitude toward Him

3b.   What's wrong with much of the teaching on prayer and intercession today?
It teaches that you have to beg God to turn from His wrath

Discipleship Questions

1. Read Genesis 18:23-25. Why was it okay for Abraham to pray the way he did?

2. In the New Covenant, what has been appeased?

3. How were Abraham and Moses acting as mediators?

4. What happened when Moses told God to repent?

5. Read Numbers 16:28-50. What is totally offensive to the Lord?

6. What's wrong with much of the teaching on prayer and intercession today?

"REPENT, GOD, REPENT!"

Answer Key

1. He was under a different covenant, and Jesus hadn't yet atoned for sin; the Lord was angry at sin in the Old Covenant

2. God's anger toward sin

3. They stood between God and the people to keep God from destroying them

4. He did

5. Praying with an adversarial, demanding, and self-righteous attitude toward Him

6. It teaches that you have to beg God to turn from His wrath

Scriptures

GENESIS 18:23-25

And Abraham drew near, and said, Wilt thou also destroy the righteous with the wicked? [24] Peradventure there be fifty righteous within the city: wilt thou also destroy and not spare the place for the fifty righteous that are therein? [25] That be far from thee to do after this manner, to slay the righteous with the wicked: and that the righteous should be as the wicked, that be far from thee: Shall not the Judge of all the earth do right?

EXODUS 32:9-14

And the Lord said unto Moses, I have seen this people, and, behold, it is a stiffnecked people: [10] Now therefore let me alone, that my wrath may wax hot against them, and that I may consume them: and I will make of thee a great nation. [11] And Moses besought the Lord his God, and said, Lord, why doth thy wrath wax hot against thy people, which thou hast brought forth out of the land of Egypt with great power, and with a mighty hand? [12] Wherefore should the Egyptians speak, and say, For mischief did he bring them out, to slay them in the mountains, and to consume them from the face of the earth? Turn from thy fierce wrath, and repent of this evil against thy people. [13] Remember Abraham, Isaac, and Israel, thy servants, to whom thou swarest by thine own self, and saidst unto them, I will multiply your seed as the stars of heaven, and all this land that I have spoken of will I give unto your seed, and they shall inherit it for ever. [14] And the Lord repented of the evil which he thought to do unto his people.

LUKE 11:5-8

And he said unto them, Which of you shall have a friend, and shall go unto him at midnight, and say unto him, Friend, lend me three loaves; [6] For a friend of mine in his journey is come to me, and I have nothing to set before him? [7] And he from within shall answer and say, Trouble me not: the door is now shut, and my children are with me in bed; I cannot rise and give thee. [8] I say unto you, Though he will not rise and give him, because he is his friend, yet because of his importunity he will rise and give him as many as he needeth.

NUMBERS 16:28-30

And Moses said, Hereby ye shall know that the Lord hath sent me to do all these works; for I have not done them of mine own mind. [29] If these men die the common death of all men, or if they be visited after the visitation of all men; then the Lord hath not sent me. [30] But if the Lord make a new thing, and the earth open her mouth, and swallow them up, with all that appertain unto them, and they go down quick into the pit; then ye shall understand that these men have provoked the Lord.

NUMBERS 16:41-50

But on the morrow all the congregation of the children of Israel murmured against Moses and against Aaron, saying, Ye have killed the people of the LORD. [42] And it came to pass, when the congregation was gathered against Moses and against Aaron, that they looked toward the tabernacle of the congregation: and, behold, the cloud covered it, and the glory of the LORD appeared. [43] And Moses and Aaron came before the tabernacle of the congregation. [44] And the LORD spake unto Moses, saying, [45] Get you up from among this congregation, that I may consume them as in a moment. And they fell upon their faces. [46] And Moses said unto Aaron, Take a censer, and put fire therein from off the altar, and put on incense, and go quickly unto the congregation, and make an atonement for them: for there is wrath gone out from the LORD; the plague is begun. [47] And Aaron took as Moses commanded, and ran into the midst of the congregation; and, behold, the plague was begun among the people: and he put on incense, and made an atonement for the people. [48] And he stood between the dead and the living; and the plague was stayed. [49] Now they that died in the plague were fourteen thousand and seven hundred, beside them that died about the matter of Korah. [50] And Aaron returned unto Moses unto the door of the tabernacle of the congregation: and the plague was stayed.

"REPENT, GOD, REPENT!"

Jesus: The Only Mediator

If you understand 1 Timothy 2:1-5, it'll change the way you pray. Notice that the beginning is obviously talking about prayer:

I exhort therefore, that, first of all, supplications, prayers, intercessions, and giving of thanks, be made for all men; [2] For kings, and for all that are in authority; that we may lead a quiet and peaceable life in all godliness and honesty. [3] For this is good and acceptable in the sight of God our Saviour; [4] Who will have all men to be saved, and to come unto the knowledge of the truth. [5] For there is one God, and one mediator between God and men, the man Christ Jesus.

EMPHASIS MINE

In the New Covenant, Jesus is the only mediator who stands between God the Father and mankind. Sin is no longer a problem with God because it's been atoned for. God's not angry. He's not ready to destroy our country like He did Sodom and Gomorrah. Abraham interceded for God to spare the city and negotiated Him down to only ten righteous people. Don't you think Jesus could do at least that well? Don't you think that Jesus could intercede and negotiate with God at least as well as Abraham? If Abraham could make Him willing to spare Sodom and Gomorrah for only ten righteous individuals, then God has been totally appeased through His Son. Jesus Christ is now the only mediator between God and man!

It was also appropriate for Moses to pray the way he did because Jesus hadn't come yet, God's wrath wasn't appeased, and sin had to be judged. However, Christ has since borne the judgment for all sin. It wasn't only for the past sins back in His day and before, but also for our day. He took the judgment not only for our past and present sins but also for our future sins as well. Jesus suffered the wrath of God for all sin and was separated from the Father on our behalf. Now He's the only mediator between God and us. If we try to be mediators like Moses or Abraham today, we are antichrist; i.e., against Christ, against His finished work, and attempting to take His place!

If you pray "O God, please have mercy. Don't pour out Your wrath!" you have just pushed the Lord aside and declared, "Jesus, I know that You atoned for us and that You dealt with sin. The Word says You are the only mediator, but I think I can help. It's also going to take my pleading and interceding to make things right!"—you're trying to add to what Jesus has already done! Jesus + anything = nothing. Jesus + nothing = everything. By attempting to intercede the way Abraham and Moses did—the way others in the Old Testament did—you aren't esteeming what Christ has done, and you're trying to become a mediator.

"WHAT HAVE YOU DONE WITH JESUS?"

The vast majority of examples and models of prayer we've been given, especially for "intercession and spiritual warfare," all go back to the Old Covenant. They're awesome examples, but not for us today! God's not ticked off or even in a bad mood. He's happy and blessed. His family is growing, and His kingdom advances daily! God's wrath toward sin was poured out on His Son. He's not angry at people anymore, because His justice was satisfied through the Lamb's perfect sacrifice.

Since God's not angry, should we still preach? Of course! God has made the provision available, but people must believe and receive for themselves. If they don't, then the wrath and judgment remain (John 3:36) because those who don't accept Jesus as their Savior will go to hell.

God prepared hell for the devil and his angels, not for man (Matt. 25:41). However, those who choose to identify with the devil and refuse to accept salvation by grace through faith (and try to work it out on their own instead) will partake of Satan's judgment. God never intended this. He doesn't will for people to go to hell, but He is just. If people don't accept God's payment in Christ, they'll go there.

Individual sins (committing a sexually immoral act, doing drugs, getting drunk, etc.) aren't what send you to hell; your sins have been forgiven. But the sin that will send you to hell is not accepting the payment for those sins. Everything revolves around how you respond to Jesus.

When you arrive in heaven, God won't ask you, "What about this sin and that sin?" No, He'll want to know, "What have you done with Jesus?" Your relationship to Jesus Christ, whether you bowed your knee and made Him Lord or not, determines if you'll be accepted or rejected. At that time, those who refused Jesus will then be held accountable for their sins because they didn't accept God's payment. They'll be judged and will have to answer for those individual sins, but really the only issue is this: What have you done with Jesus?

ASK, SEEK, KNOCK

Jesus paid for sin and satisfied God's wrath, but the church as a whole doesn't understand this yet. They still perceive God like He was in the Old Testament: angry. They think they must intercede to stop Him from doing what He really wants to do, which is to judge people for their sins. They believe they still need to beg and plead with Him for mercy. That's absolutely wrong! God's Word in the New Testament reveals the depth of His love and forgiveness through Christ.

Prayer is not so you can turn God from His wrath. It's not so you can be like the persistent person on the street at midnight (Luke 11:5-8) who says, "I know You don't have to give it to me, but I won't leave until You bless me! I'm not going anywhere until You give me what I want! You said that by Your stripes, I am healed, so I'm not going to stop until You heal me!" That's simply not esteeming Christ. You don't even have a clue that God has already provided everything you need, including healing. He loves you and wants you to have it!

God is not like the so-called "friend" in Luke 11:5-8. Jesus was making a contrast! After giving the parable, He immediately pressed His point.

> *And I say unto you, Ask, and it shall be given you; seek, and ye shall find; knock, and it shall be opened unto you. [10] For every one that asketh receiveth; and he that seeketh findeth; and to him that knocketh it shall be opened.*
>
> LUKE 11:9-10

HOW MUCH MORE!

Jesus then illustrated this truth even further by using the same logic with another human relationship.

> *If a son shall ask bread of any of you that is a father, will he give him a stone? or if he ask a fish, will he for a fish give him a serpent? [12] Or if he shall ask an egg, will he offer him a scorpion? [13] If ye then, being evil, know how to give good gifts unto your children: how much more shall your heavenly Father give the Holy Spirit to them that ask him?*
>
> LUKE 11:11-13

Do you see what He's saying? If your son wanted a piece of bread, would you give him a stone? He'd bite into it and ruin his teeth! If your daughter requested an egg, would you hand her a scorpion? If they asked for a fish, would you answer by giving them a venomous snake? Of course not! If you wouldn't even consider treating your children so cruelly, why do you think God would refuse or even hesitate to meet your needs? On the contrary! "If you, being evil, know how to give good gifts to your children, how much more will your heavenly Father give the Holy Spirit to those who ask Him?"

Most people think that God is against meeting their needs. That's why they beg and plead with Him in "prayer"—because they believe He's ticked off at their ungodliness in His sight. They visualize God with His arms folded, putting them off, saying, "I'm not giving you anything!" So, they "pray" and stay after Him until He eventually "wears down" and has to answer them. "Don't let go until He gives you what you want!" No, Jesus taught the exact opposite! It's people who have twisted these verses and called it "importunity in prayer." What a rotten attitude!

ANDREW'S RECOMMENDATIONS FOR FURTHER STUDY

My teachings entitled *Redemption; The Gospel, the Power of God*; and *Whose Righteousness?* all amplify and expound upon this truth that because of Christ's atonement, sin is no longer a problem with God. The issue is whether or not we believe on Jesus and what He's done through His death, burial, and resurrection.

Outline

I. In the New Covenant, Jesus is the only mediator who stands between God the Father and mankind:

> *I exhort therefore, that, first of all, supplications, prayers, intercessions, and giving of thanks, be made for all men; [2] For kings, and for all that are in authority; that we may lead a quiet and peaceable life in all godliness and honesty. [3] For this is good and acceptable in the sight of God our Saviour; [4] Who will have all men to be saved, and to come unto the knowledge of the truth. [5] For there is one God, and one mediator between God and men, the man Christ Jesus.*
>
> 1 TIMOTHY 2:1-5, EMPHASIS MINE

A. Sin is no longer a problem with God because Christ has borne the judgment for all sin— past, present, and future.

B. Moses had to mediate in the Old Covenant because sin still had to be judged.

C. If we try to be mediators like Moses or Abraham today, we are antichrist: against Christ, against His finished work, and attempting to take His place!

D. Jesus Christ is now the *only* mediator between God and man.

II. God's not angry at people anymore because His justice was satisfied through Jesus' sacrifice.

A. But we still need to preach because, although God has made the provision available, people must believe and receive for themselves.

B. God didn't create hell for people (Matt. 25:41), and He doesn't want them to go there.

C. Wrath and judgment remain for those who don't accept Jesus as their Savior (John 3:36).

D. God has made His provision through Jesus, but people need to properly respond to Him.

III. Jesus paid for our sins and satisfied God's wrath, but not all of us understand this yet.

A. We still perceive God like He was in the Old Testament: angry.

B. We believe we still need to beg and plead with Him for His mercy.

C. But we no longer have to pray in order to turn God from His wrath.

D. He's already provided everything we need, including healing.

E. He loves us and wants us to have it.

IV. God is not like the so-called "friend" in Luke 11:5-8.

A. Jesus used this parable as a contrast, then pressed His point by saying,

And I say unto you, Ask, and it shall be given you; seek, and ye shall find; knock, and it shall be opened unto you. [10] For every one that asketh receiveth; and he that seeketh findeth; and to him that knocketh it shall be opened.

LUKE 11:9-10

B. He illustrated this truth even further by using the same logic with another human relationship (Luke 11:11-13).

C. If we wouldn't even consider treating our children so cruelly, why do we think God would refuse or even hesitate to meet our needs?

D. Most people beg and plead with God in "prayer" because they think that He's against meeting their needs.

E. But Jesus taught the exact opposite.

ANDREW'S RECOMMENDATIONS FOR FURTHER STUDY

My teachings entitled *Redemption; The Gospel, the Power of God;* and *Whose Righteousness?* all amplify and expound upon this truth that because of Christ's atonement, sin is no longer a problem with God. The issue is whether or not we believe on Jesus and what He's done through His death, burial, and resurrection.

Teacher's Guide

1.   In the New Covenant, Jesus is the only mediator who stands between God the Father and mankind:

> *I exhort therefore, that, first of all, supplications, prayers, intercessions, and giving of thanks, be made for all men; [2] For kings, and for all that are in authority; that we may lead a quiet and peaceable life in all godliness and honesty. [3] For this is good and acceptable in the sight of God our Saviour; [4] Who will have all men to be saved, and to come unto the knowledge of the truth. [5] For there is one God, and one mediator between God and men, the man Christ Jesus.*
>
> 1 TIMOTHY 2:1-5, EMPHASIS MINE

Sin is no longer a problem with God because Christ has borne the judgment for all sin—past, present, and future. Moses had to mediate in the Old Covenant because sin still had to be judged. If we try to be mediators like Moses or Abraham today, we are antichrist: against Christ, against His finished work, and attempting to take His place! Jesus Christ is now the *only* mediator between God and man.

1a.   Why is sin no longer a problem with God?
    Because Christ has borne the judgment for all sin—past, present, and future
1b.   What does it mean to be antichrist?
    Against Christ, against His finished work, and attempting to take His place

2.   God's not angry at people anymore because His justice was satisfied through Jesus' sacrifice. But we still need to preach because, although God has made the provision available, people must believe and receive for themselves. God didn't create hell for people (Matt. 25:41), and He doesn't want them to go there. Wrath and judgment remain for those who don't accept Jesus as their Savior (John 3:36). God has made His provision through Jesus, but people need to properly respond to Him.

2a.   If God's no longer angry, why is preaching still necessary?
    Because people must believe and receive for themselves
2b.   Read John 3:36. Who does God's wrath and judgment remain for?
    Those who don't accept Jesus as their Savior

3. Jesus paid for our sins and satisfied God's wrath, but not all of us understand this yet. We still perceive God like He was in the Old Testament: angry. We believe we still need to beg and plead with Him for His mercy. But we no longer have to pray in order to turn God from His wrath. He's already provided everything we need, including healing. He loves us and wants us to have it.

3a. What is it that you may not understand yet?
That Jesus paid for your sins and satisfied God's wrath

3b. Since God loves you and wants you to have everything you need, including healing, what does this imply He has turned from?
His wrath

4. God is not like the so-called "friend" in Luke 11:5-8. Jesus used this parable as a contrast, then pressed His point by saying,

And I say unto you, Ask, and it shall be given you; seek, and ye shall find; knock, and it shall be opened unto you. [10] For every one that asketh receiveth; and he that seeketh findeth; and to him that knocketh it shall be opened.

He illustrated this truth even further by using the same logic with another human relationship (Luke 11:11-13). If we wouldn't even consider treating our children so cruelly, why do we think God would refuse or even hesitate to meet our needs? Most people beg and plead with God in "prayer" because they think that He's against meeting their needs. But Jesus taught the exact opposite.

4a. Read Luke 11:5-8. Was Jesus comparing or contrasting God to the friend in this parable?
Contrasting

4b. If you, as an imperfect human parent, wouldn't even consider treating your children so cruelly, you shouldn't think that God, your heavenly Father, would refuse or even hesitate to do what?
Meet your needs

Discipleship Questions

1. Why is sin no longer a problem with God?

2. What does it mean to be antichrist?

3. If God's no longer angry, why is preaching still necessary?

4. Read John 3:36. Who does God's wrath and judgment remain for?

5. What is it that you may not understand yet?

6. Since God loves you and wants you to have everything you need, including healing, what does this imply He has turned from?

7. Read Luke 11:5-8. Was Jesus comparing or contrasting God to the friend in this parable?

8. If you, as an imperfect human parent, wouldn't even consider treating your children so cruelly, you shouldn't think that God, your heavenly Father, would refuse or even hesitate to do what?

Answer Key

1. Because Christ has borne the judgment for all sin—past, present, and future

2. Against Christ, against His finished work, and attempting to take His place

3. Because people must believe and receive for themselves

4. Those who don't accept Jesus as their Savior

5. That Jesus paid for your sins and satisfied God's wrath

6. His wrath

7. Contrasting

8. Meet your needs

Scriptures

1 TIMOTHY 2:1-5

I exhort therefore, that, first of all, supplications, prayers, intercessions, and giving of thanks, be made for all men; [2] For kings, and for all that are in authority; that we may lead a quiet and peaceable life in all godliness and honesty. [3] For this is good and acceptable in the sight of God our Saviour; [4] Who will have all men to be saved, and to come unto the knowledge of the truth. [5] For there is one God, and one mediator between God and men, the man Christ Jesus.

JOHN 3:36

He that believeth on the Son hath everlasting life: and he that believeth not the Son shall not see life; but the wrath of God abideth on him.

MATTHEW 25:41

Then shall he say also unto them on the left hand, Depart from me, ye cursed, into everlasting fire, prepared for the devil and his angels.

LUKE 11:5-13

And he said unto them, Which of you shall have a friend, and shall go unto him at midnight, and say unto him, Friend, lend me three loaves; [6] For a friend of mine in his journey is come to me, and I have nothing to set before him? [7] And he from within shall answer and say, Trouble me not: the door is now shut, and my children are with me in bed; I cannot rise and give thee. [8] I say unto you, Though he will not rise and give him, because he is his friend, yet because of his importunity he will rise and give him as many as he needeth. [9] And I say unto you, Ask, and it shall be given you; seek, and ye shall find; knock, and it shall be opened unto you. [10] For every one that asketh receiveth; and he that seeketh findeth; and to him that knocketh it shall be opened. [11] If a son shall ask bread of any of you that is a father, will he give him a stone? or if he ask a fish, will he for a fish give him a serpent? [12] Or if he shall ask an egg, will he offer him a scorpion? [13] If ye then, being evil, know how to give good gifts unto your children: how much more shall your heavenly Father give the Holy Spirit to them that ask him?

A Ploy of the Devil

Luke 18:1-8 is another passage often used to teach "importunity in prayer."

And he spake a parable unto them to this end, that men ought always to pray, and not to faint; [2] Saying, There was in a city a judge, which feared not God, neither regarded man: [3] And there was a widow in that city; and she came unto him, saying, Avenge me of mine adversary. [4] And he would not for a while: but afterward he said within himself, Though I fear not God, nor regard man; [5] Yet because this widow troubleth me, I will avenge her, lest by her continual coming she weary me.

LUKE 18:1-5

They teach that God is like this unjust judge who wasn't prone to answer the first time, but this woman just kept after him until he finally relented and said, "I must give her what she wants or she won't let me rest." They interpret this passage to mean that that's the way the Lord is. We have to go in, grab hold of the horns of the altar, and shake it until He comes out. We just have to make the power of God operate! That's not what this passage is saying. God is not like the unjust judge. This parable is another contrast, not a comparison!

Personally, I don't have much respect for our judicial system here in the United States. In recent years, they've been doing some serious reinterpreting of the Constitution. However, even these liberals would treat someone better than this. I just can't imagine something this bad, this far beyond reason, going on in our society today.

Jesus was using an absurd example to illustrate His point. Even if you could visualize such injustice happening, the woman wore him out until he finally gave in to her. In other words, you expect to receive better service from the imperfect judicial system than what you believe you're getting from the Lord. Most people put more faith in an earthly judge to treat them well! This parable shows the absurdity of such thinking.

ADVOCATE OR ADVERSARY?

And the Lord said, Hear what the unjust judge saith. [7] And shall not God avenge his own elect, which cry day and night unto him, though he bear long with them?

LUKE 18:6-7

Some people interpret these verses to mean that God will avenge you, but He'll *"bear long"* with you first. They say, "Sometimes it takes Him a while. You just have to ask and ask, but eventually He'll answer." If that's the way to interpret this, then verse 8 means the passage makes no sense at all!

I tell you that he will avenge them speedily. Nevertheless when the Son of man cometh, shall he find faith on the earth?

LUKE 18:8

God is not like this unjust judge, making you wait a long time for His answer; He avenges speedily! The problem isn't His willingness or ability to give, but rather your ability to believe and receive: *"Shall he find faith on the earth?"*

If you approach God as if He's an adversary who doesn't want to answer your prayer, you approach Him with less respect than you have for your own mom and dad. You expect your parents, your friends, and a judge to treat you better than you expect God to.

Such a bad picture of the Lord has been so widely presented that we think He's willing to let babies be born with birth defects. We believe that God puts cancer on people to teach them something. We declare that it was the Lord who burned a building to the ground with people in it because they owned a pornography shop and He judged them for it.

With this twisted view in mind, many Christians believe they must stand in between God and their country to beg for His mercy so He won't judge them. Millions of people have signed up for "prayer chains" to plead with God and take the place that Christ already occupies. That's simply not what God wants them to do!

"THAT'S NOT RIGHT!"

Do you have this image and attitude in prayer? If so, you're approaching God in an adversarial relationship and in unbelief, slandering His character, not esteeming Christ, and believing that what Jesus did wasn't enough. "Jesus, I know You made intercession, but get out of the way—I'm doing it now!" Then you ask yourself, "Why are my prayers not working?" It's a wonder you're not a pile of ashes! The only reason God's not ticked off at you is because Jesus did such an effective job.

We believe the devil's lies and ignorantly embrace religion's warped views. Considering the Lord our adversary, we try to force Him to answer our prayers. We attempt to twist His arm and make Him heal people while vainly imagining ourselves to be more compassionate than the Healer Himself!

During an all-night prayer meeting when we bombarded the gates of heaven, I remember screaming (at the time I thought God was deaf, so louder was better) and beating the wall. I actually yelled, "God, if You loved the people in Arlington, Texas, half as much as I do, we'd have revival!" Immediately, my lightning-fast mind realized there was something seriously wrong with my theology. I stopped dead in my tracks and said, "That's not right!" But this is where most "intercessors" are today.

Many intercessors plead with the Lord, praying, "O God, please love these people as much as I do." They wouldn't use those exact words, but it's what they're doing. They believe that God is angry and that He'd just let people die and go to hell if it weren't for their great prayers. They think that apart from them, He wouldn't heal anybody, that their begging is making Him turn and extend mercy. Nothing could be further from the truth.

God loves people infinitely more than you do. If you want to see your country turned around or someone saved, healed, and delivered, it's because God Himself has already touched your heart so you have that desire. It's definitely not human nature! The nature of people is to be selfish and not care for anyone but themselves. If you have compassion to see others touched, it's because God is already working on you. He's the one who gave you that compassion. He stirred you up, not so you could plead with Him to become as merciful as you are, but so that motivated by love, you would start releasing the power of God by going out and doing something about it.

ACT ON THE TRUTH

I'd love to see the same hunger, desire, and passion for the Lord here in America that I've seen in other countries. It's not because God hasn't poured out His Spirit on America; it's because America's so preoccupied with all its DVDs, televisions, video games, shopping malls, and beaches. Our nation spends more on entertainment, sports equipment, and related leisure items than the gross national product of many countries. Lusting for all kinds of material things, we just don't have time for God!

God isn't holding back His Spirit; He's trying to work in the U.S.A. It's just that the Holy Spirit doesn't move independently of us. He told us as believers to go out and heal the sick, cleanse the lepers, raise the dead, and cast out demons. Instead of doing what He's commanded us to do, we're asking God to do what He told us to do. God has already released His power. It's in us. Now we must release His power to others.

God has already placed inside us the same power that raised Jesus from the dead. It's not time for Him to pour out His Spirit. The Lord already has, and He's indwelling every one of us born-again believers. We just need to start speaking the truth and encouraging each other to act on it!

You could raise someone from the dead tomorrow, and then ask all of the people standing around when it occurred if they would like to go to a meeting and find out how they can raise someone from the dead too. You'd pack places out! You don't need to pray for God's power to be poured out; He wants it manifested, but you must first start believing, going, and doing. As you do, the signs will follow!

CONSIDER THE FRUIT

Satan is behind much of the teaching on "prayer" floating around in the body of Christ today. Consider the fruit. You are being driven into your closet, not valuing what the Lord has done, trying to take His position, telling Him to repent from wrath He no longer has, begging for the Holy Spirit who's already been poured out, and pleading with God to become as merciful as you are. All of this just destroys your understanding and impression of God.

Meanwhile, your family, coworkers, and neighbors may be going to hell. You ought to be out there, speaking God's Word and demonstrating it by commanding healing into their broken bodies, not busy "interceding" in your closet for an hour or more each day. What a ploy of the devil!

Outline

I.   Luke 18:1-8 is another passage often used to teach "importunity in prayer."

   A. God is not like the unjust judge.

      i.   In this passage, Jesus is making another contrast, not a comparison.

      ii. He was using an absurd example to illustrate His point.

   B. Most of us put more faith in an earthly judge to treat us well than in God!

   C. This parable is a contrast showing us the absurdity of such thinking.

II. God is not like this unjust judge, making us wait a long time for His answer (Luke 18:6-8); He avenges speedily.

   A. The problem isn't God's willingness or ability to give but, rather, our ability to believe and receive.

   B. We shouldn't approach God like an adversary who doesn't want to answer our prayers, but as an advocate.

   C. This mindset has led many of us to believe we must stand in between God and our country to beg for His mercy so He won't judge us.

III. When we approach God in an adversarial relationship, we are in unbelief, we slander His character, we don't esteem Christ, and we don't believe that what He did was enough.

   A. Instead, we're believing the devil's lies and embracing religion's views.

   B. Many intercessors believe that God is angry and that He'd just let people die and go to hell if it weren't for their prayers.

   C. God gives us the desire to see our country and others changed so we would start releasing His power, not so we can plead with Him for His mercy.

IV. Instead of doing what He's commanded us to do, we're asking God to do what He told us to do.

    A. God has already placed inside us the same power that raised Jesus from the dead.

    B. We just need to start speaking the truth and encouraging each other to act on it.

    C. We must start believing, going, and doing—as we do, the signs will follow.

V. Satan tries to get us to take God's position, telling Him to repent from the wrath that He no longer has, begging for the Holy Spirit who's already been poured out, and pleading for God to become as merciful as we are.

    A. We should be speaking God's Word and demonstrating it by commanding healing, not busy "interceding" in our closets for an hour or more each day.

    B. This is a ploy of the devil.

Teacher's Guide

1.   Luke 18:1-8 is another passage often used to teach "importunity in prayer." God is not like the unjust judge. In this passage, Jesus is making another contrast, not a comparison. He was using an absurd example to illustrate His point. Most of us put more faith in an earthly judge to treat us well than in God! This parable is a contrast showing us the absurdity of such thinking.

1a.   Read Luke 18:1-5. Why did the judge finally change his mind about helping the widow?
He decided to help her because she kept coming to him and troubling him

1b.   What is the point of this parable?
It's a contrast showing you the absurdity of such thinking

2.   God is not like this unjust judge, making us wait a long time for His answer (Luke 18:6-8); He avenges speedily. The problem isn't God's willingness or ability to give but, rather, our ability to believe and receive. We shouldn't approach God like an adversary who doesn't want to answer our prayers, but as an advocate. This mindset has led many of us to believe we must stand in between God and our country to beg for His mercy so He won't judge us.

2a.   Read Luke 18:6-8. How does God avenge?
Speedily

2b.   If the problem isn't with God's willingness or ability to give, what is it with?
Your ability to believe and receive

3.   When we approach God in an adversarial relationship, we are in unbelief, we slander His character, we don't esteem Christ, and we don't believe that what He did was enough. Instead, we're believing the devil's lies and embracing religion's views. Many intercessors believe that God is angry and that He'd just let people die and go to hell if it weren't for their prayers. God gives us the desire to see our country and others changed so we would start releasing His power, not so we can plead with Him for His mercy.

3a.   When you consider the Lord as your adversary, whose lies are you believing?
The devil's

3b.   Why does God give you the desire to see others changed?
So you can start releasing His power

4.   Instead of doing what He's commanded us to do, we're asking God to do what He told us to do. God has already placed inside us the same power that raised Jesus from the dead. We just need to start speaking the truth and encouraging each other to act on it. We must start believing, going, and doing—as we do, the signs will follow.

4a.   What are you possibly doing instead of what God has commanded you to do?
        Asking Him to do what He told you to do

4b.   What will happen when you start believing, going, and doing?
        Signs will follow

5.   Satan tries to get us to take God's position, telling Him to repent from the wrath that He no longer has, begging for the Holy Spirit who's already been poured out, and pleading for God to become as merciful as we are. We should be speaking God's Word and demonstrating it by commanding healing, not busy "interceding" in our closets for an hour or more each day. This is a ploy of the devil.

5a.   Who tries to get you to take God's position?
        Satan

5b.   Instead of speaking and demonstrating God's Word, what does the devil have you doing?
        Interceding in your closet

Discipleship Questions

1. Read Luke 18:1-5. Why did the judge finally change his mind about helping the widow?

2. What is the point of this parable?

3. Read Luke 18:6-8. How does God avenge?

4. If the problem isn't with God's willingness or ability to give, what is it with?

5. When you consider the Lord as your adversary, whose lies are you believing?

6. Why does God give you the desire to see others changed?

7. What are you doing instead of what God has commanded you to do?

8. What will happen when you start believing, going, and doing?

9. Who tries to get you to take God's position?

10. Instead of speaking and demonstrating God's Word, what does the devil have you doing?

Answer Key

1.   He decided to help her because she kept coming to him and troubling him

2.   It's a contrast showing you the absurdity of such thinking

3.   Speedily

4.   Your ability to believe and receive

5.   The devil's

6.   So you can start releasing His power

7.   Asking Him to do what He told you to do

8.   Signs will follow

9.   Satan

10.   Interceding in your closet

Scriptures

LUKE 18:1-8

And he spake a parable unto them to this end, that men ought always to pray, and not to faint; [2] Saying, There was in a city a judge, which feared not God, neither regarded man: [3] And there was a widow in that city; and she came unto him, saying, Avenge me of mine adversary. [4] And he would not for a while: but afterward he said within himself, Though I fear not God, nor regard man; [5] Yet because this widow troubleth me, I will avenge her, lest by her continual coming she weary me. [6] And the Lord said, Hear what the unjust judge saith. [7] And shall not God avenge his own elect, which cry day and night unto him, though he bear long with them? [8] I tell you that he will avenge them speedily. Nevertheless when the Son of man cometh, shall he find faith on the earth?

A PLOY OF THE DEVIL

Come Out of the Closet!

Literally thousands of people have come up to me and asked, "How come [insert name of unsaved person here] isn't saved? I've been praying for [him/her/them] for over twenty years now and God hasn't answered my prayer!" What a sorry attitude! If I were God, the spirit of slap would come all over me. You can't get another person saved on your faith!

> *And they said, Believe on the Lord Jesus Christ, and thou shalt be saved, and thy house.*
>
> ACTS 16:31

This scripture from the Philippian jailer passage is commonly taught as "claim your relatives—your whole house—for salvation." But you can't "claim" someone else's salvation. This verse doesn't mean that. It's saying, "Believe on the Lord Jesus Christ, and you'll be saved. Your house will, too, if they believe. It'll work for anyone!"

If "claiming" another's salvation really worked, then we should quit teaching anything else and focus on this one thing. We could organize the churches to "claim" all of their relatives and then, once they're saved, immediately lead them in "claiming" all of theirs too. If this were true, we could "claim" and win the whole world in no time flat! This simply cannot be done, because people must personally believe in Christ for themselves.

> *Being born again, not of corruptible seed, but of incorruptible, by the word of God, which liveth and abideth for ever.*
>
> 1 PETER 1:23

The seed of God's Word must be planted in people's hearts before they can be born again. Salvation simply cannot be conceived without the Word entering first.

Presently, more believers are holed up in their closets interceding and "claiming" others' salvations than there are believers out planting the seed of God's Word into hearts. Brothers and sisters, this should not be!

NO NEW TESTAMENT MODEL

Jesus never organized "prayer warriors" and "intercessors" the way it's modeled today. He never sent His disciples out to "intercede and do spiritual warfare" over a city to "prepare the ground." He did send them forth in advance to publicize His coming, and that was because they didn't have radio, television, newspapers, the internet, billboards, and so on back then. These disciples spread the word of His miracles, but Jesus never ordained any "prayer warriors" or "intercessors." There's simply no scriptural, New Testament model for such things.

Paul never had any "intercessors" either. He asked his friends to pray for him, but he never organized "prayer warriors" to "hold up his hands." People inquire of me all the time, "Who are your intercessors?" Honestly, I don't know! I'm sure many of my ministry partners and friends do pray for me (and I very much appreciate it), but I don't have any "intercessors" the way it's commonly meant today. Nobody in Scripture who changed the world ever had paid "prayer warriors." It's a new thing in our day and age—and it's foolish!

The logic behind all of this states that demonic powers are holding certain areas captive. Before going in and preaching the Gospel, the "strongman" must be bound and his power broken. Although that sounds spiritual, Jesus didn't do it this way and neither did Paul. Am I disputing the fact that there are demonic powers at work in the world today? No! I've seen demons come out of people. I'm also fully aware that there are demonic powers over cities.

Demons are even present in church services! Some may say, "Well, they shouldn't be. Plead the blood and keep them out!" You can't do that! Satan attended the Last Supper with Jesus. After the Lord dipped the bread into the sop and handed it to Judas, the devil entered him (John 13:26-27). If Christ couldn't keep Satan away from His communion table, what makes you think you can?

HALF-SUPERSTITIOUS

I visited a church once that aggressively "pled the blood" over all their thresholds, doors, and windows. The preacher declared, "If the devil could've attended that meeting, he'd have been a 'saved' devil." Why? "He'd have had to come in through the blood!" That's just religious foolishness! Only Christians would fall for something like that. Nonbelievers sure wouldn't. You have to be half-superstitious to believe some of the weird stuff that goes on in churches today.

If "pleading the blood" actually kept demons out of church services, they'd be empty! God's Word doesn't make a distinction between "oppressed" and "possessed." The Greek word simply means "demonized." If you're depressed, you're demonized. Satan is messing with you. Many sicknesses are also demonic. Most believers have evil spirits hovering around, constantly harassing and afflicting them. If all the demons were truly bound and kept out of church services, there wouldn't be anyone left. You just can't do that!

If it were truly possible to keep evil spirits out of church services, then we should round up all of the believers in the community together into one large meeting. We could use our corporate faith to increase our range as we bound all of the demons within a five-mile radius. Then we could go out and blitz that area with the Gospel so that all the people would become born again and Spirit filled. Then we could have them agree with us to bind all of the demons from out of the rest of town. Once the whole city was saved, we could bind the demons from our state and then our nation!

It just doesn't work that way. You can't "claim" people and, through prayer, force them to be born again against their wills. Neither can you cast demons out of people against their wills. However, this is what's being popularly taught as "prayer." "Claim people's salvations and bind the demons over this and that." In the process, we aren't preaching the Word.

DEALING WITH DIANA

We don't understand that God's Word must come to people and enter them in order to change their lives. We think our prayers cause people to receive salvation. When they don't respond, we wonder, *Why hasn't God saved them? I've been praying!* Really! Have you ever taken into account the fact that these people may not want to be saved? Maybe they're truly enjoying their sin. Perhaps they're under demonic deception and believe that being a Christian is a bad thing. Have you ever told them the truth and countered their unbelief? Telling people the truth of God's Word isn't properly emphasized. Instead, it's more like, "Let's have everybody pray for an outpouring of God's Spirit so we won't have to witness. Then we won't have to go out and suffer the possibility of rejection. Let's just ask the Lord to do what He's told us to do!"

God isn't the one who's led the body of Christ into a hundred million "intercessors" begging Him to pour out His Spirit. Ten believers out doing the work of the ministry—raising the dead, healing the sick, and speaking the Truth—would accomplish more good than all of those people pleading with God to do what He's already done!

Colorado Springs, where we're based, is a center for much of this "intercession-and-spiritual-warfare" stuff. I remember hearing about an international group of approximately 20,000 intercessors being organized to meet at the amphitheater in Ephesus in order to "bind" a demonic entity named "Diana." They believed that this was the spirit holding Muslims in bondage, so they spent a ton of money traveling to Turkey. Their expressed goal for being there was to "tear down" Diana of the Ephesians, thus ending her "reign" and paving the way for many Muslims to come to Jesus.

When Paul dealt with this "Diana," multitudes of people regularly came to worship her image (which was reputed to have fallen down from Jupiter) in the temple at Ephesus. Paul never told the disciples to pray against her, never led a praise service to bind her, and never did "spiritual warfare" or "spiritual mapping." They didn't go back into the history of Ephesus to repent and apologize for all of the different sins so that God could finally move.

What did Paul and his fellow laborers do? They preached the Truth: there's no other god but God the Father, His Son—the Lord Jesus Christ—and the Holy Spirit. In a relatively short period of time, the entire worship of "Diana of the Ephesians" was on the verge of being completely abandoned because someone dared to tell the people the Truth. The subsequent religious, political, and primarily economic aftershocks nearly caused Paul to be stoned to death (Acts 19:23-41). Am I arguing that there wasn't a demonic power operating through this worship of Diana of the Ephesians? No, I believe there was. However, Paul and his companions didn't deal with it in prayer. They boldly spoke the truth of God's Word with Holy Spirit power demonstrated to the people.

Paul destroyed Diana of the Ephesians through the power of the Truth. She hasn't been a factor for nearly 2,000 years, until the "intercessors" resurrected her.

WHO BROUGHT WHOM?

How do demonic entities over cities derive their power? They get it from the people who believe and act on their lies! Evil spirits aren't able to dominate or control people against their wills. Human beings are the ones who empower demons by believing their lies and cooperating with their unholy desires.

It's often been said, "Homosexual spirits control the San Francisco area. We need intercessors to come and bind these demonic powers so that the people can be set free!" Who came to San Francisco first: the demons or the homosexuals? When individuals who favored homosexuals were elected into government positions, they started passing laws that benefited them (access to special tax breaks, welfare, marital benefits, and social status). Due to this, homosexuals flocked to San Francisco and brought the evil spirits with them. It wasn't the demons who brought the homosexuals; it was the homosexuals who brought the demons!

I don't doubt the reality of demonic powers of homosexuality over San Francisco, but rebuking them in prayer and intercession is not the way to deal with them. Lovingly tell the homosexuals the Truth and see them born again. Let them know that God made them Adam and Eve, not Adam and Steve. As they're set free, the homosexual demons will have to go somewhere else.

I know I've stepped on some toes with these things I'm sharing. You love God, and you're as sincere as you can possibly be. Yet you've bought into some of these misconceptions I've been disproving. You're probably feeling offended, like I'm saying you're all wrong. Really, I'm just encouraging you to recognize and root out these wrong attitudes and approaches in prayer. You can be sincere but still be sincerely wrong!

BELIEVE, GO, AND DO!

God loves you! He's seen your heart. He's been taking what He can and is using it, but there's a better way to pray!

Instead of all that other junk, honor God by praying, "Father, thank You that You love my country much more than I ever could. Forgive me for feeling like I have to make You love people as much as I do. Forgive me for my arrogance and self-righteous attitude. Forgive me for taking the place of Christ and trying to become a mediator between You and others. I see it now for what it really is, and I repent!

"I know that You passionately love my family, friends, coworkers, and neighbors, so I offer myself as a willing vessel for You to work through. Show me who You want me to speak Your Word to today. Give me wisdom and I'll boldly proclaim Your Truth and love! Thank You, Father. You're so good! Amen."

Now take a step of faith and come on out of that closet. The Holy Spirit is leading, but it's up to you to actually believe, go, and do!

Outline

I. Salvation works by planting the seed of God's Word into people's hearts (see 1 Peter 1:23).

    A. We cannot get other people saved on our faith.

    B. Acts 16:31 is saying that a person's entire household can be saved because salvation is for everyone, but each person must receive salvation personally.

    C. We cannot "claim" salvation for someone else.

    D. More believers are in their prayer closets "claiming" others' salvations than there are believers out planting God's Word.

II. There is no New Testament model for today's form of intercession.

    A. Jesus never organized "prayer warriors" and "intercessors" the way it's modeled today.

        i. Neither Jesus nor Paul sent intercessors ahead of them to "prepare the ground" or to bind the "strongman" over certain areas.

    B. We can't "claim" people and force them to be born again against their wills, and we can't cast demons out of people against their wills, even though most believers have evil spirits that harass and afflict them.

III. God's Word is what changes lives, yet telling people the truth of God's Word isn't properly emphasized.

    A. Ten believers out doing the work of the ministry—raising the dead, healing the sick, and speaking the Truth—would accomplish more good than a hundred million intercessors pleading with God to do what He's already done!

    B. Paul destroyed the demonic power behind Diana of the Ephesians by proclaiming the truth with Holy Spirit power demonstrated, not through intercession.

IV. Demonic entities over cities derive their power from the people who believe and act on their lies.

    A. Human beings are the ones who empower demons by believing their lies and cooperating with their unholy desires.

        i. It's often been said that homosexual spirits control the San Francisco area, so intercessors need to go in and bind those demonic powers so that the people can be set free.

        ii. But it wasn't the demons who brought the homosexuals; it was the homosexuals who brought the demons.

    B. If we've fallen for this wrong type of intercession instead of sharing God's Word, we need to ask for God's forgiveness and for Him to lead us to people to talk to.

    C. The Holy Spirit leads, but we have to believe, go, and do.

Teacher's Guide

1.   Salvation works by planting the seed of God's Word into people's hearts (see 1 Peter 1:23). We cannot get other people saved on our faith. Acts 16:31 is saying that a person's entire household can be saved because salvation is for everyone, but each person must receive salvation personally. We cannot "claim" salvation for someone else. More believers are in their prayer closets "claiming" others' salvations than there are believers out planting God's Word.

1a.   Read Acts 16:31 and 1 Peter 1:23. Why can't you get others saved on your faith?
People must receive salvation for themselves—salvation comes as you plant God's Word into people's hearts, not by praying for them

1b.   Instead of planting God's Word into people's hearts, what are many believers doing?
"Claiming" others' salvation from their prayer closets

2.   There is no New Testament model for today's form of intercession. Jesus never organized "prayer warriors" and "intercessors" the way it's modeled today. Neither Jesus nor Paul sent intercessors ahead of them to "prepare the ground" or to bind the "strongman" over certain areas. We can't "claim" people and force them to be born again against their wills, and we can't cast demons out of people against their wills, even though most believers have evil spirits that harass and afflict them.

2a.   How do you know that today's form of intercession is not correct?
There is no New Testament model for it

2b.   What can you not do against people's wills?
Force them to be born again or cast demons out of them

3.   God's Word is what changes lives, yet telling people the truth of God's Word isn't properly emphasized. Ten believers out doing the work of the ministry—raising the dead, healing the sick, and speaking the Truth—would accomplish more good than a hundred million intercessors pleading with God to do what He's already done! Paul destroyed the demonic power behind Diana of the Ephesians by proclaiming the truth with Holy Spirit power demonstrated, not through intercession.

3a.   What isn't properly emphasized?
Telling people the truth of God's Word

3b.   How did Paul destroy the demonic power behind Diana of the Ephesians?
By speaking the truth of God's Word with Holy Spirit power demonstrated

4. Demonic entities over cities derive their power from the people who believe and act on their lies. Human beings are the ones who empower demons by believing their lies and cooperating with their unholy desires. It's often been said that homosexual spirits control the San Francisco area, so intercessors need to go in and bind those demonic powers so that the people can be set free. But it wasn't the demons who brought the homosexuals; it was the homosexuals who brought the demons. If we've fallen for this wrong type of intercession instead of sharing God's Word, we need to ask for God's forgiveness and for Him to lead us to people to talk to. The Holy Spirit leads, but we have to believe, go, and do.

4a. Who empowers demons and how?
Human beings empower them by believing their lies and cooperating with their unholy desires

4b. The Holy Spirit will lead, but you have to what?
Believe, go, and do

Discipleship Questions

1. Read Acts 16:31 and 1 Peter 1:23. Why can't you get others saved on your faith?

2. Instead of planting God's Word into people's hearts, what are many believers doing?

3. How do you know that today's form of intercession is not correct?

4. What can you not do against people's wills?

5. What isn't properly emphasized?

6. How did Paul destroy the demonic power behind Diana of the Ephesians?

7. Who empowers demons and how?

8. The Holy Spirit will lead, but you have to what?

Answer Key

1. People must receive salvation for themselves—salvation comes as you plant God's Word into people's hearts, not by praying for them

2. "Claiming" others' salvation from their prayer closets

3. There is no New Testament model for it

4. Force them to be born again or cast demons out of them

5. Telling people the truth of God's Word

6. By speaking the truth of God's Word with Holy Spirit power demonstrated

7. Human beings empower them by believing their lies and cooperating with their unholy desires

8. Believe, go, and do

Scriptures

ACTS 16:31

And they said, Believe on the Lord Jesus Christ, and thou shalt be saved, and thy house.

1 PETER 1:23

Being born again, not of corruptible seed, but of incorruptible, by the word of God, which liveth and abideth for ever.

JOHN 13:26-27

Jesus answered, He it is, to whom I shall give a sop, when I have dipped it. And when he had dipped the sop, he gave it to Judas Iscariot, the son of Simon. [27] And after the sop Satan entered into him. Then said Jesus unto him, That thou doest, do quickly.

ACTS 19:23-41

And the same time there arose no small stir about that way. [24] For a certain man named Demetrius, a silversmith, which made silver shrines for Diana, brought no small gain unto the craftsmen; [25] Whom he called together with the workmen of like occupation, and said, Sirs, ye know that by this craft we have our wealth. [26] Moreover ye see and hear, that not alone at Ephesus, but almost throughout all Asia, this Paul hath persuaded and turned away much people, saying that they be no gods, which are made with hands: [27] So that not only this our craft is in danger to be set at nought; but also that the temple of the great goddess Diana should be despised, and her magnificence should be destroyed, whom all Asia and the world worshippeth. [28] And when they heard these sayings, they were full of wrath, and cried out, saying, Great is Diana of the Ephesians. [29] And the whole city was filled with confusion: and having caught Gaius and Aristarchus, men of Macedonia, Paul's companions in travel, they rushed with one accord into the theatre. [30] And when Paul would have entered in unto the people, the disciples suffered him not. [31] And certain of the chief of Asia, which were his friends, sent unto him, desiring him that he would not adventure himself into the theatre. [32] Some therefore cried one thing, and some another: for the assembly was confused; and the more part knew not wherefore they were come together. [33] And they drew Alexander out of the multitude, the Jews putting him forward. And Alexander beckoned with the hand, and would have made his defence unto the people. [34] But when they knew that he was a Jew, all with one voice about the space of two hours cried out, Great is Diana of the Ephesians. [35] And when the townclerk had appeased the people, he said, Ye men of Ephesus, what man is there that knoweth not how that the city of the Ephesians is a worshipper of the great goddess Diana, and of the image which fell down from Jupiter? [36] Seeing then that these things cannot be spoken against, ye ought to be quiet, and to do nothing rashly. [**37**] For ye have brought hither these men, which are neither robbers of churches, nor yet blasphemers of your goddess. [**38**] Wherefore if Demetrius, and the craftsmen which are with him, have a matter against any man, the law is open, and there are deputies: let them implead one another. [**39**] But if ye enquire any thing concerning other matters, it shall be determined in a lawful assembly. [**40**] For we are in danger to be called in question for this day's uproar, there being no cause whereby we may give an account of this concourse. [**41**] And when he had thus spoken, he dismissed the assembly.

Roadblocks to Hell

I'd like to offer you some scriptural suggestions for effectively praying for those who are lost.

God's Word reveals the presence of demonic deception in unbelievers' lives:

In whom the god of this world hath blinded the minds of them which believe not, lest the light of the glorious gospel of Christ, who is the image of God, should shine unto them.

2 CORINTHIANS 4:4

In view of this truth, begin praising God, and then bind their blindness by praying, "Father, You would not have any perish but for all to come to repentance and the knowledge of You (2 Pet. 3:9). You love these people more than I do, so I don't have to beg. Thank You for loving them. Since I know that there's demonic deception involved, I bind this blindness, in the name of Jesus!" This doesn't remove the blindness, but it'll provide temporary relief. The people you're praying for have more control over their lives than you do, but if they're in deception, break it!

VOIDING PRAYER

Since lost people have the right to void your prayer, you may need to pray it several times. It's different from when you request something for yourself, like healing. When praying for yourself, you only ask once. If you ask twice, then at least one of the two times was in unbelief. However, in praying for others to be saved, the deception of praying only once exists. You rebuke it, but they can then void your prayer. As the Lord begins convicting them, they could think, *Man, what's this? I feel like I should go to church, start studying the Bible, and begin fellowshipping with God. Must be the devil*—"Give me another drink!" When they turned from the Holy Spirit's prompting, they negated your prayer. It's not that God didn't answer. He did, but they voided it. So, you must pray that prayer again and keep on praying until you see the manifestation. Don't doubt that God has answered, but realize that they are negating your prayer.

After binding the blindness and deception over them, remember that they must be born again of the incorruptible seed of God's Word (1 Pet. 1:23). Pray Matthew 9:38: "Father, I ask You to send laborers across their paths. They need to hear Your Word, so I speak my faith and release Your power to have them tune in to You through television, radio, the internet, audio messages, books, billboards, and people. Let a Spirit-filled believer walk into the bar right now and start ministering to them. Let there be an on-fire Christian in the next cubicle at work who will speak Your Word to them."

God wants to do all of these things, but He must flow through people. He needs someone here on earth with a physical human body to do it. If the unsaved individuals aren't inviting God into their lives, they need someone to pray for them who will. They don't need someone pleading with God as if He doesn't already love them; they need someone who will speak and release these things by faith!

Once you've done that, then offer yourself as a laborer! Don't ever pray for someone else to do what you could do. If you can talk to the unbelievers, do it! Speak the truth in love. They must hear God's Word because that's what will set them free. Pray that the Truth will cross their paths.

> *But the Comforter, which is the Holy Ghost, whom the Father will send in my name, he shall teach you all things, and bring all things to your remembrance, whatsoever I have said unto you.*
>
> JOHN 14:26

God has been dealing with lost people throughout their entire lives. He's put roadblocks on their highways to hell by speaking to them as much as He can. Pray that He'd bring back to their minds those things that they've already received. Perhaps it's scriptures they learned as children. Maybe it's John 3:16 from a placard in the end zone of their favorite football team. As the Holy Spirit quickens these verses ("laborers" that crossed their paths), they'll come under conviction.

REMITTANCE

You can't receive forgiveness for someone else's sins, but you can remit them.

> *Whose soever sins ye remit, they are remitted unto them; and whose soever sins ye retain, they are retained.*
>
> JOHN 20:23

Remittance speaks of the effects of sin. You can't stop sin or pray forgiveness over someone, but you can deal with sin's negative repercussions.

If people are living sexually immoral lives, they could be opening themselves up to many different kinds of sexually transmitted diseases. You could pray, "Father, I recognize that they must receive forgiveness for their sins on their own from You, but I'm going to stand against the negative effects of those sins, according to John 20:23. Satan, even though they have opened up a door, you are not going to give them any sexually transmitted diseases. I rebuke AIDS. They will not reap it, in Jesus' name!"

Your prayer can grant them a measure of protection, but they can void it. If they do, you'll have to pray it again. Just keep releasing His power and protection into their lives until they respond favorably. Ultimately, you can't make them receive the Lord, but you can put positive spiritual pressure on them by releasing the power of God into their lives. Even Jesus, the perfect intercessor, couldn't convince people or set them free through His faith alone:

> *O Jerusalem, Jerusalem, thou that killest the prophets, and stonest them which are sent unto thee, how often would I have gathered thy children together, even as a hen gathereth her chickens under her wings, and ye would not!*
>
> MATTHEW 23:37

"Many times I wanted to bless and minister to you, but you wouldn't allow it!" All you can do is be a channel for God's power to flow through and touch people because, ultimately, they must choose the Lord for themselves.

Paul echoed this truth in 1 Corinthians 7:16:

> *For what knowest thou, O wife, whether thou shalt save thy husband? or how knowest thou, O man, whether thou shalt save thy wife?*

Don't leave your unbelieving mate! How do you know whether or not your influence will persuade your mate to be saved? If you stay, loving and praying for him or her, your mate just might receive the Lord. You can't "claim" your spouse or force him or her into salvation, but God will use you to convict him or her. Your mate will see and hear the Truth through you, but he or she alone must choose whether to go to hell or not, because God doesn't force anyone to receive His Son.

BARBECUED

Before teaching what prayer is, our Lord Jesus Christ spent quite a bit of time revealing what prayer is not. That's exactly what I've been doing so far in this study. I had wanted to be kinder, gentler, and more polite, but regarding all of this weirdness and perversity in the body of Christ concerning prayer today, the Lord said, "There's simply no easy way to kill it—so kill it!"

When ministering in foreign countries, I've found it important to separate myself from the religious culture. In northern India, where our faith isn't very strong yet, there are many religious expressions of Christianity that are just as pagan and ungodly as the predominant Hinduism. While visiting, I saw people worshiping at shrines that had little figurines of Krishna, Buddha, and Jesus all sitting there together. Since literally millions of gods are worshiped in India, many people will readily "accept" Jesus simply because they don't want to miss out on another deity. In pagan cultures like this, I distance myself from what isn't true Christianity before sharing what it is.

Here in the West, we have plenty of religious expressions of Christianity as well. It may not be as obvious to us because we've grown up with it, but they are false nonetheless. Some of these attitudes and misconceptions have even crept into charismatic circles. Much effort is expended while very little—if any—real benefit is experienced. In light of this reality, something must be wrong!

Up until this point, I've primarily been countering that which is wrong. Now that I've separated myself from the predominant religious culture by thoroughly barbecuing all these sacred cows, I'd like to shift gears and begin showing you what prayer really is!

Outline

I.   God's Word reveals the presence of demonic deception in unbelievers' lives:

In whom the god of this world hath blinded the minds of them which believe not, lest the light of the glorious gospel of Christ, who is the image of God, should shine unto them.

2 CORINTHIANS 4:4

A. In view of this truth, we should begin praising God and then bind their blindness, in the name of Jesus.

B. Since lost people have the right to void our prayers, we may need to pray several times.

C. God may convict them, but if they ignore the Holy Spirit's prompting, they've negated our prayers.

i.   Unlike praying for ourselves, we need to keep praying for an unbeliever until we see the manifestation.

ii. God has answered our prayer, but they are negating it by not responding to Him.

II. After binding the blindness and deception over them, we need to remember that unbelievers must be born again of the incorruptible seed of God's Word:

Being born again, not of corruptible seed, but of incorruptible, by the word of God, which liveth and abideth for ever.

1 PETER 1:23

A. We should pray Matthew 9:38 and ask for laborers to be sent to them.

i.   God wants to reach them, but He must flow through people.

ii. If the unsaved aren't inviting God into their lives, they need someone to pray for them who will.

iii. They need someone who will speak and release these things by faith.

B. After doing that, we should offer ourselves as laborers to share God's Word with them.

C. Also, we need to pray that God would bring back to their minds the Word they've already received (John 14:26).

III. We can't receive forgiveness for someone else's sins, but we can remit them:

Whose soever sins ye remit, they are remitted unto them; and whose soever sins ye retain, they are retained.

JOHN 20:23

A. Remittance speaks of the effects of sin.

    i. We can't stop sin or pray forgiveness over someone, but we can deal with sin's negative repercussions.

    ii. We can keep releasing God's power and protection into their lives until they respond favorably.

B. We can't make people receive the Lord, but we can put positive spiritual pressure on them by releasing the power of God into their lives (Matt. 23:37 and 1 Cor. 7:16).

C. Even Jesus, the perfect intercessor, couldn't convince people or set them free through His faith alone (Matt. 23:37).

D. All we can do is be a channel for God's power to flow through and touch people because, ultimately, they must choose the Lord for themselves.

Teacher's Guide

1.   God's Word reveals the presence of demonic deception in unbelievers' lives:

> *In whom the god of this world hath blinded the minds of them which believe not, lest the light of the glorious gospel of Christ, who is the image of God, should shine unto them.*
>
> 2 CORINTHIANS 4:4

In view of this truth, we should begin praising God and then bind their blindness, in the name of Jesus. Since lost people have the right to void our prayers, we may need to pray several times. God may convict them, but if they ignore the Holy Spirit's prompting, they've negated our prayers. Unlike praying for ourselves, we need to keep praying for an unbeliever until we see the manifestation. God has answered our prayer, but they are negating it by not responding to Him.

1a.   How can you counter the presence of demonic deception in unbelievers' lives?
By praising God and binding the unbelievers' blindness

1b.   What may you need to do, since lost people have the right to void your prayers?
Keep praying until you see the manifestation

2.   After binding the blindness and deception over them, we need to remember that unbelievers must be born again of the incorruptible seed of God's Word:

> *Being born again, not of corruptible seed, but of incorruptible, by the word of God, which liveth and abideth for ever.*
>
> 1 PETER 1:23

We should pray Matthew 9:38 and ask for laborers to be sent to them. God wants to reach them, but He must flow through people. If the unsaved aren't inviting God into their lives, they need someone to pray for them who will. They need someone who will speak and release these things by faith. After doing that, we should offer ourselves as laborers to share God's Word with them. Also, we need to pray that God would bring back to their minds the Word they've already received (John 14:26).

2a.   Read 1 Peter 1:23 and Matthew 9:38. People must be born again of what?
The incorruptible seed of God's Word

2b.   What should you do once you've prayed for someone, speaking and releasing these things by faith?
      Offer yourself as a laborer

3.   We can't receive forgiveness for someone else's sins, but we can remit them:

> *Whose soever sins ye remit, they are remitted unto them; and whose soever sins ye retain, they are retained.*
>
> JOHN 20:23

Remittance speaks of the effects of sin. We can't stop sin or pray forgiveness over someone, but we can deal with sin's negative repercussions. We can keep releasing God's power and protection into their lives until they respond favorably. We can't make people receive the Lord, but we can put positive spiritual pressure on them by releasing the power of God into their lives (Matt. 23:37 and 1 Cor. 7:16). Even Jesus, the perfect intercessor, couldn't convince people or set them free through His faith alone (Matt. 23:37). All we can do is be a channel for God's power to flow through and touch people because, ultimately they must choose the Lord for themselves.

3a.   Read John 20:23, Matthew 23:37, and 1 Corinthians 7:16. Although you can't stop sin in other people's lives, what can you do for them?
      Deal with the sin's negative repercussions

3b.   How do you put positive spiritual pressure on someone?
      By releasing the power of God into that person's life

Discipleship Questions

1. How can you counter the presence of demonic deception in unbelievers' lives?

2. What may you need to do, since lost people have the right to void your prayers?

3. Read 1 Peter 1:23 and Matthew 9:38. People must be born again of what?

4. What should you do once you've prayed for someone, speaking and releasing these things by faith?

5. Read John 20:23, Matthew 23:37, and 1 Corinthians 7:16. Although you can't stop sin in other people's lives, what can you do for them?

6. How do you put positive spiritual pressure on someone?

Answer Key

1. By praising God and binding the unbelievers' blindness

2. Keep praying until you see the manifestation

3. The incorruptible seed of God's Word

4. Offer yourself as a laborer

5. Deal with the sin's negative repercussions

6. By releasing the power of God into that person's life

Scriptures

2 CORINTHIANS 4:4

In whom the god of this world hath blinded the minds of them which believe not, lest the light of the glorious gospel of Christ, who is the image of God, should shine unto them.

2 PETER 3:9

The Lord is not slack concerning his promise, as some men count slackness; but is longsuffering to us-ward, not willing that any should perish, but that all should come to repentance.

1 PETER 1:23

Being born again, not of corruptible seed, but of incorruptible, by the word of God, which liveth and abideth for ever.

MATTHEW 9:38

Pray ye therefore the Lord of the harvest, that he will send forth labourers into his harvest.

JOHN 14:26

But the Comforter, which is the Holy Ghost, whom the Father will send in my name, he shall teach you all things, and bring all things to your remembrance, whatsoever I have said unto you.

JOHN 3:16

For God so loved the world, that he gave his only begotten Son, that whosoever believeth in him should not perish, but have everlasting life.

JOHN 20:23

Whose soever sins ye remit, they are remitted unto them; and whose soever sins ye retain, they are retained.

MATTHEW 23:37

O Jerusalem, Jerusalem, thou that killest the prophets, and stonest them which are sent unto thee, how often would I have gathered thy children together, even as a hen gathereth her chickens under her wings, and ye would not!

1 CORINTHIANS 7:16

For what knowest thou, O wife, whether thou shalt save thy husband? or how knowest thou, O man, whether thou shalt save thy wife?

The Primary Purpose of Prayer

Prayer is communion with God. It's fellowship, relationship, and intimacy with Him. Prayer is conversation. It's a dialogue (two-way), not a monologue (one-way). Prayer is both talking and listening. Ninety-five percent of the time I spend in prayer, I'm just thanking, loving, praising, appreciating, and hanging out with the Lord—nothing special or dramatic. The vast majority of prayer is simply visiting with God!

There have been times when I've stood and taken authority over the devil, done warfare, bound and loosed, and seen miracles happen because of it. But all of this is just a tiny part of my prayer life as a whole. Yet these things are normally taught as if they are so very important! People hear me minister on prayer as primarily loving God and immediately respond, "Oh, no, that's too simple. We need to be strong in 'prayer' by regularly doing all of these other things." I totally disagree.

Most teaching on prayer today centers on how to request and receive something from God. It's all about getting your prayers answered and, if you're really spiritual, how to receive answers for other people too (intercession). Although it's appropriate to ask for your needs to be met (John 16:24), this should only be a very small part of your prayer life. If it's your primary focus, then it's also one of the main reasons your prayers aren't very effective. Asking and receiving is one purpose of prayer, but it's definitely not the purpose of prayer. God wants to meet your needs, but seeking to receive something from Him shouldn't dominate your prayer life.

ADDED—SUPERNATURALLY

If you made the main thing the main thing—loving, worshiping, and fellowshipping with God as your primary purpose in prayer—you'd soon discover that you wouldn't have as many needs. When you seek first God's kingdom, things are just supernaturally added to you.

> *Therefore I say unto you, Take no thought for your life, what ye shall eat, or what ye shall drink; nor yet for your body, what ye shall put on. Is not the life more than meat, and the body than raiment?*
>
> MATTHEW 6:25

Lost people are completely occupied with the pursuit of what to eat, what to wear, where to live, etc., but believers shouldn't be that way. God is fully aware of your need for these physical things, but He's commanded you to *"seek ye first the kingdom of God, and his righteousness."* As you do, *"all these things shall be added unto you"* (Matt. 6:33). When you're passionately in love with God, He takes care of you—supernaturally—better than you could ever take care of yourself.

By literally living to love Him, you release powerful spiritual dynamics that positively affect the flow of provision in your life. Most people can't wrap their brains around this truth because it's simply too far outside their realm of experience. It just floats right over their heads! I'm not talking about making your family or career the main thing and loving God on the side, or merely having Him add an "extra quality" to your lifestyle. I mean that God is your complete focus, the very center of your life!

For most Christians, the Lord is just another addition to their already busy lives. Their focus is on making a living, raising their kids, maintaining their residences, acquiring more creature comforts, and doing many other temporal activities. On the side, they try to add God into the mix, but He's definitely not the center. They work their tails off because the burden of producing wealth remains on their shoulders. Stressed out, they constantly struggle under cares because they're the ones always trying to make ends meet.

However, when God is truly the center of your life, everything else works out. The Lord makes it work supernaturally. I can't explain how, but it's a kingdom principle. When God prospers you, it's effortless, yet I've met very few Christians who are truly in this divine flow. When your whole heart is simply "God, I love You!" you'll find that He has many ways of working things out.

PRAISE CHANGES PERSPECTIVE

People tell me, "Andrew, it doesn't seem like your feathers ever get ruffled about anything. Things go wrong, but it just doesn't faze you!" It's true! When we were in the process of purchasing a new facility, the contract appeared to be falling through—again. I wasn't bothered by it, because I love God and knew He'd work it out somehow. It was just another annoyance, hindrance, and pain. All the devil can do is aggravate you. He can't stop anything. Staying up half the night bombarding heaven wouldn't have helped, so I just went to bed. I wasn't going to let it change my life! The next day, I was informed that things had worked out, and we were back on track. Hallelujah!

Your perspective changes when you put God first by praising Him. Many of your cares cease to be problems anymore. As you spend time with the King of kings and Lord of Lords, His attitude becomes your attitude. The entire way you think changes because of His influence. You aren't even bothered by the things that upset others and cause them to spend days, weeks, months, and even years praying about it!

When problems arise, many people feel like they have to fix them. Personally, I don't feel like I have to fix a thing. God is my source, and I keep my focus on Him. In the face of adversity, I tell my staff, "You hide and watch—I'll seek first His kingdom, and everything will work out. When the dust settles, we'll look back and say, 'God blessed us—and it was awesome how He did it!'"

"I NEVER ASK GOD FOR MONEY!"

If you put God first and just loved Him, you wouldn't have to spend much time asking Him for finances. There's just a supernatural divine flow. In the summer of 2005, Andrew Wommack Ministries needed $720,000 a month just to break even. That's $24,000 a day! Just to do what we were doing, it took $1,000 an hour every hour of every day of every week—and that was years ago! Our costs have increased since then, yet it's been decades since I've asked the Lord for any money.

I never ask God for money. I don't pray for Him to increase our income. I just say, "God, since we need more money, I must be thinking too small. I need to start increasing my vision!" Then I meditate on the scriptures about God supplying my needs, but I don't pray, push, pull, beg, or plead with Him for more money.

If we run into a financial bind, I'll make sure that I'm not doing something in my flesh. Once I'm convinced that I'm doing what He's told me to do, I'll just start encouraging myself that God is my source. I'll tell myself, "God is faithful!" I'll even use Scripture and preach to myself, but I don't ever ask Him for money.

That might seem weird to you, but the Word says, "Seek first the kingdom of God, and all of these things will be added to you." I've spent decades without asking the Lord for a penny, yet He's blessing our ministry more than ever before. It's working a whole lot better than my asking and begging. In prayer, I just say, "Father, I love You! You're the center of my life." If you would just worship and fellowship with Him, He would supernaturally add everything you need. You wouldn't have to know how to "bind poverty" and all of these other things, because you'd do better accidentally than you've ever done on purpose!

BLESSED OR STRESSED?

Stress wouldn't be a part of your life if you were constantly in God's presence, loving and worshiping Him. I don't have any stress in my life; I'm too blessed to be stressed! I'm not bothered by things, because it's just not worth it. People criticize me and say all kinds of mean things, but nobody's going to rent space in my mind! I have more important things to think about than their criticism. Compared to fulfilling the vision God has put in my heart, critics just aren't that important to me. I love them, and I'm not trying to be mean; but I have something bigger than them, bigger than me, and bigger than what they say about me, consuming my thoughts. When people criticize me, I just stay focused on loving God. I don't have to pray, "Father, did You hear what they said about me?" It simply doesn't matter, because I'm seeking first His kingdom and righteousness. I'm not burdened, depressed, or defeated. I seek God and I'm a happy guy. I really am!

"Well, Andrew, that's because you don't have any problems!" I have problems just like anybody else! As a matter of fact, ministers usually have more problems than others because they have big targets drawn on them in the spirit. The devil hits preachers with all kinds of things. If I wanted to, I could obsess as much as anybody else because I've had some pretty bad stuff happen to me. But the words of a popular song say it so well: "Turn your eyes upon Jesus, Look full in His wonderful face, And the things of earth will grow strangely dim, In the light of His glory and grace." Looking into the brightness of God's glory blinds you to other things. I don't have the worries and cares that other people have, because I don't see what they see. One reason for this is because my prayer life is 99 percent, "Father, I love You. You're awesome!" I just fellowship and visit with God, which is what prayer is all about. I really don't ask Him for much.

ANOINTED!

I never pray over meetings. Many ministers have intercessors agonizing and travailing to "clear the air." They ask God to bring the people and beg, "Oh, please let Your anointing be there!" That's an insult to God!

If the Lord has called me to minister His Word, He'd be unjust not to give me the equipment I need to get the job done. Jesus declared,

> *The Spirit of the Lord is upon me, because he hath* [past tense—already has] *anointed me.*
>
> LUKE 4:18, EMPHASIS AND BRACKETS MINE

I never ask God to anoint me, because His Word says He already has (1 John 2:20). I pray, "Father, thank You that we are going to have a good meeting because I'll speak the truth You have spoken to my heart." God's Word is already anointed!

The Lord wants to change people's lives even more than I do. I don't have to ask Him to become concerned about a series of meetings; He already is. I try to get myself as concerned about those meetings as He is. In prayer, I remind myself, "God, You love these people and want to see them set free!" I encourage and talk to myself in this manner.

Large or small, the size of the audience doesn't bother me. For the first two years I preached, the largest crowd I ever had was fifteen people! Three out of five nights a week, I would minister to Jamie, Joshua (our oldest son), and this other couple who was with us at the time. Every once in a while, someone else would come, but it didn't matter to me. I preached my heart out! Today I look back on that as good training. I don't really care about the size of a meeting. If it's over ten or fifteen people, I consider it a crowd!

UNIMPORTANT OBSESSIONS

Martha obsessed over serving, but Mary sat at the Lord's feet, fellowshipping with and listening to Him. Martha was concerned about the food and wanted Jesus to coerce her sister into helping, but instead, He told her that Mary had chosen wisely and that it wouldn't be taken away from her (Luke 10:38-42). Are you still obsessing over serving, or have you chosen wisely?

Prayer is primarily for loving God, not getting your needs met. Don't just barge into His presence with your grocery cart, ready to tramp up and down the aisles of heaven, saying, "Gimme, gimme, gimme. My name is Jimmy. My middle name is More. Gimme more, gimme more!" Instead of that, spend ten minutes loving God and you'd wonder *What was that problem I had?* because it just leaves.

When you magnify God, you discover how insignificant your problems really are. "Father, I had something I was going to ask You, but I forgot what it was. It's really not worth bothering You because it'll pass. No big deal!" You'll find out that 90 percent of what you've been obsessing over is unimportant!

People use prayer in an effort to secure God's attention and twist His arm into giving them useless things. For instance, when you attend a Bible conference, Satan does things to try to steal the Word away from you. Something happens back home, with your car, with your hotel room, with the air conditioner, with the toilet, etc. You obsess over these things and start aggressively using your faith to fix them. However, in a week, you won't even remember what had you so bothered! If you kept a journal and looked back on it a year from now, you'd think, *That wasn't such a big deal, yet I spent an hour in prayer asking God to help me through it!*

We often act like immature, spoiled brats seeking God's help. "Father, these people said something about my clothes. They didn't like the way I looked!" Who gives a rip? "I have bags under my eyes. Until God heals me, I can't go on!" It's just your earth suit. Get over it! Is God not concerned about these kinds of things? Sure, He is. But if you focused your attention on loving Him, you'd discover that they really aren't that important. If you'd just center your thoughts and affections upon the Lord, you'd be better off accidentally than you've ever been on purpose!

I've had people come up to me in prayer lines bawling and squalling. After blubbering out their answer when I ask what's wrong, many times I've literally had to bite my lip to keep from bursting out in laughter. Inside, I wonder, *Is that really what you're crying about? I have worse things happen to me on my good days!*

LOVING GOD

Your life will become stable as you enter God's presence and primarily use prayer to love and worship Him. You'll have a whole new outlook. You'll think differently than those who don't love and worship Him. If you'd quit asking for things and just start loving Him, you'd start seeing everything in your life change for the better. The Lord did say "Ask, and you shall receive," but it's not what prayer is all about!

Prayer is simply loving God! It's saying, "Father, You're a good God! I adore You! You are awesome!" Enter His presence with generous amounts of praise and thanksgiving. Singing and worship should also be a huge part of prayer, but most people give God so very little. Instead, their prayers are consumed with taking. "God, I have nothing to give You, but I need this and that and this and that. Please, send it quickly!" If loving and communing with God isn't your primary purpose in prayer, you're missing out on what Christianity is all about!

Outline

I. Prayer is simply communion with God, involving fellowship, relationship, and intimacy with Him.

    A. Prayer is both talking and listening; it must be a two-way dialogue.

    B. Most teaching on prayer today centers on how to request and receive from God.

    C. While asking and receiving is *one* purpose of prayer, it is not *the* purpose of prayer.

    D. When we seek first God's kingdom by loving, worshiping, and fellowshipping with Him, we'll soon discover that we don't have as many needs and that things are supernaturally added to us.

II. Our perspective changes when we put God first by praising Him.

    A. Many of our cares cease being problems anymore.

    B. As we spend time with Him, His attitude becomes our attitude, and the entire way we think will change.

    C. When God is our source, we won't have to worry about fixing our own problems.

III. When we put God first and love Him, there will be a supernatural flow in our finances, and we won't have to ask Him for financial help.

    A. Instead of pleading or even asking God for money, we should meditate on scriptures regarding finances, and worship and fellowship with Him.

    B. He will supernaturally add everything we need.

IV. Stress wouldn't be a part of our lives if we were constantly in God's presence, loving and worshiping Him.

A. It's possible to be too blessed to be stressed!

B. Looking into the brightness of God's glory blinds us to other things.

C. We don't have to have the worries and cares that other people have when we don't see what they see.

V. Ministers often ask God to bring the people to their meetings, then beg Him for His anointing to be present.

A. That's an insult to God!

B. We shouldn't have to ever ask God to anoint us, because His Word says in Luke 4:18 and 1 John 2:20 that He already has.

C. We must realize that God wants to change people's lives more than we do, and His anointing is always present to do so.

VI. Prayer is primarily for loving God, not getting our needs met.

A. When we magnify God, we discover how insignificant our problems really are and that 90 percent of what we've been obsessing over is unimportant.

B. If we'd quit asking Him for things and just start loving Him, we'd start seeing everything in our lives change for the better.

C. The Lord did say "Ask, and you shall receive," but it's not what prayer is all about.

D. If loving and communing with God isn't our primary purpose in prayer, we're missing out on what Christianity is all about!

Teacher's Guide

1.   Prayer is simply communion with God, involving fellowship, relationship, and intimacy with Him. Prayer is both talking and listening; it must be a two-way dialogue. Most teaching on prayer today centers on how to request and receive from God. While asking and receiving is *one* purpose of prayer, it is not *the* purpose of prayer. When we seek first God's kingdom by loving, worshiping, and fellowshipping with Him, we'll soon discover that we don't have as many needs and that things are supernaturally added to us.

1a.   What is prayer?
Communion with God, which is fellowship, relationship, and intimacy with Him—both talking and listening
1b.   How do you seek first God's kingdom?
By loving, worshiping, and fellowshipping with Him

2.   Our perspective changes when we put God first by praising Him. Many of our cares cease being problems anymore. As we spend time with Him, His attitude becomes our attitude, and the entire way we think will change. When God is our source, we won't have to worry about fixing our own problems.

2a.   What are some results of praising God?
Your perspective changes, your cares will cease being problems, God's attitude will become your attitude, and the way you think will change
2b.   When can you stop worrying about fixing your own problems?
When God is your source

3.   When we put God first and love Him, there will be a supernatural flow in our finances, and we won't have to ask Him for financial help. Instead of pleading or even asking God for money, we should meditate on scriptures regarding finances, and worship and fellowship with Him. He will supernaturally add everything we need.

3a.   Why shouldn't you have to ask God for finances?
Because when you put Him first and love Him, there will be a supernatural flow in your finances
3b.   Instead of pleading with God for financial help, what should you do?
Meditate on scriptures regarding finances, and worship and fellowship with Him

4.   Stress wouldn't be a part of our lives if we were constantly in God's presence, loving and worshiping Him. It's possible to be too blessed to be stressed! Looking into the brightness of God's glory blinds us to other things. We don't have to have the worries and cares that other people have when we don't see what they see.

4a.   How can you stay free of stress?
By staying in God's presence, loving and worshiping Him

4b.   What blinds you to other things?
Looking into the brightness of God's glory

5.   Ministers often ask God to bring the people to their meetings, then beg Him for His anointing to be present. That's an insult to God! We shouldn't have to ever ask God to anoint us, because His Word says in Luke 4:18 and 1 John 2:20 that He already has. We must realize that God wants to change people's lives more than we do, and His anointing is always present to do so.

5a.   Read Luke 4:18 and 1 John 2:20. What does God's Word say you already are?
Anointed

5b.   Who wants to change people's lives more than you do?
God

6.   Prayer is primarily for loving God, not getting our needs met. When we magnify God, we discover how insignificant our problems really are and that 90 percent of what we've been obsessing over is unimportant. If we'd quit asking Him for things and just start loving Him, we'd start seeing everything in our lives change for the better. The Lord did say "Ask, and you shall receive," but it's not what prayer is all about. If loving and communing with God isn't our primary purpose in prayer, we're missing out on what Christianity is all about!

6a.   What do you discover when you magnify God?
How insignificant your problems really are

6b.   When do you miss out on what Christianity is all about?
When your primary purpose in prayer isn't loving God and communing with Him

Discipleship Questions

1. What is prayer?

2. How do you seek first God's kingdom?

3. What are some results of praising God?

4. When can you stop worrying about fixing your own problems?

5. Why shouldn't you have to ask God for finances?

6. Instead of pleading with God for financial help, what should you do?

7. How can you stay free of stress?

8. What blinds you to other things?

9. Read Luke 4:18 and 1 John 2:20. What does God's Word say you already are?

10. Who wants to change people's lives more than you do?

11. What do you discover when you magnify God?

12. When do you miss out on what Christianity is all about?

Answer Key

1. Communion with God, which is fellowship, relationship, and intimacy with Him—both talking and listening

2. By loving, worshiping, and fellowshipping with Him

3. Your perspective changes, your cares will cease being problems, God's attitude will become your attitude, and the way you think will change

4. When God is your source

5. Because when you put Him first and love Him, there will be a supernatural flow in your finances

6. Meditate on scriptures regarding finances, and worship and fellowship with Him

7. By staying in God's presence, loving and worshiping Him

8. Looking into the brightness of God's glory

9. Anointed

10. God

11. How insignificant your problems really are

12. When your primary purpose in prayer isn't loving God and communing with Him

Scriptures

JOHN 16:24

Hitherto have ye asked nothing in my name: ask, and ye shall receive, that your joy may be full.

MATTHEW 6:25

Therefore I say unto you, Take no thought for your life, what ye shall eat, or what ye shall drink; nor yet for your body, what ye shall put on. Is not the life more than meat, and the body than raiment?

MATTHEW 6:33

But seek ye first the kingdom of God, and his righteousness; and all these things shall be added unto you.

LUKE 4:18

The Spirit of the Lord is upon me, because he hath anointed me to preach the gospel to the poor; he hath sent me to heal the brokenhearted, to preach deliverance to the captives, and recovering of sight to the blind, to set at liberty them that are bruised.

1 JOHN 2:20

But ye have an unction from the Holy One, and ye know all things.

LUKE 10:38-42

Now it came to pass, as they went, that he entered into a certain village: and a certain woman named Martha received him into her house. [39] And she had a sister called Mary, which also sat at Jesus' feet, and heard his word. [40] But Martha was cumbered about much serving, and came to him, and said, Lord, dost thou not care that my sister hath left me to serve alone? bid her therefore that she help me. [41] And Jesus answered and said unto her, Martha, Martha, thou art careful and troubled about many things: [42] But one thing is needful: and Mary hath chosen that good part, which shall not be taken away from her.

Intimacy: The Heart of Salvation

For God so loved the world, that he gave his only begotten Son, that whosoever believeth in him should not perish, but have everlasting life.

JOHN 3:16

Most Christians are so familiar with John 3:16 that they don't really know what it says. It's often used to proclaim, "God came and forgave your sins so that you could be born again and escape hell!" However, a closer look reveals that "not perishing" isn't really the goal of salvation—eternal life is!

Unfortunately, eternal life to most people is just a religious cliché meaning "to live forever in heaven." However, eternal life truly begins the moment you're born again (John 3:36). It's a present-tense—not future-tense—reality. If you're a believer, eternal life is now!

INTIMATE, PERSONAL KNOWLEDGE

What is eternal life? Jesus, its Author, defined it as,

And this is life eternal, that they might know thee the only true God, and Jesus Christ, whom thou hast sent.

JOHN 17:3

Eternal life is knowing God the Father and His Son, Jesus Christ!

Knowing, in the original Greek, speaks of personal, intimate, experiential knowledge. It's not referring to simply "knowing about." That's when you can describe certain facts about something or someone, like knowing famous people's names, where they're from, and the color of their hair without ever having met them face to face. *Knowing* in John 17:3 is knowledge in the biblical sense. (In Genesis 4:1, Adam knew his wife, Eve, who then conceived and bore a child.) It's the most intimate of all relationships. Jesus Christ died to produce knowing both Him and the Father intimately, now in this life, not just at some future time in heaven. This is the goal of salvation!

The church has cheapened, weakened, and cut the heart right out of the Gospel by preaching "Repent or burn!" and "Avoid hell—be born again!" It's true that those who don't receive Christ will go to hell. That alone is reason enough for us to lay down our lives in aggressive evangelism. However, it's not what Scripture reveals as the true goal of the Gospel.

Jesus gave His life so that you and I could know Him in an intimate, close, and personal way. If all you've ever received is forgiveness of sins so you won't go to hell, you haven't yet experienced the true goal of salvation. Although missing hell is a wonderful benefit, it's not the heart of the Gospel. If all you've received is forgiveness of your sins, you've missed the main purpose of salvation.

Complete salvation is being able to be so intimate with God that He's your very best friend. He's the closest person to you—more real than even your spouse and children. If you aren't yet experiencing this kind of relationship with God, you're missing out on what eternal life is all about.

Sin wasn't the object of Christ's coming; it was simply the barrier that stood between mankind and God. Jesus took man's sin upon the cross and forever removed that barrier. However, His ultimate purpose wasn't to overcome sin but to restore man to a close, personal, intimate relationship with God. This is the eternal life Jesus came to provide.

HUNGRY LIONS & FLAMING STAKES

The reason the first-century church had much better results than this century's church is because they experienced this eternal life! Without the assistance of modern media, this ragtag group of mostly uneducated servants changed the world. The Gospel spread like wildfire throughout the entire known world due to their aggressive witness those first thirty years. What caused this greater impact? The infectious quality of their intimacy with God!

When I was eighteen years old, my mother took me to Rome. I saw the catacombs, the Coliseum, and the Circus Maximus (location of the Ben-Hur chariot race). In the Circus Maximus, the Romans would kill people by burning them at the stake or throwing them to the lions (among other things). Since they hated Christians so very much, they would also desecrate their graves. That's why many believers took their dead and buried them in underground passageways called the "catacombs."

One of the inscriptions I read in the catacombs profoundly impacted me as a young believer. It said, "Here lies my wife and six-month-old daughter who gave their lives today for the glory of God in the Circus Maximus." This man's pride and joy came through loud and clear to me. His wife and daughter were killed for the glory of God!

Before being burnt alive, sharp stakes were driven up into believers' bodies. Impaled and in pain, the joyful songs of these Christians caused the cruel emperor, Nero, to literally stick his fingers in his ears and scream, "My God, why do these Christians sing?" Believers actually fought each other to see who would receive the honor of being chosen to die that day for the glory of God. Most Western Christians today would be so full of self-love and fear that they'd be thinking, *My life!*

For every Christian killed, up to seven Romans jumped out of the stands and took their place. They, too, were immediately slaughtered by the lions or put to the stake. It was the joy, the peace, and the love emanating from these believers' faces as they gladly died for their Beloved that provoked these Romans to give up their lives in order to have a relationship with Someone like that. It's also one of the main reasons they stopped doing these things in the Circus Maximus.

"GOD, MEET MY NEEDS!"

Today hardly one Christian in a thousand would have that kind of attitude! Most believers' relationship with God is so superficial and self-centered. Their constant cry is "God, meet my needs!" I'm not suggesting that God wants all of us to be martyrs, but our focus definitely needs realignment.

As you seek Him first with a heart full of love, worship, and gratitude, you'll experience the joy and peace of God to such a degree that it wouldn't even bother you if they foreclosed on your house or repossessed your car. You'd say, "Who cares? God will take care of me. Besides, I have a mansion up there where the streets are paved with gold!" If you could get that kind of attitude, prosperity would be no problem. You wouldn't have to spend any time praying about your own needs!

Salvation has been cheapened to the point where it's just an opportunity for us to look at our big Father up in the sky to meet all of our needs. When most people came to the Lord, they came for selfish reasons—especially those who were just escaping judgment.

We ought to be telling people of God's greatness, goodness, and grace. He's not angry with us anymore, because His own Son bore the sin, judgment, and punishment we deserved so that we could be intimate with Him. That's how much God loves us! If we preached that, people would jump out of the stands by the droves to join us.

Instead, "turn or burn" is preached, and people look at God as their "fire insurance." Once new converts have been assured that they've truly escaped hell, most don't give God much time or effort beyond that. They're instructed to "hang in there," serving the Lord just enough to make it to heaven.

Faith comes by hearing, and hearing by the Word of God. When people are taught that the reason they should be saved is to escape hell and then get all of their needs met, that's what they'll have faith for. If that's the goal, they'll serve Him just enough to get what they need. Then, as they enter into prosperity, He is forgotten. Sound familiar? That's the way salvation has been preached.

CHASED OR CHASING?

God loves you so very much that He gave His own Son for you. He's not mad at you but desires intimacy with you more than you could ever imagine. He's not holding your sins against you but views you through your righteous, born-again spirit. Almighty God wants to hang out with you because He loves you!

Since most believers are ignorant of this truth, they aren't enjoying a very intimate relationship with God. Their whole Christian life—specifically, prayer—has been reduced to "How can I make God do this? How can I receive that from God? How can I make Him do this for someone else?" We aren't using prayer for what it's really for.

Prayer is communion and fellowship with God. What prayer should be about is "Father, I love You" and hearing Him answer "I love you too!" It's listening to Him in your heart and feeling His pleasure as you spend time with Him. If you did that, you wouldn't have to spend much time asking for things, because they'd just supernaturally show up.

The Word reveals that all of God's blessings should be coming upon us and overtaking us (Deut. 28:2). I haven't seen very many Christians with blessings chasing them, but there sure are lots of believers chasing blessings! People come to my meetings with their tongues hanging out, saying, "I'm here at another service trying to make God do something." We need to just stop, and start loving God by saying, "I'm sorry, Father. Yes, there are things I need in my life, but it's no big deal. The main thing I need is just to love You, fellowship with You, and know that You love me. I worship You!" Our lives would transform tremendously!

On the other hand, the Christian life is a painful, difficult struggle when 95 percent of your prayer life is asking for things, repenting, bawling and squalling, griping and complaining, telling God what the doctor said, informing Him of your bills, and such. You're missing out on what Christianity is all about: knowing and loving Him!

GOD WANTS YOU!

God isn't as concerned about what we do as much as He is who we are. He wants our fellowship more than our service, but the church has emphasized "Do a work for God!" We've equated His love and acceptance of us to be proportional to how well we think we're performing. We've become "human doings" instead of "human beings." We feel obligated and duty bound to serve Him because we feel we owe Him. This debtor mentality is what gives us the concept *I have to do something for God!*

If you give God your heart, He'll have no problem getting your service. But your service can never replace intimate fellowship! If the Lord has your heart, He'll also have your wallet. However, your giving alone will never be a substitute for your worship. What God wants is you!

I once heard a minister passionately preach, "The sole justification for our existence is to lead others to the Lord!" If that were true, then what would have been the justification for Adam and Eve's existence? They didn't have anyone to lead to the Lord! In fact, they had no demons to cast out, or clothes or food to believe for. *"Give us this day our daily bread"* (Matt. 6:11) didn't apply, because the climate was perfect and the provision was plentiful. Neither did they pray to receive healing for their broken hearts, painful memories, or dysfunctional families. Adam and Eve didn't have all this stuff that occupies our entire Christianity, yet they met with God every day in the cool of the evening to fellowship with Him.

> *Thou art worthy, O Lord, to receive glory and honour and power: for thou hast created all things, and for thy pleasure they are and were created.*
> REVELATION 4:11

You were created for God's pleasure! He loves you and wants to show you how much He loves you so you can then say, "I love You too!" That's what God created you for, not just to do something. It's true that He wants things done, but your service is a byproduct of your intimate relationship with Him.

Many scriptures reveal God's displeasure when we give Him our service but not our hearts. "Your offerings are a stench in My nostrils. I can't stand it—away with them!" These were things God had commanded to be done, but they stank because His people had attempted to substitute sacrifices for their hearts. It profits us nothing to give all our goods to feed the poor—even our bodies to be burned—if we don't have a heart of love behind it (1 Cor. 13:1-3). We could speak with the tongues of men and of angels or have faith to move mountains, but if our hearts aren't in union with God, it'll profit us nothing. We haven't understood how much God wants us. He desires us much more than our service!

PURPOSE FOR LIVING

After hearing me minister this message on the radio over twenty-five years ago, a woman in prison sent me this tear-stained letter:

Dear Andrew,

I'm on death row for murder. Since committing this crime, I've been born again and Spirit-filled. I live in solitary confinement without anyone to talk to. They slip me my food under the door, and I never leave my cell. I've spent years asking God to kill me, saying "Please, just let me die and go home!"

All my life I've been nothing but a problem! I disgraced my family and ruined my marriage. My own kids are ashamed and refuse to see me. Not only that, but I killed someone and hurt their family. Even though I'm born again now and love God, I'm still just a drain on the taxpayers. For so long, it seemed to me that it would be better if this leech were dead and gone. Who could I witness to? There's no guard or any other prisoners here. I simply had no purpose!

Then I heard your teaching on the radio. For the first time in my life, I understand that I am born again because God loves me. I can really bless and minister to Him by saying, "Father, I love You!" Now I have a purpose for living!

For the first time in my life, I'm free. I am more free in this jail cell than I ever thought I could be!

This sister in solitary confinement experienced more liberty than most people who aren't in prison, simply because she discovered that eternal life is all about knowing God intimately.

When you are intimate with God, He's blessed and you change. You're infused with stability and strength. Instead of falling apart at the slightest little thing, you can boldly and honestly declare, "Come what may, I'll make it through because God loves me!" If this doesn't describe your Christian life, then it's time to change your primary focus in prayer from getting your needs met to loving and worshiping God!

Outline

I. "Not perishing" isn't really the goal of salvation—eternal life is!

    For God so loved the world, that he gave his only begotten Son, that whosoever believeth in him should not perish, but have everlasting life.
    JOHN 3:16

    A. Eternal life truly begins the moment we're born again (John 3:36).

    B. It's a present-tense—not future-tense—reality.

    C. Eternal life is knowing God the Father and His Son, Jesus Christ:

    And this is life eternal, that they might know thee the only true God, and Jesus Christ, whom thou hast sent.
    JOHN 17:3

II. *Knowing* means to have a personal, intimate, experiential knowledge of someone (see Gen. 4:1).

    A. Jesus Christ died to produce *knowing* both Him and the Father intimately now in this life, not just at some future time in heaven—this is the goal of salvation!

        i. Complete salvation is being able to be so intimate with God that He's our very best friend.

    B. If all we've received is forgiveness of our sins, we've missed the main purpose of salvation.

    C. Sin wasn't the object of Christ's coming; it was simply the barrier that stood between mankind and God.

    D. His ultimate purpose wasn't to overcome sin, but to restore man to a close, personal, intimate relationship with Him—this is the eternal life Jesus came to provide.

III. The first-century church experienced true eternal life and shared it with the world.

    A. The Gospel spread like wildfire due to their aggressive witness and infectious quality of intimacy with God.

    B. Early martyrs considered it an honor to die for the glory of God.

    C. The joy, peace, and love emanating from these believers' faces as they gladly died for their Beloved provoked others to also give up their own lives to have a relationship with Someone like that.

IV. Unlike the early martyrs, most believers today are too selfish to give their lives for the Gospel.

    A. Salvation has been cheapened to the point where it's just an opportunity for us to look to God to meet all of our needs.

    B. If we would tell people about God's greatness, goodness, and grace and that He's not angry with man anymore, people would want to join us.

    C. Instead, "turn or burn" is preached, and people look at God as their "fire insurance."

        i. When people are taught that the reason they should be saved is to escape hell and then get all of their needs met, that's what they'll have faith for.

        ii. If that's the goal, they'll serve Him just enough to get what they need, and then they'll forget about Him.

    D. That's the way salvation has been preached.

V. God loves us so very much that He gave His own Son for us!

    A. He's not mad at us but desires intimacy with us more than we could ever imagine.

    B. He's not holding our sins against us but views us through our righteous, born-again spirits.

        i. Almighty God wants to hang out with us because He loves us!

C. Instead of using prayer to try to make God do something, we should use it for communion and fellowship with Him.

    i.   When we do, the things we want will just supernaturally show up.

D. When 95 percent of our prayer life is spent asking for things or complaining, we're missing out on what Christianity is all about: knowing and loving God.

VI. God isn't as concerned about what we do as much as He is about who we are.

A. He wants our fellowship more than our service.

    i.   We're supposed to be "human beings," not "human doings."

    ii. We've equated His love and acceptance of us to be proportional to how well we think we're performing.

B. We feel obligated to serve him because we feel we owe Him.

C. If we give God our hearts, He'll have no problem getting our service, but our service can never replace intimate fellowship with Him.

    i.   Our service is a byproduct of our intimate relationship with Him—He does not want our service without our hearts.

D. When we are intimate with God, He's blessed and we change!

Teacher's Guide

1.   "Not perishing" isn't really the goal of salvation—eternal life is!

> *For God so loved the world, that he gave his only begotten Son, that whosoever believeth in him should not perish, but have everlasting life.*
>
> **JOHN 3:16**

Eternal life truly begins the moment we're born again (John 3:36). It's a present-tense—not future-tense—reality. Eternal life is knowing God the Father and His Son, Jesus Christ:

> *And this is life eternal, that they might know thee the only true God, and Jesus Christ, whom thou hast sent.*
>
> **JOHN 17:3**

1a.   Read John 3:16 and 36. What is the goal of salvation?
Eternal life

1b.   When does eternal life truly begin?
The moment you're born again

2.   *Knowing* means to have a personal, intimate, experiential knowledge of someone (see Gen. 4:1). Jesus Christ died to produce *knowing* both Him and the Father intimately now in this life, not just at some future time in heaven—this is the goal of salvation! Complete salvation is being able to be so intimate with God that He's our very best friend. If all we've received is forgiveness of our sins, we've missed the main purpose of salvation. Sin wasn't the object of Christ's coming; it was simply the barrier that stood between mankind and God. His ultimate purpose wasn't to overcome sin, but to restore man to a close, personal, intimate relationship with Him—this is the eternal life Jesus came to provide.

2a.   What does knowing, as it's used in Genesis 4:1, mean?
To have a personal, intimate, experiential knowledge of someone

2b.   What was Christ's ultimate purpose in coming?
To restore you to a close, personal, intimate relationship with God

3.   The first-century church experienced true eternal life and shared it with the world. The Gospel spread like wildfire due to their aggressive witness and infectious quality of intimacy with God. Early martyrs considered it an honor to die for the glory of God. The joy, peace, and love

emanating from these believers' faces as they gladly died for their Beloved provoked others to also give up their own lives to have a relationship with Someone like that.

3a.   Why did the first-century church have much better results than this century's church?
Because they experienced true eternal life

3b.   What was the early martyrs' attitude toward death?
They considered it an honor to die for the glory of God

4.   Unlike the early martyrs, most believers today are too selfish to give their lives for the Gospel. Salvation has been cheapened to the point where it's just an opportunity for us to look to God to meet all of our needs. If we would tell people about God's greatness, goodness, and grace and that He's not angry with man anymore, people would want to join us. Instead, "turn or burn" is preached, and people look at God as their "fire insurance." When people are taught that the reason they should be saved is to escape hell and then get all of their needs met, that's what they'll have faith for. If that's the goal, they'll serve Him just enough to get what they need, and then they'll forget about Him. That's the way salvation has been preached.

4a.   How are most believers today different from the early martyrs?
They're too selfish to give their lives for the Gospel

4b.   What would people want to do if you told them about God's greatness, goodness, and grace?
Join you

5.   God loves us so very much that He gave His own Son for us! He's not mad at us but desires intimacy with us more than we could ever imagine. He's not holding our sins against us but views us through our righteous, born-again spirits. Almighty God wants to hang out with us because He loves us! Instead of using prayer to try to make God do something, we should use it for communion and fellowship with Him. When we do, the things we want will just supernaturally show up. When 95 percent of our prayer life is spent asking for things or complaining, we're missing out on what Christianity is all about: knowing and loving God.

5a.   How does God view you?
Through your righteous, born-again spirit

5b.   How do people miss out on what Christianity is all about?
By spending their prayer lives asking God for things or complaining

6.   God isn't as concerned about what we do as much as He is about who we are. He wants our fellowship more than our service. We're supposed to be "human beings," not "human doings." We've equated His love and acceptance of us to be proportional to how well we think we're

performing. We feel obligated to serve him because we feel we owe Him. If we give God our hearts, He'll have no problem getting our service, but our service can never replace intimate fellowship with Him. Our service is a byproduct of our intimate relationship with Him—He does not want our service without our hearts. When we are intimate with God, He's blessed and we change!

6a. What have people equated God's love and acceptance to?
How well they think they're performing

6b. What can your acts of service never replace?
Intimate fellowship with God

Discipleship Questions

1. Read John 3:16 and 36. What is the goal of salvation?

2. When does eternal life truly begin?

3. What does knowing, as it's used in Genesis 4:1, mean?

4. What was Christ's ultimate purpose in coming?

5. Why did the first-century church have much better results than this century's church?

6. What was the early martyrs' attitude toward death?

7. How are most believers today different from the early martyrs?

8. What would people want to do if you told them about God's greatness, goodness, and grace?

9. How does God view you?

10. How do people miss out on what Christianity is all about?

11. What have people equated God's love and acceptance to?

12. What can your acts of service never replace?

Answer Key

1. Eternal life

2. The moment you're born again

3. To have a personal, intimate, experiential knowledge of someone

4. To restore you to a close, personal, intimate relationship with God

5. Because they experienced true eternal life

6. They considered it an honor to die for the glory of God

7. They're too selfish to give their lives for the Gospel

8. Join you

9. Through your righteous, born-again spirit

10. By spending their prayer lives asking God for things or complaining

11. How well they think they're performing

12. Intimate fellowship with God

Scriptures

JOHN 3:16
For God so loved the world, that he gave his only begotten Son, that whosoever believeth in him should not perish, but have everlasting life.

JOHN 3:36
He that believeth on the Son hath everlasting life: and he that believeth not the Son shall not see life; but the wrath of God abideth on him.

JOHN 17:3
And this is life eternal, that they might know thee the only true God, and Jesus Christ, whom thou hast sent.

GENESIS 4:1
And Adam knew Eve his wife; and she conceived, and bare Cain, and said, I have gotten a man from the LORD.

DEUTERONOMY 28:2
And all these blessings shall come on thee, and overtake thee, if thou shalt hearken unto the voice of the LORD thy God.

MATTHEW 6:11
Give us this day our daily bread.

REVELATION 4:11
Thou art worthy, O Lord, to receive glory and honour and power: for thou hast created all things, and for thy pleasure they are and were created.

1 CORINTHIANS 13:1-3
Though I speak with the tongues of men and of angels, and have not charity, I am become as sounding brass, or a tinkling cymbal. [2] And though I have the gift of prophecy, and understand all mysteries, and all knowledge; and though I have all faith, so that I could remove mountains, and have not charity, I am nothing. [3] And though I bestow all my goods to feed the poor, and though I give my body to be burned, and have not charity, it profiteth me nothing.

You're a Good Dad!

Bless the LORD, O my soul: and all that is within me, bless his holy name.

PSALM 103:1

Merely saying the words "Bless the Lord" doesn't necessarily bless the Lord.

A pagan cocktail waitress in Las Vegas became born again and started hearing people talk about the baptism in the Holy Spirit. She asked, "What's that?" They described it as being filled with God's power and then speaking in tongues. "Sounds good to me. How do I get it?" she asked them. They told her, "Just ask for it, and then start blessing the Lord." So, she went home knowing only this tiny little bit.

Since it was a "baptism," she filled her bathtub with water and lit candles all around the room. From the tub, she asked for this "baptism in the Holy Spirit" and began saying, "Bless the Lord! Bless the Lord!" That's how she understood what they had told her to do. She thought simply repeating those particular words was what it meant to bless the Lord. God did honor her childlike faith by baptizing her in the Holy Spirit and giving her a brand-new prayer language in the bathroom that day. But there's much more to blessing the Lord than simply saying those words.

MINISTER TO GOD

"Blessing the Lord" is ministering to Him. When you say from your heart "Father, I love You. You're a good God," it blesses Him! The prophets and teachers in Antioch *ministered to the Lord*" (Acts 13:2). They weren't preaching at Him or exhorting Him to repent. They were praising, worshiping, and loving Him. Anyone who loves has a need to be loved in return. If the object of your love doesn't love you back, it's miserable. God is love (1 John 4:8) and He loves you. When you love Him, it blesses and ministers to Him!

I took my sons and some of their friends out one Saturday when they were about five and seven years old. We spent all day riding horses, playing in the creek, and eating junk food (a special treat while away from Mom). At the end of the day, I cleaned them up and put them to bed after having devotions together. As I turned out the light and was leaving the room, my youngest said, "Dad, you're a good dad!" That blessed me! He didn't say "Bless you, Dad!" but he communicated "Thanks!" and "I love you!" in his own way. It made me want to drag him right out of that bed to go horseback riding all over again!

That's the way it is with your heavenly Father. You may not realize it, but God needs ministry. He wants you to bless Him because it's the purpose you were originally created for. Pray, "Father, You're a good Dad and an awesome God! Thank You for my health, for letting me live here in this country, for my opportunities, and for my job." Instead of cursing your life and making it worse, thank Him that it's as good as it is! God will be so blessed by your love and worship that He'll want to drag you out of bed and give you everything He can think of to bless you! It'll just come upon and overtake you. All these other people will still be begging and pleading with God for these things that are just flowing in your life because you love Him.

Spend 95 percent of your prayer time singing, praising, and worshiping. "Father, I love You!" Then every once in a while say, "Oh, yeah, the doctor thinks I'm going to die, but that's not so bad. It'd be awesome to be with You. I'm actually having trouble deciding whether I should stay or not because of how wonderful You are!" Instead of spending all of your time rebuking fear and white-knuckling it with "O God, help me believe!" you'd say, "Either way, Father. If I die, I win. If I'm healed, I win. I can't lose!" That's the attitude you ought to have. Nothing else would matter!

This isn't just for "super-saints"; this is entry-level, baby Christianity! As soon as people are born again, they should be told, "You were created for intimacy with God. Now that you're saved, you can fulfill your calling by returning the awesome love He's shown. As you continue receiving His love and giving Him yours, raise someone from the dead, cast out some devils, heal the sick, and get your needs met." Really, those things are incidental. If you developed this kind of attitude, you'd be unstoppable!

FOOT-TAPPIN' GOOD

And a vision appeared to Paul in the night; There stood a man of Macedonia, and prayed him, saying, Come over into Macedonia, and help us.

ACTS 16:9

God supernaturally directed Paul and Silas to Philippi (in the province of Macedonia) by the vision recorded in Acts 16:9. Within forty-eight hours of arriving, they were beaten within an inch of their lives and thrown into the deepest part of the jail. It was from this rat- and disease-infested, absolutely dark place that they started to sing. Even though stocks on their hands and feet prevented them from soothing their wounds, these men praised God!

When in bad situations, some Christians discipline themselves to "praise" God through gritted teeth. They know that praising the Lord is strength to *"still the enemy and the avenger"* (Ps. 8:2). Although they may not truly mean it from their hearts, they're doing "spiritual warfare." Since praise drives out demons, they exercise themselves to "praise" those problems right out of their lives. Hey, if that's the best reason you've got, it's better to praise God like that than to gripe and complain!

As Paul and Silas worshiped the Lord, it's like He must have started tapping His foot, because an earthquake resulted, breaking off their stocks and opening up all the prison cell doors. However, instead of running away, Paul and Silas stayed. How could this be? Here's a radical truth: They weren't praising God just to escape their problem; they really loved Him! Backs beaten to shreds and ankle-deep in filth, they just continued worshiping and enjoying the Lord's glorious presence.

Most Christians today would have run out of that prison just as soon as they could have. They just don't love God that way! On another occasion, the disciples left the Jewish council after being beaten, thanking the Lord and praising Him that they had been counted worthy to suffer shame for His name (Acts 5:41). Peter was crucified upside down for his faith. He thought he was unworthy to be hung in the same position as Jesus. We love self and would be thinking of our own loss to such a degree that we wouldn't care about anyone else. We need to get beyond that, recognizing that Christianity is all about loving God.

RAISED FROM THE DEAD!

Prayer is primarily for loving and worshiping God. If you would seek first His kingdom and just fellowship with Him, you'd find your needs already provided for. You wouldn't have any "problems," because nothing would bother you. Instead of being depressed, the joy of the Lord would be your strength!

> *Thou wilt shew me the path of life: in thy presence is fulness of joy; at thy right hand there are pleasures for evermore.*
>
> PSALM 16:11

If you're depressed, you're not in the presence of the Lord. He's with you, but you're not with Him, because something else has you occupied. Get back in God's presence, and you'll find fullness of joy!

After an international ministry trip, Jamie and I had finally arrived home and gotten to bed around midnight. Four hours later, the telephone rang. It was our oldest son, Joshua, calling about our youngest son. He said, "Dad, I'm sorry to have to tell you this, but Peter is dead."

"Dead? What happened?" He told me, and I declared, "The first report is not the last report!" After hanging up the phone, Jamie and I spent about thirty seconds taking authority and commanding life back into our son. Then we just praised, worshiped, and loved on God all the way into Colorado Springs.

I had the same thoughts and feelings anybody else would. However, since my heart was so fixed on the Lord, I couldn't help but pray, "Father, I know You didn't kill my son, because You're a good God! This is not Your will. I love You so much! Thank You for being such a good God!"

I just kept on praising, worshiping, and thanking Him all the way into the Springs. Peter had turned black from being dead for five hours, but five minutes after we started praying, he just sat right up. God raised our son from the dead! Hallelujah! Thank You, Jesus!

My prayer life is all about loving God. I don't ask for very much or do very much, but great things are happening. My Christian life is fun, and I don't fret about things. Worry is blasphemy against God's promises anyway. It stems from not being very intimate with Him. I realize this way of praying may not fit your present mold, but until you get better results, maybe you ought to try it!

"WELL, THANK YOU, ANDREW!"

What I'm sharing is simple, but it's very profound. Of course, it takes effort to set aside self and focus on loving God. However, I've found that as I minister to Him, I get more blessed than He does! I'm not sure exactly how it works, but God won't ever let me out-give Him! As I bless the Lord, I have all of the emotion I can handle. He takes care of me and treats me well—much better than I deserve. I spend my time loving Him.

Sometimes I'll just pray in tongues for an hour or two. Usually, that's because I need wisdom in some area, and I pray in the Spirit to draw it out. Even then, I praise God because I know the answer is coming.

You shouldn't ever need to bawl and squall, because you're always praising and thanking Him. *"With thanksgiving let your requests be made known unto God"* (Phil. 4:6). This approach to prayer shrinks problems down so small that they're literally no big deal.

Normally, this kind of message doesn't sell very many books. If I offered one entitled *Seven Steps to Make God Do Something*, everybody and their brother would buy a copy because that's really what they want to know. However, the best results come from loving, thanking, praising, blessing, and worshiping God as the highest priority in life. It's simply staying in communication with Him all day long.

Nothing this world has to offer can even compare to experiencing God's pleasure. I remember sitting with Jamie after a Kathryn Kuhlman meeting. We were the last two people there, but we just couldn't get up and walk out, because of His presence. People's lives had been miraculously transformed, both physically and emotionally, right before my eyes. Hurting individuals had been put in touch with the living, loving, healing God. I was completely overwhelmed!

I've been overwhelmed just like that many times since. While driving back to the motel after one of my meetings, I remember thanking God for how awesome He'd been and the way He'd moved through me to touch people's lives. Then I heard Him answer, "Well, thank you, Andrew! I appreciate your letting Me use you." That blessed me! You might think, *God would never say anything like that!* Sure, He would! You just don't know Him very well. God is good, and He loves and appreciates us.

READY TO CHANGE?

God doesn't just love you; He likes you too! You might not have heard Him tell you that before, but it's true. He isn't just your Creator who felt obligated to provide salvation; God appreciates you. It's a joy to experience telling Him how much you love Him and then have Him turn right around and do the same!

Your entire prayer life would be transformed if you'd get the heart of what I'm communicating. Everything in your life would change, and you'd become a totally different person. Loving God is all that matters. Everything else is incidental.

Have you missed the real purpose of salvation? Were you born again just to avoid hell? Have you ever truly understood God's love and desire for intimacy? Sure, you say "Thank You" every once in a while, but praising and worshiping God isn't what you primarily use prayer for. Your focus has been something else. Friend, if this is you, then you need to repent and go on to receive the true goal of salvation. You need to start loving and worshiping God.

Everybody can love God more, but have you ever made this your heart's commitment? Are you primarily dedicated to yourself and praying for your own needs to be met? Perhaps you even pray for others sometimes, too, but the truth is you don't love God in this way. Is that you? Are you ready to change?

> *For I know whom I have believed, and am persuaded that he is able to keep that which I have committed unto him.*
>
> 2 TIMOTHY 1:12B

God has promised to keep what you commit. No committing means no keeping. "But, Andrew, I'm not sure I can live up to this!" Don't worry—you can't! You'll fail at times, but if you make the commitment, God will faithfully remind you of it.

It's important that you take a moment to humble yourself and respond. I encourage you to do so right now, before going on in this study or doing something else. The Holy Spirit has been dealing with you. Now is the time to yield and say, "Yes, Lord!" Believe me—you'll be so glad you did!

Outline

I.   Psalm 103 instructs us to bless the Lord:

> *Bless the Lord, O my soul: and all that is within me, bless his holy name.*
> **PSALM 103:1**

   A.   But merely saying the words "Bless the Lord" doesn't necessarily bless the Lord.

   B.   We can bless the Lord by ministering to Him and loving Him back.

       i.   The prophets and teachers in Antioch showed us an example of ministering to the Lord in Acts 13:2 when they praised, worshiped, and loved Him.

   C.   God wants us to bless Him, because it's the purpose we were originally created for.

II.   It's good to praise God in all circumstances.

   A.   Some Christians discipline themselves to "praise" God in tough situations, but they don't really mean it from their hearts.

   B.   Since praise drives out demons (Ps. 8:2), they exercise themselves to "praise" those problems right out of their lives.

   C.   Paul and Silas genuinely praised God from prison.

   D.   They didn't just praise Him to escape their problem; they really loved Him!

   E.   Likewise, the disciples left the Jewish council after being beaten, thanking the Lord and praising Him that they had been counted worthy to suffer shame for His name (Acts 5:41).

   F.   Most Christians love self too much and don't recognize that Christianity is all about loving God.

III. Prayer is primarily for loving and worshiping God.

   A. If we would seek first His kingdom and just fellowship with Him, we'd find our needs already provided for.

   B. We wouldn't have any "problems," because nothing would bother us.

   C. Being depressed means that we're not in the presence of the Lord and that something else has us occupied.

   D. In God's presence, we'll find fullness of joy (Ps. 16:11).

      i. Because Andrew was living in God's presence, he was able to continue praising and worshiping God and believe for a miracle when he learned his son had died.

   E. Intimacy with God will keep us from worrying.

      i. Worry is blasphemy against God's promises.

IV. Our main focus should be loving God.

   A. It takes effort, though, to set aside self and focus on loving Him.

   B. Our best results will come from loving, thanking, praising, blessing, and worshiping God as our highest priority in life and staying in communication with Him all day long.

   C. This approach to prayer shrinks problems down so small that they're no big deal.

   D. Nothing this world has to offer can even compare to experiencing God's pleasure.

   E. God doesn't just love us; He also likes us and appreciates us.

   F. We must make it our hearts' commitment to stop being primarily dedicated to ourselves in prayer and instead make it our priority to love and worship God.

Teacher's Guide

1.   Psalm 103 instructs us to bless the Lord:

Bless the Lord, O my soul: and all that is within me, bless his holy name.

PSALM 103:1

But merely saying the words "Bless the Lord" doesn't necessarily bless the Lord. We can bless the Lord by ministering to Him and loving Him back. The prophets and teachers in Antioch showed us an example of ministering to the Lord in Acts 13:2 when they praised, worshiped, and loved Him. God wants us to bless Him, because it's the purpose we were originally created for.

1a.   Read Psalm 103:1 and Acts 13:2. What are some good ways to bless the Lord?
       Ministering to Him, loving Him, praising and worshiping Him
1b.   Why is it important for you to bless the Lord?
       It's the purpose you were created for

2.   It's good to praise God in all circumstances. Some Christians discipline themselves to "praise" God in tough situations, but they don't really mean it from their hearts. Since praise drives out demons (Ps. 8:2), they exercise themselves to "praise" those problems right out of their lives. Paul and Silas genuinely praised God from prison. They didn't just praise Him to escape their problem; they really loved Him! Likewise, the disciples left the Jewish council after being beaten, thanking the Lord and praising Him that they had been counted worthy to suffer shame for His name (Acts 5:41). Most Christians love self too much and don't recognize that Christianity is all about loving God.

2a.   What do some Christians discipline themselves to do?
       "Praise" God in tough situations
2b.   How was the disciples' approach to praise different than many Christians?
       They praised God because they genuinely loved Him and because He counted them worthy to suffer for His name

3.   Prayer is primarily for loving and worshiping God. If we would seek first His kingdom and just fellowship with Him, we'd find our needs already provided for. We wouldn't have any "problems," because nothing would bother us. Being depressed means that we're not in the presence of the Lord and that something else has us occupied. In God's presence, we'll find

fullness of joy (Ps. 16:11). Because Andrew was living in God's presence, he was able to continue praising and worshiping God and believe for a miracle when he learned his son had died. Intimacy with God will keep us from worrying. Worry is blasphemy against God's promises.

3a. What is prayer primarily for?
Loving and worshiping God

3b. Read Psalm 16:11. What are the benefits of being in God's presence?
You won't be depressed, and there's fullness of joy

4. Our main focus should be loving God. It takes effort, though, to set aside self and focus on loving Him. Our best results will come from loving, thanking, praising, blessing, and worshiping God as our highest priority in life and staying in communication with Him all day long. This approach to prayer shrinks problems down so small that they're no big deal. Nothing this world has to offer can even compare to experiencing God's pleasure. God doesn't just love us; He also likes us and appreciates us. We must make it our hearts' commitment to stop being primarily dedicated to ourselves in prayer and instead make it our priority to love and worship God.

4a. What will happen when you make God your highest priority in life?
Your best results will come

4b. Nothing this world has to offer can even compare to experiencing what?
God's pleasure

Discipleship Questions

1. Read Psalm 103:1 and Acts 13:2. What are some good ways to bless the Lord?

2. Why is it important for you to bless the Lord?

3. What do some Christians discipline themselves to do?

4. How was the disciples' approach to praise different than many Christians?

5. What is prayer primarily for?

6. Read Psalm 16:11. What are the benefits of being in God's presence?

7. What will happen when you make God your highest priority in life?

8. Nothing this world has to offer can even compare to experiencing what?

Answer Key

1. Ministering to Him, loving Him, praising and worshiping Him

2. It's the purpose you were created for

3. "Praise" God in tough situations

4. They praised God because they genuinely loved Him and because He counted them worthy to suffer for His name

5. Loving and worshiping God

6. You won't be depressed, and there's fullness of joy

7. Your best results will come

8. God's pleasure

Scriptures

PSALM 103:1
Bless the LORD, O my soul: and all that is within me, bless his holy name.

ACTS 13:2
As they ministered to the Lord, and fasted, the Holy Ghost said, Separate me Barnabas and Saul for the work whereunto I have called them.

1 JOHN 4:8
He that loveth not knoweth not God; for God is love.

ACTS 16:9
And a vision appeared to Paul in the night; There stood a man of Macedonia, and prayed him, saying, Come over into Macedonia, and help us.

PSALM 8:2
Out of the mouth of babes and sucklings hast thou ordained strength because of thine enemies, that thou mightest still the enemy and the avenger.

ACTS 5:41
And they departed from the presence of the council, rejoicing that they were counted worthy to suffer shame for his name.

PSALM 16:11
Thou wilt shew me the path of life: in thy presence is fulness of joy; at thy right hand there are pleasures for evermore.

PHILIPPIANS 4:6
Be careful for nothing; but in every thing by prayer and supplication with thanksgiving let your requests be made known unto God.

2 TIMOTHY 1:12
For the which cause I also suffer these things: nevertheless I am not ashamed: for I know whom I have believed, and am persuaded that he is able to keep that which I have committed unto him against that day.

Answer That Fig Tree!

Mark 11 contains some tremendous lessons about how to receive from God in prayer.

And on the morrow, when they were come from Bethany, he [Jesus] was hungry: [13] And seeing a fig tree afar off having leaves, he came, if haply he might find any thing thereon: and when he came to it, he found nothing but leaves; for the time of figs was not yet. [14] And Jesus answered and said unto it, No man eat fruit of thee hereafter for ever. And his disciples heard it.

MARK 11:12-14, BRACKETS MINE

For a fig tree to have leaves, it should also have had figs! Fig trees produce fruit prior to or at the same time as when they leaf out. Seeing the leaves and being hungry, Jesus went over to it, expecting to pick some figs. When none were to be found, He cursed the tree and commanded it to die.

Many people wonder why the Lord would be upset with this fig tree if it wasn't time yet for figs. It's because Jesus was the Creator of fig trees. He's the one who made them to produce figs before they produced leaves. This fig tree had violated His command. It was a pervert. It was hypocritical. It professed something that it didn't possess. So, Jesus became angry and cursed it.

Notice that the Lord *"answered"* the fig tree. It had been talking to Him! You can't answer unless you've been communicated with first. This tree had been telling Jesus it had figs when, in fact, it didn't. It was a liar. So, Jesus spoke directly to it, *"No man eat fruit of thee hereafter for ever"* (Mark 11:14).

And in the morning, as they passed by, they saw the fig tree dried up from the roots.

MARK 11:20

In Matthew 21:19, the Bible records that the fig tree died immediately when Jesus spoke to it, even though the disciples didn't see the results until the next day. At the very moment Christ spoke, the miracle took place and the fig tree perished. However, since the tree died in its roots, it took approximately twelve hours for what had happened below the ground to be manifest above the ground. That's a beautiful picture of what takes place in prayer!

MORE THAN MEETS THE EYE

God is a Spirit, and He moves in the spirit realm. It often takes a period of time before what God has done in the spiritual world manifests in the physical world. I'm amazed by how many people don't know this. Most Christians think that if God wants something done, then—BAM—it's done. They don't understand the limitations and restrictions God deals with in order to answer prayer.

The Lord put certain laws in motion when He created the heavens and the earth. He Himself abides by these laws. That's why it often takes some time before what's true in the spirit manifests itself in the physical. For instance, God commanded one of His greatest angels, Gabriel, to answer Daniel's prayer in Daniel 9. It took about three minutes for Gabriel to appear and perform what the Lord had commanded. In Daniel 10, it took twenty-one days for God's messenger to appear with Daniel's answer. Why did God answer one prayer in three minutes and the next prayer in three weeks? He didn't! God answered both prayers instantly, but it took three minutes for the first messenger to appear and three weeks for the next. God wasn't the variable. He's consistent. Both times, the decree immediately went forth from His throne as soon as the request was made in prayer. There's simply more happening here than we've previously understood.

God's Word promises your recovery, but not that it'll manifest instantly. Mark 16:18 declares, *"They shall lay hands on the sick, and they shall recover."* However, the idea that says "If God wanted to, I would be healed and these symptoms would leave immediately!" cannot be verified by Scripture. Many things govern how quickly you experience your healing.

After praying with a woman who had AIDS, I could tell that it had left her body. I then released the anointing of God to restore her body from the damage the disease had done. I told her, "I believe you are completely healed of AIDS. Even though there is now no trace of it in you, your body will have to recover from the damage the disease did while it was still there. I don't know what all is involved in that, but you should give your body some time to build itself back up. It might take a few days to fully recover."

If you receive prayer and don't see instantaneous results, resist the temptation to think, *Well, nothing happened.* Even though you still feel weak, the junk could be totally kicked out of your system! Much is happening below the surface that you cannot see. If you try to use only your five senses to discern whether or not He's moved, you'll miss out on the things of God!

FAITH IN GOD

Although Jesus cursed this fig tree and instantly it was done, the results weren't visible until twelve hours later. Sometimes it takes time for what God has already accomplished to manifest itself in the physical realm.

> *And Peter calling to remembrance saith unto him, Master, behold, the fig tree which thou cursedst is withered away.*

> MARK 11:21

ANSWER THAT FIG TREE!

Peter was shocked the next morning when he saw that fig tree. In reading the Scriptures, people often have a tendency to overlook how it must have felt for those living it. You'd be pretty impressed if, as we were walking along, I commanded a tree "Die, in the name of Jesus!" and the next day you found it shriveled up dead. You'd say something, wouldn't you? Peter didn't just mention this—he was overwhelmed: "Jesus, look at this fig tree!"

The Lord used this teachable moment to illustrate how prayer works:

And Jesus answering saith unto them, Have faith in God.

MARK 11:22

This happened through faith in God. Faith is a powerful force, but you must believe in order to reap its benefits.

Faith is governed by law (Rom. 3:27). Just like the natural realm, the spirit realm operates according to God's divinely instituted order. Ignorance asks, "Why didn't God help these people? Why did He let them die?" Healing, deliverance, prosperity, and salvation don't "just happen." Spiritual laws must be obeyed in order to receive the desired results.

SELF-IMPOSED RESTRAINTS

Natural laws govern electricity. For instance, electrical power flows better through copper than rubber. That's just the way God made it to work. By using the laws of electricity, we are able to tame and harness its power for our benefit. However, before we understood and applied these laws, we did without electricity.

People lived thousands of years without the benefit of electricity. This was due to ignorance, not stupidity. Many brilliant individuals lived throughout the centuries, but they simply didn't know what electrical power was or how it worked. Even though electricity has been on the earth since God created it, people had to discover the laws that governed it before they could use it.

Imagine if electricity had been used back in the heyday of Egypt, in Solomon's time, or when Jesus walked the earth. It was already here, but man's ignorance kept him from operating in it. For example, the components that make a cell phone work have been around forever, but it's only been recently that man has been able to develop the technology to use them. Many things today could have been done long before, had it not been for ignorance.

Technological advancements are made possible as we discover the laws that govern them. Someday, we'll be able to drive cars with water. That's when we'll look back and think that using gasoline for fuel was ignorant. The only reason we aren't enjoying these things already is because we haven't discovered the laws yet.

God controls Himself and the universe He created by the laws He spoke into existence. These laws govern how He works. It simply wouldn't make sense for the one who created this physical world with so much order (i.e., the laws of electricity, gravity, etc.) to be Himself random and disorganized. Christians tell me often, "Well, I prayed!" But did you pray correctly? "I don't know if I did it all right, but if God wanted to, He could just heal me!" They don't think there are any restraints on God. Granted, the restraints are self-imposed, but they're restraints nonetheless. God follows His own laws!

FOLLOW HIS GUIDELINES

My covenant will I not break, nor alter the thing that is gone out of my lips.

PSALM 89:34

When God gives His word, He never violates it. He never says something He doesn't mean, and He always means what He says. For example, the Lord gave you a tremendous privilege by saying, "You resist the devil, and he'll flee from you" (James 4:7). However, He also just limited Himself, because now it's your responsibility to resist the devil, not His.

Since the authority has been given to you, God won't rebuke the Enemy for you. Praying "O God, please get the devil off my back!" isn't going to work. The Lord set down a law by speaking His Word. You must resist the devil, and he'll flee from you. Be as sincere as you want, but freedom from demonic oppression won't come until you follow His guidelines. You must exercise the authority God gave you, or it won't work.

Another law is you will have what you speak:

> *A man's belly shall be satisfied with the fruit of his mouth; and with the increase of his lips shall he be filled. [21] Death and life are in the power of the tongue: and they that love it shall eat the fruit thereof.*
>
> PROVERBS 18:20-21

Life and death are in the power of the tongue. You will have what you say! (See also Matt. 12:34, Mark 11:23, and James 3:2-12.)

Many people desire to be healed, but speak forth all kinds of negative things. They say what the doctor told them, what their bodies feel like, and what other people's opinions are, and then they wonder why they aren't seeing God's healing power manifest in their lives. Spiritual laws are in place and functioning!

DON'T KILL YOURSELF!

The same laws that bring benefit can also kill! If you touch an exposed wire that has electricity running through it, you'll get shocked. Depending on how much power was flowing through it, you could even be killed. It's not that the electric company doesn't like you and says, "We'll punish you for touching this bare wire!" No! It's not personal; it's just the law. The electric company generates power to benefit you, not kill you.

God created gravity for your benefit. It causes you to be able to sit in your chair without having to bolt it down and strap yourself in. Instead of having to exert constant, strenuous effort to keep from floating away, you could just fall asleep in that chair if you wanted. However, if you violate the law of gravity by jumping off the top of the Empire State Building and flapping your arms in a feeble attempt to fly, the same law (which was intended for your benefit) will kill you. It wasn't personal. Whether you lacked understanding or willfully chose not to cooperate doesn't really matter. The results are the same because you violated the law. God didn't do it; you killed yourself!

It's ignorant to say "Oh, man, I'm feeling worse. The doctor says I'll be dead in two weeks. I'm dying!" and then turn around and pray "God, please heal me if it be Thy will, for Jesus' sake, amen." After doing that, people often get mad at God and wonder why they aren't healed. They're violating the laws of faith and killing themselves by speaking those words of unbelief.

God isn't going to violate His word! He won't suspend gravity for one person trying to jump off the Empire State Building. It doesn't matter how sincere or how good that person is; gravity is a natural law. If the Lord suspended gravity for this one jumper, millions of other people would die who were depending on it. God will not suspend His laws—natural or spiritual—just because you mean well!

YOU TALK TO IT!

And Jesus answering saith unto them, Have faith in God. [23] For verily I say unto you, That whosoever shall say unto this mountain, Be thou removed, and be thou cast into the sea; and shall not doubt in his heart, but shall believe that those things which he saith shall come to pass; he shall have whatsoever he saith.

MARK 11:22-23

The Lord commands us to speak to our problems. This is a truth about prayer most people have missed—speak to the mountain!

A lot of people speak to God about their mountains instead of speaking to their mountains about God. The "mountain" represents whatever your problem is. Jesus declared, "Speak to your mountain, and command it to be cast into the sea!" Most Christians pray, "God, I have this mountain. Would You please move it for me?" The Lord told you to talk to it, not to Him. Whatever it is—speak to it!

The whole thing that occasioned all of this was that dead, dried-up fig tree. The day before, it had talked to Jesus. He answered and it talked no more. Have faith in God!

ANDREW'S RECOMMENDATIONS FOR FURTHER STUDY

I have a great teaching entitled "What to Do When Your Prayers Seem Unanswered." It'll encourage and instruct you on how to actively stand in faith during the time between when you pray and when the answer manifests in the physical realm.

Outline

I. Mark 11:12-14 paints a perfect picture of what happens when we pray.

    A. When Jesus spoke to the fig tree and cursed it because it had no fruit, it died immediately at its roots, but it didn't appear dead until the following day (Mark 11:20).

    B. God responds immediately to our prayers as well, but it often takes a period of time before what God has done in the spiritual world manifests in the physical world.

    C. Even though Mark 16:18 declares *"They shall lay hands on the sick, and they shall recover,"* we may not see our healing manifest immediately because many things affect the timing of our healing.

    D. Just because we can't discern with our five senses that anything's happened doesn't mean God hasn't answered our prayers.

    E. There's a lot happening beneath the surface that we do not see.

II. The Lord used this incident with the fig tree to illustrate how prayer works (Mark 11:22).

    A. Faith is a powerful force, but we must believe in order to reap its benefits.

    B. Faith is governed by law (Rom. 3:27).

    C. God has set spiritual laws in motion just like He did natural laws, and both must be obeyed to receive the desired results.

    D. God controls Himself and the universe He created by the laws He spoke into existence—these laws govern how He works.

III. God follows His own laws.

    A. He will never violate His own Word (Ps. 89:34).

    B. Because God has given us His authority, we are the ones who must exercise that authority or it won't work—He won't do it for us.

C. Another law is that we will have what we say (Prov. 18:20-21, Matt. 12:34, Mark 11:23, and James 3:2-12).

D. What we speak out will come to pass—for good or bad.

E. God will not suspend His laws—natural or spiritual—just because we mean well!

IV. The Lord commands us to speak to our problems (Mark 11:22-23).

A. A lot of people speak to God about their mountains (problems) instead of speaking to their mountains about God.

B. Most Christians pray, "God, I have this mountain. Would You please move it for me?"

C. The Lord told us to talk to the mountain, not to Him about the mountain.

D. This means that whatever it is, we can speak to it.

ANDREW'S RECOMMENDATIONS FOR FURTHER STUDY

I have a great teaching entitled "What to Do When Your Prayers Seem Unanswered." It'll encourage and instruct you on how to actively stand in faith during the time between when you pray and when the answer manifests in the physical realm.

Teacher's Guide

1.   Mark 11:12-14 paints a perfect picture of what happens when we pray. When Jesus spoke to the fig tree and cursed it because it had no fruit, it died immediately at its roots, but it didn't appear dead until the following day (Mark 11:20). God responds immediately to our prayers as well, but it often takes a period of time before what God has done in the spiritual world manifests in the physical world. Even though Mark 16:18 declares *"They shall lay hands on the sick, and they shall recover,"* we may not see our healing manifest immediately because many things affect the timing of our healing. Just because we can't discern with our five senses that anything's happened doesn't mean God hasn't answered our prayers. There's a lot happening beneath the surface that we do not see.

1a.   What happened when Jesus spoke to the fig tree?
       It died immediately
1b.   If you don't see your healing manifest immediately after you pray, does that mean it didn't happen? Why or why not?
       No, because many things can affect the timing of your healing

2.   The Lord used this incident with the fig tree to illustrate how prayer works (Mark 11:22). Faith is a powerful force, but we must believe in order to reap its benefits. Faith is governed by law (Rom. 3:27). God has set spiritual laws in motion just like He did natural laws, and both must be obeyed to receive the desired results. God controls Himself and the universe He created by the laws He spoke into existence—these laws govern how He works.

2a.   Read Mark 11:22. What did Jesus use the incident with the fig tree to teach?
       How prayer works
2b.   How are spiritual laws like natural laws?
       They both must be obeyed to receive the desired results

3.   God follows His own laws. He will never violate His own Word (Ps. 89:34). Because God has given us His authority, we are the ones who must exercise that authority or it won't work—He won't do it for us. Another law is that we will have what we say (Prov. 18:20-21, Matt. 12:34, Mark 11:23, and James 3:2-12). What we speak out will come to pass—for good or bad. God will not suspend His laws—natural or spiritual—just because we mean well!

3a.   Read Psalm 89:34. What won't God do?
       Violate His own Word

3b. What happens if you do not exercise the authority God has given you?
It (your prayers) won't work

4. The Lord commands us to speak to our problems (Mark 11:22-23). A lot of people speak to God about their mountains (problems) instead of speaking to their mountains about God. Most Christians pray, "God, I have this mountain. Would You please move it for me?" The Lord told us to talk to the mountain, not to Him about the mountain. This means that whatever it is, we can speak to it.

4a. Read Mark 11:22-23. What has the Lord commanded you to speak to?
Your mountains, or problems

4b. What do a lot of people do concerning their problems?
They talk to God about them

Discipleship Questions

1.   What happened when Jesus spoke to the fig tree?

2.   If you don't see your healing manifest immediately after you pray, does that mean it didn't happen? Why or why not?

3.   Read Mark 11:22. What did Jesus use the incident with the fig tree to teach?

4.   How are spiritual laws like natural laws?

5.   Read Psalm 89:34. What won't God do?

6.   What happens if you do not exercise the authority God has given you?

7.   Read Mark 11:22-23. What has the Lord commanded you to speak to?

8.   What do a lot of people do concerning their problems?

Answer Key

1. It died immediately

2. No, because many things can affect the timing of your healing

3. How prayer works

4. They both must be obeyed to receive the desired results

5. Violate His own Word

6. It (your prayers) won't work

7. Your mountains, or problems

8. They talk to God about them

Scriptures

MARK 11:12-14

And on the morrow, when they were come from Bethany, he was hungry: [13] And seeing a fig tree afar off having leaves, he came, if haply he might find any thing thereon: and when he came to it, he found nothing but leaves; for the time of figs was not yet. [14] And Jesus answered and said unto it, No man eat fruit of thee hereafter for ever. And his disciples heard it.

MARK 11:20-23

And in the morning, as they passed by, they saw the fig tree dried up from the roots. [21] And Peter calling to remembrance saith unto him, Master, behold, the fig tree which thou cursedst is withered away. [22] And Jesus answering saith unto them, Have faith in God. [23] For verily I say unto you, That whosoever shall say unto this mountain, Be thou removed, and be thou cast into the sea; and shall not doubt in his heart, but shall believe that those things which he saith shall come to pass; he shall have whatsoever he saith.

MATTHEW 21:19

And when he saw a fig tree in the way, he came to it, and found nothing thereon, but leaves only, and said unto it, Let no fruit grow on thee henceforward for ever. And presently the fig tree withered away.

MARK 16:18

They shall take up serpents; and if they drink any deadly thing, it shall not hurt them; they shall lay hands on the sick, and they shall recover.

ROMANS 3:27

Where is boasting then? It is excluded. By what law? of works? Nay: but by the law of faith.

PSALM 89:34

My covenant will I not break, nor alter the thing that is gone out of my lips.

JAMES 4:7

Submit yourselves therefore to God. Resist the devil, and he will flee from you.

PROVERBS 18:20-21

A man's belly shall be satisfied with the fruit of his mouth; and with the increase of his lips shall he be filled. [21] Death and life are in the power of the tongue: and they that love it shall eat the fruit thereof.

MATTHEW 12:34

O generation of vipers, how can ye, being evil, speak good things? for out of the abundance of the heart the mouth speaketh.

JAMES 3:2-12

For in many things we offend all. If any man offend not in word, the same is a perfect man, and able also to bridle the whole body. [3] Behold, we put bits in the horses' mouths, that they may obey us; and we turn about their whole body. [4] Behold also the ships, which though they be so great, and are driven of fierce winds, yet are they turned about with a very small helm, whithersoever the governor listeth. [5] Even so the tongue is a little member, and boasteth great things. Behold, how great a matter a little fire kindleth! [6] And the tongue is a fire, a world of iniquity: so is the tongue among our members, that it defileth the whole body, and setteth on fire the course of nature; and it is set on fire of hell. [7] For every kind of beasts, and of birds, and of serpents, and of things in the sea, is tamed, and hath been tamed of mankind: [8] But the tongue can no man tame; it is an unruly evil, full of deadly poison. [9] Therewith bless we God, even the Father; and therewith curse we men, which are made after the similitude of God. [10] Out of the same mouth proceedeth blessing and cursing. My brethren, these things ought not so to be. [11] Doth a fountain send forth at the same place sweet water and bitter? [12] Can the fig tree, my brethren, bear olive berries? either a vine, figs? so can no fountain both yield salt water and fresh.

Speak to Your Mountain

Therefore I say unto you, What things soever ye desire, when ye pray, believe that ye receive them, and ye shall have them.

MARK 11:24

When Jesus prayed over the fig tree, there was never any type of petition or request made to God (Mark 11:14). Instead, taking His authority, believing, and speaking to the problem is what He called "prayer."

The purpose of prayer is not to inform "poor, misinformed" God! Your heavenly Father already knows what you need (Matt. 6:8). Telling Him what the doctor said, how bad you feel, and that dear old Aunt Suzie died of it is counterproductive. Don't just sit there griping and complaining; the Lord's already done it! By His stripes, you were healed (1 Pet. 2:24)!

You're probably wondering, *If God has already healed me in the spiritual realm, then how do I pray to see that healing manifest here in the physical realm, where I need it?* First of all, enter His gates with thanksgiving (Ps. 100:4). Begin to praise and magnify Him for the fact that it's already done. This builds your faith and encourages you. Say, "Father, I thank You that by Jesus' stripes, I was healed. I receive it now by faith!" Then turn to whatever the issue is in your body and talk to it. Don't just speak to God about it. Praise the Lord for what His Word says He's already done, and then speak directly to your problem.

"WHY DIDN'T IT LEAVE?"

Mary Hill is a classic example of this truth in action. In September 2001, I ministered in Charlotte, North Carolina. While there, I gave a copy of the video *Niki Ochenski: The Story of a Miracle!* to the family who was hosting me in their home. I encouraged them to watch this inspiring story of a young lady's healing. When I arrived back from being out that day, the woman was sitting there on the couch, crying after watching the video. She asked, "Would you pray for my friend who has the exact same thing as Niki?" After answering "Sure," my hostess informed me that she was already on the way!

Ten minutes later, Mary Hill arrived wrapped in magnet-lined blankets. Additional magnets were taped all over her body. The doctors who diagnosed her in 1994 stated that on a scale of one to ten, Mary's pain was a constant eleven. She hurt and couldn't do anything!

As we began talking, Mary told me that she knew God had a purpose in this and that He was receiving glory from it. I spent about thirty minutes countering her religious doctrine with God's Word. Finally, she was ready for me to pray for her.

Grabbing Mary's hands, I commanded all the pain to leave her body in Jesus' name. BOOM! Instantly, she was pain free for the first time in seven years!

Amazed, she started praising God. Then she stopped and remarked, "I still have a burning here across the back of my waist. Why didn't it leave?"

"I didn't speak to 'burning.' You told me you had 'pain.' Watch this!" Grabbing her hands again, I spoke to burning and commanded it to leave.

She exclaimed "It's gone!" and started praising God some more!

YOU PRAY!

Then I trained Mary on how to minister to herself using Mark 11:23. I told her, "If another pain comes back, it's not that God didn't heal you; it's the devil knocking on your door to see if you'll open it back up again. If you say 'Oh, no, I wasn't healed' or 'I lost my healing,' then you open the door, and Satan will come back in. But if you say 'No! By His stripes, I was healed. The gifts and callings of God are without repentance. I command this pain to leave!' you'll retain your healing, and everything will be just fine."

As Mary prepared to go, she said, "That burning is back."

"Well, I've been teaching you what to do. I'll join hands with you and agree, but you pray."

"Father, I thank You that it's Your will for me to be healed. By the stripes of Jesus, I was healed, and I thank You for it. I claim my healing now in Jesus' name." Just forty minutes earlier, this lady had been a Presbyterian who believed her disease had been sent from God so that He could be glorified. She had come a long way! However, even though that's a pretty good prayer, you can't receive healing praying that way. It simply doesn't work.

So, after she finished, I asked, "Do you have any burning?"

"Yes, it's still there."

"Do you know why?"

"No."

"You didn't do what I told you to do.

"What's that?"

"You didn't speak to your mountain. You talked to God and praised Him. What you said was good, but you didn't do what the Word told you to do."

"You mean I'm supposed to say, 'Burning, in the name of Jesus…'?"

"Yes!"

"Okay."

We joined hands again, and Mary declared "Burning! In the name of Jesus…" and then stopped right there, exclaiming, "It left! It's gone! I'm healed!" I heard from her two years later and she's been fine. In fact, she is causing "no small stir" in the Presbyterian church. What an awesome example!

DIRECT YOUR FAITH

The Bible says, "Speak to those problems!"

"Well, Andrew, I don't believe you have to be so technical. God knows what I mean."

That's just like the person who grabs a live electrical wire, saying, "How dare this kill me! I intended good, but I didn't know it was live!" It doesn't matter what our intentions are. There are laws that govern how things work. God said "Talk to things!" and we don't do it. Then we wonder why we aren't healed.

You have faith, but it needs to be directed. Use it in cooperation with the laws that govern how it works. Resist the devil. Talk directly to him. Speak to your problem and command it to change. Direct your faith with your words.

Although your words are very important, your actions must also be consistent with your faith. If you believe one way and act another, you cancel out your faith!

If you have a headache, don't say, "O God, I've got a headache. Please take it away. I believe that by Your stripes, I am healed, in Jesus' name." That's not sufficient! It's not what the Lord told you to do. If the problem is pain, speak to it, saying, "Pain, in the name of Jesus, I command you to leave my body. Whatever is causing this pain, I speak to that part of my body and command it to respond so that this thing can stop, in the name of Jesus." Talk to it!

JAMIE'S FOOT

I remember when Jamie smashed her foot with a heavy, metal chair we have in our study. She was barefoot when it fell over and landed on the bridge of her foot. Instantly, it turned black and blue and began swelling up. After praying over it for five minutes, she hobbled in to where I was and asked, "Will you agree with me?"

We prayed and I talked to it, saying, "Foot, in the name of Jesus, I command you to respond to this. Bones, if any of you are broken, I command you to be healed." Within a minute, the swelling left and the color returned to normal. That's how you speak to the problem!

Although I've known about this a long time, for some reason it just didn't register with me. However, since starting to apply this principle more deliberately in the past five years, I've probably seen four times as many instant manifestations of healing as before. It's a real simple principle!

YOU MUST COOPERATE

Many people just don't understand that Jesus laid down spiritual laws. They say, "Well, if God loved me, He would just heal me." No, it doesn't work that way. You receive according to your faith!

> *O Jerusalem, Jerusalem, which killest the prophets, and stonest them that are sent unto thee;* how often would I have *gathered thy children together, as a hen doth gather her brood under her wings,* and ye would not!
>
> LUKE 13:34, EMPHASIS MINE

The Lord Himself lamented over His beloved people. He wanted to bless, minister to, and comfort them, but they wouldn't receive it. In His own hometown of Nazareth, unbelief kept Jesus from doing more (Mark 6:5-6). You must cooperate with God's spiritual laws governing faith in order to receive.

Do what the Word says! When you pray, praise God that your problem has been taken care of. Then, exercise your authority, and speak directly to the problem. If you don't, you won't see your desired results. Like it or not, that's just the way it works!

Your job is to discover the laws and cooperate with them—not pick and choose which ones you'll obey, or make them up! You might think it's cheaper and easier to wire your house with wood, but I guarantee you that it won't conduct electricity the same as copper. It doesn't matter that you like wood better. You just need to discover what conducts electricity, and then go with the flow. Learn what God's Word says about how His power works and then cooperate!

GOD ANSWERS INSTANTLY

Therefore I say unto you, What things soever ye desire, when ye pray, believe that ye receive them, and ye shall have them.

MARK 11:24

Believe you receive when you pray, and you shall (future tense) have what you prayed for. Believe that you have received God's answer the instant you pray, and you shall (future tense) see the visible manifestation of it.

Most people don't have a clue what's going on in prayer! They pray, ask, and then passively wait. When something—anything—works out, they think, *God must have answered my prayer.* If what they asked for doesn't happen, then it's *He must have said no.* That's simply not true!

More than you realize, you have a larger degree of control over how long it takes between "amen" and "there it is." The amount of time before manifestation could be one second, one hour, one day, one week, or longer. However, the very moment you pray and believe, God moves and releases His power. Instantly, like the fig tree, it's done! Apart from a hindrance inside or outside of yourself, you should be able to see an immediate manifestation when you use God's power correctly.

Speak directly to the problem. God has already done everything about healing that He's ever going to do. Don't just pray for someone who's sick and then passively wait for something to happen. Take control and make them manifest healing!

You may say, "You can't do that!" Yes, you can! That's how we're praying, and good things are happening. It's up to you when your healing manifests!

As a basic rule, God answers prayer instantly. Regardless of what you see (or don't see) manifest immediately, believe that you received when you prayed. As you speak to your mountain, you cooperate with an important spiritual law and expedite the manifestation of your answer.

ANDREW'S RECOMMENDATIONS FOR FURTHER STUDY

To find out more about Niki's awesome miracle, be sure to check out our *Niki Ochenski: The Story of a Miracle!* DVD. This will bless you tremendously!

Outline

I.   When Jesus prayed over the fig tree, there was never any type of petition or request made to God (Mark 11:14 and 24).

   A. Instead, taking His authority, believing, and speaking to the problem is what He called "prayer."

   B. The purpose of prayer is not to inform God of our needs.

   C. Our heavenly Father already knows what we need (Matt. 6:8).

   D. Let's not just sit there griping and complaining; the Lord has already done it!

II. Jesus has already healed us (1 Pet. 2:24), but we need to bring our healings from the spirit realm into the physical realm where we need them.

   A. We can start by entering His gates with thanksgiving (Ps. 100:4).

   B. Then, we praise and magnify Him for the fact that it's already done.

   C. Finally, we must talk specifically to whatever the issues are in our bodies.

   D. We should praise the Lord for what His Word says He's already done and speak directly to our problems.

III. Sometimes our problems may try to return.

   A. If that happens, it's not that God didn't heal us, but the devil is knocking on our doors to see if we'll open back up again.

   B. We can open to him by saying that we haven't been healed or that we've lost our healings.

   C. But God's gifts and callings are without repentance, so if we stand firm and say "No! By His stripes I have been healed," we'll keep our healings.

IV.   The Bible says, "Speak to those problems!"

    A.   We have faith, but it needs to be directed.

    B.   We must use it in cooperation with the laws that govern how it works.

    C.   We can direct our faith with our words by resisting the devil, talking directly to him, and speaking to our problems to command them to change.

    D.   We also need to make our actions consistent with our faith.

    E.   If we believe one way and act another, we'll cancel our faith.

V.   We must cooperate with God's spiritual laws governing faith in order to receive (Rom. 3:27).

    A.   Just because God loves us and wants us healed, we still must receive by faith.

    B.   We must do what the Word says.

    C.   Our job is to discover the laws and cooperate with them—not pick and choose which ones we'll obey, or make them up!

    D.   Jesus wanted to bless, minister to, and comfort Jerusalem, but the people wouldn't receive from Him (Luke 13:34).

    E.   In His own hometown of Nazareth, unbelief kept Jesus from doing more (Mark 6:5-6).

VI.   If we believe we receive when we pray, we shall (future tense) have what we prayed for (Mark 11:24).

    A.   More than we realize, we have a larger degree of control over how long it takes between "amen" and "there it is."

    B.   The very moment we pray and believe, God moves and releases His power.

    C.   Apart from a hindrance inside or outside of ourselves, we should be able to see an immediate manifestation when we use God's power correctly.

D. We don't have to passively wait for the healing to come; we can take control and bring about the manifestation.

ANDREW'S RECOMMENDATIONS FOR FURTHER STUDY

To find out more about Niki's awesome miracle, be sure to check out our *Niki Ochenski: The Story of a Miracle!* DVD. This will bless you tremendously!

Teacher's Guide

1.   When Jesus prayed over the fig tree, there was never any type of petition or request made to God (Mark 11:14 and 24). Instead, taking His authority, believing, and speaking to the problem is what He called "prayer." The purpose of prayer is not to inform God of our needs. Our heavenly Father already knows what we need (Matt. 6:8). Let's not just sit there griping and complaining; the Lord has already done it!

1a.   Read Mark 11:14, 24; and Matthew 6:8. How did Jesus "pray"?
He took His authority, believed, and spoke to the problem

1b.   Why should you not use prayer to inform God of your needs?
He already knows what you need

2.   Jesus has already healed us (1 Pet. 2:24), but we need to bring our healings from the spirit realm into the physical realm where we need them. We can start by entering His gates with thanksgiving (Ps. 100:4). Then, we praise and magnify Him for the fact that it's already done. Finally, we must talk specifically to whatever the issues are in our bodies. We should praise the Lord for what His Word says He's already done and speak directly to our problems.

2a.   You need to bring your healing from where to where?
From the spiritual into the physical realm

2b.   What do you do after praising the Lord for what His Word says He's already done?
Speak directly to your problems

3.   Sometimes our problems may try to return. If that happens, it's not that God didn't heal us, but the devil is knocking on our doors to see if we'll open back up again. We can open to him by saying that we haven't been healed or that we've lost our healings. But God's gifts and callings are without repentance, so if we stand firm and say "No! By His stripes I have been healed," we'll keep our healings.

3a.   How do you open the door to the devil when your problems try to return?
By saying that you haven't been healed or that you've lost your healing

3b.   How can you keep your healing?
By standing firm and saying "No! By His stripes I have been healed"

4.   The Bible says, "Speak to those problems!" We have faith, but it needs to be directed. We must use it in cooperation with the laws that govern how it works. We can direct our faith with our words by resisting the devil, talking directly to him, and speaking to our problems to command them to change. We also need to make our actions consistent with our faith. If we believe one way and act another, we'll cancel our faith.

4a.   Your faith must be used in cooperation with what?
        God's laws that govern how it works
4b.   How do you direct your faith with your words?
        By resisting the devil, talking directly to him, and speaking to your problems

5.   We must cooperate with God's spiritual laws governing faith in order to receive (Rom. 3:27). Just because God loves us and wants us healed, we still must receive by faith. We must do what the Word says. Our job is to discover the laws and cooperate with them—not pick and choose which ones we'll obey, or make them up! Jesus wanted to bless, minister to, and comfort Jerusalem, but the people wouldn't receive from Him (Luke 13:34). In His own hometown of Nazareth, unbelief kept Jesus from doing more (Mark 6:5-6).

5a.   Read Romans 3:27. You must cooperate with God's spiritual laws in order to what?
        Receive
5b.   Read Luke 13:34. What happened when Jesus wanted to bless Jerusalem?
        The people wouldn't receive from Him

6.   If we believe we receive when we pray, we shall (future tense) have what we prayed for (Mark 11:24). More than we realize, we have a larger degree of control over how long it takes between "amen" and "there it is." The very moment we pray and believe, God moves and releases His power. Apart from a hindrance inside or outside of ourselves, we should be able to see an immediate manifestation when we use God's power correctly. We don't have to passively wait for the healing to come; we can take control and bring about the manifestation.

6a.   When does God move and release His power?
        The very moment you pray
6b.   Instead of passively waiting for healing to come, what can you do?
        Take control and bring about the manifestation

Discipleship Questions

1.   Read Mark 11:14, 24; and Matthew 6:8. How did Jesus "pray"?

2.   Why should you not use prayer to inform God of your needs?

3.   You need to bring your healing from where to where?

4.   What do you do after praising the Lord for what His Word says He's already done?

5.   How do you open the door to the devil when your problems try to return?

6.   How can you keep your healing?

7.   Your faith must be used in cooperation with what?

8.   How do you direct your faith with your words?

9.   Read Romans 3:27. You must cooperate with God's spiritual laws in order to what?

10. Read Luke 13:34. What happened when Jesus wanted to bless Jerusalem?

11. When does God move and release His power?

12. Instead of passively waiting for healing to come, what can you do?

Answer Key

1. He took His authority, believed, and spoke to the problem

2. He already knows what you need

3. From the spiritual into the physical realm

4. Speak directly to your problems

5. By saying that you haven't been healed or that you've lost your healing

6. By standing firm and saying "No! By His stripes I have been healed"

7. God's laws that govern how it works

8. By resisting the devil, talking directly to him, and speaking to your problems

9. Receive

10. The people wouldn't receive from Him

11. The very moment you pray

12. Take control and bring about the manifestation

Scriptures

MARK 11:23-24

For verily I say unto you, That whosoever shall say unto this mountain, Be thou removed, and be thou cast into the sea; and shall not doubt in his heart, but shall believe that those things which he saith shall come to pass; he shall have whatsoever he saith. [24] Therefore I say unto you, What things soever ye desire, when ye pray, believe that ye receive them, and ye shall have them.

MARK 11:14

And Jesus answered and said unto it, No man eat fruit of thee hereafter for ever. And his disciples heard it.

MATTHEW 6:8

Be not ye therefore like unto them: for your Father knoweth what things ye have need of, before ye ask him.

1 PETER 2:24

Who his own self bare our sins in his own body on the tree, that we, being dead to sins, should live unto righteousness: by whose stripes ye were healed.

PSALM 100:4

Enter into his gates with thanksgiving, and into his courts with praise: be thankful unto him, and bless his name.

LUKE 13:34

O Jerusalem, Jerusalem, which killest the prophets, and stonest them that are sent unto thee; how often would I have gathered thy children together, as a hen doth gather her brood under her wings, and ye would not!

MARK 6:5-6

And he could there do no mighty work, save that he laid his hands upon a few sick folk, and healed them. [6] And he marvelled because of their unbelief. And he went round about the villages, teaching.

Shoot Him Again!

Many people struggle with what I'm teaching, wondering, *How can I believe? I have pain in my body right now, but you're telling me to believe that I'm healed without any physical evidence of it*. Others respond, "Oh, I understand! You're saying to act like it's so, when it really isn't so, and then it'll become so!" No, that's not what I'm teaching. I'm not encouraging you into some "mind game" of trying to believe something is real when it isn't so that it'll become real. I'm challenging you to look beyond just the natural realm.

God is a Spirit (John 4:24). When He moves, He does so in the spirit realm. When you ask for healing, God gives it to you in spiritual form inside your spirit the very instant you believe Him for it. As a New Testament believer, the same virtue, anointing, and power that raised Jesus Christ from the dead is already living inside of you. The moment you believe, God releases that power in your spirit. Therefore, you did receive. God did everything He's going to do about your miracle the instant you prayed—He gave the command and released His power, and it's a done deal!

"But I need it out here in my body!" Faith is the bridge from the spiritual realm into the physical realm. It's how what has already happened in the spirit transfers over into the natural. Faith gives substance to things hoped for and evidence—tangibility, physical proof—to something unseen (Heb. 11:1). Just because something is in an unseen realm doesn't mean it's nonexistent!

If you think the physical world—what you can see, taste, hear, smell, and feel—is the only realm of reality there is, you'll argue, "I hurt, so I don't care what you say! I'd be a liar to confess that God has healed me when I'm still in pain and have this (rash, tumor, whatever). You're just one of those 'name-it-and-claim-it,' 'blab-it-and-grab-it' guys, trying to 'make it so.'" The truth is, there really is a spiritual realm, and there's a real spiritual you!

DRAW IT OUT

The spiritual world is the parent force (Col. 1:16 and Heb. 11:3). It created everything you see and will still be in existence long after this physical world is gone (2 Cor. 4:18). It's not wrong to acknowledge that there are things beyond what your five natural senses can detect. There are radio and television signals where you are right now. You can't see them, but they're there. With the help of a receiver, you could prove it. Saying "They aren't here, because I can't see or feel them!" just means you aren't very smart. They're there, but you're ignorant of it.

There are spiritual entities—angels, demons, and the Holy Spirit—right where you are. There's a reality within you—your spirit—that you can't come into contact with through your five senses. You just have to believe God's Word, which says, "When you pray, you receive." If you start feeling in your body or looking in the mirror to see if it happened, you'll miss it. Your healing comes in the spiritual world. How does it get from the supernatural to the natural? By somebody believing!

Declare by faith, "Even though I can't see it, I know God's Word says in Mark 11:24 that when I pray and believe that I receive the answer right now, it will (future tense) manifest. So, I believe God did it. In the spirit realm, there's tremendous activity and power being released. The virtue of God is flowing through me right now. I haven't seen it yet, but I know it's there." Then, make your answer manifest by putting these laws into motion. Start speaking to things and commanding them to work.

When Jamie hurt her foot, we believed that God had already provided her healing long before she ever knocked the chair over. We praised God that it was already accomplished, saying, "Thank You, Father, that You have done it. Right now it's ours!" Her foot still looked bad, so I turned to it and commanded, "Foot, I speak to you, in the name of Jesus." I was drawing out the healing that Jamie had already received in her spirit.

It's like being thirsty and standing next to a well. All the water you'll ever need is already down there, but you could die of thirst if you don't know how to stick a bucket in and draw it out. There are things you can do that draw out the supernatural power of God already present in the spiritual well within you.

TALKING TO TREES

Use your words to speak life instead of death (Prov. 18:21). Direct them specifically toward your problem (Mark 11:23). Jesus Himself answered the fig tree (Mark 11:14). If your checkbook is always in the red, talk to it! If every time you pick it up, you hear "God's Word doesn't work! You never have enough!" then look right at it and say, "I command all of this red to leave and for black to take its place, in the name of Jesus!" You need to talk to your wallet, your investments, and so on.

I talk to my trees. We live in a semi-arid climate, and our property is like a forest. I quote scriptures to it regarding how God makes water flow in the mountains. Every time I see the wrong kind of bug, I curse it and bless the tree. There's a row of dead trees just over the property line, but all of mine look good. People think this is weird, but it works!

God taught me to speak to trees way back in my poverty days. While Jamie and I were struggling along, there were times when my mother kept us alive. I'm not sure if she knew it or not, but sometimes the meals she gave us would be the only meals we'd eat in a week or two. We never told her we needed anything, but she'd feed us whenever we visited. I'd pitch in by mowing her lawn.

Our family had twenty-three pecan trees. When my dad was still alive, he took good care of them by fertilizing and spraying. They'd yield anywhere from 300 to 400 pounds of nuts each year. After he died, we just let them go. Finally, the bagworms were so bad one year that the entire yield was only 50 pounds of pecans!

During that next year, I blessed those trees each time I cut the grass. As I walked around them with the lawnmower, I'd place one hand on the tree and say, "Bagworms, I curse you, in the name of Jesus and command you to die. Tree, you are blessed. I command you to be fruitful and produce!" That year, we harvested over 500 pounds of pecans!

HOW THE KINGDOM WORKS

Speak to your body—it'll respond to you! Scientists have discovered a part of the brain that's voice activated. They've found that if you say "I'm tired," your brain will hear it and tell your body to prepare for a rest. You'll become more tired as you talk "tired." If you say "Man, I feel good!" that same part of the brain will start sending endorphins through your body to energize you. The scientific community is just now discovering what God has said all along!

Your body has the ability to kill pain. Medicines don't really relieve it; they just stimulate your body to produce endorphins. It's the endorphins that alleviate your pain. There's even a technology available now for people with chronic pain that sends an electrical shock to the part of the brain that produces endorphins. It kills pain ten times better than morphine! "Second wind" for athletes is simply their endorphins chasing pain and tiredness away.

Use your words to command pain to leave. You can speak to your body and make it recover. I've commanded toothaches to leave and my eyesight to work. After we spoke to it, a rash all over my friend's hands left. Don't just automatically turn to a pill; speak to your body!

This is how the kingdom works. We've made it too hard, praying, "O God, here's my need. If You love me, do something!" When nothing happens, we become bitter at God and wonder, *Why haven't You done anything?* God has given you the power, but you're ignorant of how to use it. The anointing is already inside you to heal the sick, cleanse the lepers, and raise the dead. If you aren't seeing it manifest, it's not God's giver that's broken; it's your receiver that needs to be turned on and tuned in. Get into the Word, and then use it to speak to your mountain!

FAITH IS DISCERNIBLE

Putting all of this back into perspective, I don't spend much time asking for things. Ninety percent of my prayer is spent loving God. He keeps me in perfect peace because my mind is stayed on Him (Is. 26:3). When I heard the bad report about our building contract falling through, it was no big deal. I'd been fellowshipping with Almighty God. As important as that building was, I knew it wasn't eternal. Besides, I had something better to do that night than worry—I went to bed and slept. I never even prayed about it, yet this situation took care of itself and worked out just fine.

When loving and worshiping God is your top priority, you'll find that you won't have to spend much time praying over things. However, when you do need to pray over something important, start by praising, glorifying, and thanking Him. Say "Father, I thank You that You've already taken care of this before I even had it. Thank You that by Your stripes, I was healed." Colossians 2:7 reveals that you abound in faith with thanksgiving. Until you know you're not in fear or worry anymore and faith has been quickened inside, just keep praising and thanking God for what the Word says has already happened in the spirit.

Faith is discernible. I know when I'm in faith. The first time I ever said "I know I'm operating in faith, and I can raise the dead!" was in 1976. In my heart, I knew it. I don't always feel stirred up, but I know how to get there. I'll start praising and thanking God until my faith is quickened.

If you're still in fear, don't pray about your situation yet. Just like you don't pull the trigger on a gun unless it's aimed and loaded, neither should you pray your prayer unless you know you're in faith! Draw near to God, and deal with the fear. Praise Him for His awesome love until it casts out all that fear (1 John 4:18). Once you're rid of it and know you're in faith, come back and do what you need to do to pray over the situation—but don't speak words in fear!

Don't speak words in hope alone either. Wishing and trying aren't faith. True faith must be present in order to give substance to your hope.

Once I know my faith is quickened and I truly believe it's already done in the spirit realm, I take that faith and speak to whatever needs to be spoken to: my body, my finances, demons, etc. Then I use praise to still the Enemy. Drawing on everything God's ever shown me, I keep blasting the devil and my situation until I see results. It's not unbelief for me to continue praying this way about something. I believed God did it the very instant I asked. I received His answer when I prayed, but I'm not willing to let it stay there in the spirit realm. I make it manifest in the physical world, where I need it.

KEEP PRAYING UNTIL MANIFESTATION!

When I minister healing to people, I'll pray for them two, three, four, or more times. I don't care! I'm willing to pray for them until I rub all the hair off their heads! However, I'm not going back to God and saying, "Father, it didn't work the first time. Let it work now, please!" No! I believe it happened because God is faithful. He gave, but something's wrong with our receivers. So, I work on it. If the devil withstands one dose of the Holy Spirit, I'll shoot him again! Just like Jesus did with the blind man of Bethsaida (Mark 8:22-26), I pray until I see the answer manifest!

You need to get this attitude that God is faithful and that He's already met your need before you ever had it. Boldness, confidence, and faith will rise in your heart as you realize that God's supply is always greater than your need.

Sometimes I pray for the other people's benefit as much as my own. I'm normally ready to go, but they aren't always ready right at that moment. While ministering to a lady with AIDS, I realized by talking to her that she still had some fear about it. So, I started praying, "Father, we thank You that You are exalted above every name. AIDS has a name. AIDS, you bow the knee to the name of Jesus!" Right then, I sensed that her faith had quickened, so I continued, "AIDS, you are nothing but a loser! You have no power, no might, and no dominion!" In this manner, both my faith and the faith of the person I'm praying for are strengthened. Then, by speaking to the situation and releasing God's power, I've seen thousands of instant manifestations!

Another lady received prayer for her two swollen feet. One returned to normal, but the other stayed swollen. Some wonder, *Why didn't God heal them both?* He did! It's just that she only received healing in one of them. What do you do then? Keep praying until the other healing manifests. If you can move the devil an inch, you can move him a mile—an inch at a time if you must!

YOUR RESULTS WILL IMPROVE

People think that God heals in mysterious ways. If He wants someone healed—BOOM—they are! If there's any delay or problem or if they have to stand in faith speaking to and rebuking something, they wonder, *Why didn't it work?*

God is using imperfect people. We'd all see greater and quicker manifestations if we weren't so full of unbelief! It's a miracle we see anything happen while bathing our minds in murder, adultery, and sexual immorality for "entertainment" and listening to the (bad) "news" each day. We're baptized in unbelief.

Since Jesus has to use imperfect vessels like you and me, sometimes His power doesn't flow through us as easily. Each of us has some unbelief and other junk that haven't been worked out yet, but we shouldn't let that stop us from doing it. Our conductivity for God's power often increases through use. We can't just give up if we try a few times and don't yet see the results we desire. Even Jesus was limited in what He could do in His own hometown, because of their unbelief (Matt. 13:58). We have to keep at it.

As you begin to understand, believe, and practice some of these things, your results will greatly improve!

Outline

I.   God is a Spirit (John 4:24)—when He moves, He does so in the spirit realm.

   A.   When we ask for healing, God gives it to us in spiritual form inside our spirits the very instant we believe Him for it.

      i.   The moment we pray and believe, God releases His power in our spirits.

      ii.   He gives the command and releases His power, and it's a done deal!

   B.   Faith is the bridge from the spiritual realm into the physical—it transfers what has happened in the spirit to the natural.

   C.   It gives substance to things hoped for and evidence to something unseen (Heb. 11:1).

   D.   Just because something is unseen doesn't mean it's nonexistent!

II.   The spiritual world is the parent force (Col. 1:16 and Heb. 11:3).

   A.   It created everything we see and will still be in existence long after this physical world is gone (2 Cor. 4:18).

   B.   There's a reality within our spirits that we can't come into contact with through our five senses.

   C.   But we can draw out God's supernatural power and cause it to manifest through faith by speaking to things and commanding them to work.

III.   We can use our words to speak life instead of death (Prov. 18:21) and direct them specifically toward our problems (Mark 11:23).

   A.   Jesus Himself answered the fig tree (Mark 11:14).

   B.   Our bodies will even respond to us when we speak to them.

        i.   Scientists have discovered what God has said all along—our bodies are voice activated!

   C. God has given us this power, but we're ignorant of how to use it.

   D. The anointing is already inside us to heal the sick, cleanse the lepers, and raise the dead.

   E. If we aren't seeing it manifest, it's not God's giver that's broken; it's our receivers that need to be turned on and tuned in.

IV. When loving and worshiping God is our top priority, we'll find that we won't have to spend much time praying over things.

   A. However, when we do need to pray over something important, we should start by praising, glorifying, and thanking Him (Col. 2:7).

   B. We should keep praising and thanking God for what the Word says has already happened in the spirit until we know we're no longer in fear but in faith.

   C. Until we're in faith, we need to draw near to God until His awesome love casts out all fear (1 John 4:18).

   D. Then we can pray over the situation, being sure to speak words of faith, not fear.

   E. Hope is not faith; true faith must be present in order to give substance to our hopes.

V. It's okay to keep praying for something until it manifests.

   A. We can use our praise to still the Enemy and then to keep blasting him and our situation until we see results.

        i.   If the devil withstands one dose of the Holy Spirit, let's shoot him again (Mark 8:22-26)!

        ii.   It's not unbelief to continue praying when we know we received God's answer the instant we prayed.

   B. We need to get this attitude that God is faithful and He's already met our needs before we ever had them.

C. If we can move the devil an inch, we can move him a mile—an inch at a time if we must!

D. Since Jesus has to use imperfect vessels like us, sometimes His power doesn't come through into manifestation as quickly (Matt. 13:58).

E. We'd all see greater and quicker manifestations if we weren't so full of unbelief!

Teacher's Guide

1.   God is a Spirit (John 4:24)—when He moves, He does so in the spirit realm. When we ask for healing, God gives it to us in spiritual form inside our spirits the very instant we believe Him for it. The moment we pray and believe, God releases His power in our spirits. He gives the command and releases His power, and it's a done deal! Faith is the bridge from the spiritual realm into the physical—it transfers what has happened in the spirit to the natural. It gives substance to things hoped for and evidence to something unseen (Heb. 11:1). Just because something is unseen doesn't mean it's nonexistent!

1a.   Where does God's healing first take place when you pray?
        In your spirit
1b.   How does faith connect the spirit realm to the natural realm?
        It acts as a bridge, transferring what has happened in the spirit to the natural

2.   The spiritual world is the parent force (Col. 1:16 and Heb. 11:3). It created everything we see and will still be in existence long after this physical world is gone (2 Cor. 4:18). There's a reality within our spirits that we can't come into contact with through our five senses. But we can draw out God's supernatural power and cause it to manifest through faith by speaking to things and commanding them to work.

2a.   What is the spiritual world?
        It's the parent force that created everything
2b.   How can you draw out God's supernatural power?
        By using your faith to speak to things and command them to work

3.   We can use our words to speak life instead of death (Prov. 18:21) and direct them specifically toward our problems (Mark 11:23). Jesus Himself answered the fig tree (Mark 11:14). Our bodies will even respond to us when we speak to them. Scientists have discovered what God has said all along—our bodies are voice activated! God has given us this power, but we're ignorant of how to use it. The anointing is already inside us to heal the sick, cleanse the lepers, and raise the dead. If we aren't seeing it manifest, it's not God's giver that's broken; it's our receivers that need to be turned on and tuned in.

3a.   Read Proverbs 18:21; Mark 11:14, and 23. How can you use your words?
        To speak life instead of death and direct them specifically toward your problems

3b. If you're not seeing God's power manifest in your life, what's the problem?
Your receiver needs to be turned on and tuned in

4. When loving and worshiping God is our top priority, we'll find that we won't have to spend much time praying over things. However, when we do need to pray over something important, we should start by praising, glorifying, and thanking Him (Col. 2:7). We should keep praising and thanking God for what the Word says has already happened in the spirit until we know we're no longer in fear but in faith. Until we're in faith, we need to draw near to God until His awesome love casts out all fear (1 John 4:18). Then we can pray over the situation, being sure to speak words of faith, not fear. Hope is not faith; true faith must be present in order to give substance to our hopes.

4a. How long should you keep praising and thanking God for what has already happened in the spirit realm?
Until you know you're no longer in fear but in faith

4b. What do you need to do once you begin praying over your situation?
Speak words of faith not fear

5. It's okay to keep praying for something until it manifests. We can use our praise to still the Enemy and then to keep blasting him and our situation until we see results. If the devil withstands one dose of the Holy Spirit, let's shoot him again (Mark 8:22-26)! It's not unbelief to continue praying when we know we received God's answer the instant we prayed. We need to get this attitude that God is faithful and He's already met our needs before we ever had them. If we can move the devil an inch, we can move him a mile—an inch at a time if we must! Since Jesus has to use imperfect vessels like us, sometimes His power doesn't come through into manifestation as quickly (Matt. 13:58). We'd all see greater and quicker manifestations if we weren't so full of unbelief!

5a. What should your attitude in prayer be?
That God is faithful and He's already met your needs

5b. Why doesn't God's power always manifest quickly?
Because He has to use imperfect vessels

Discipleship Questions

1. Where does God's healing first take place when you pray?

2. How does faith connect the spirit realm to the natural realm?

3. What is the spiritual world?

4. How can you draw out God's supernatural power?

5. Read Proverbs 18:21; Mark 11:14, and 23. How can you use your words?

6. If you're not seeing God's power manifest in your life, what's the problem?

7. How long should you keep praising and thanking God for what has already happened in the spirit realm?

8. What do you need to do once you begin praying over your situation?

9. What should your attitude in prayer be?

10. Why doesn't God's power always manifest quickly?

Answer Key

1. In your spirit

2. It acts as a bridge, transferring what has happened in the spirit to the natural

3. It's the parent force that created everything

4. By using your faith to speak to things and command them to work

5. To speak life instead of death and direct them specifically toward your problems

6. Your receiver needs to be turned on and tuned in

7. Until you know you're no longer in fear but in faith

8. Speak words of faith not fear

9. That God is faithful and He's already met your needs

10. Because He has to use imperfect vessels

Scriptures

JOHN 4:24
God is a Spirit: and they that worship him must worship him in spirit and in truth.

HEBREWS 11:1
Now faith is the substance of things hoped for, the evidence of things not seen.

COLOSSIANS 1:16
For by him were all things created, that are in heaven, and that are in earth, visible and invisible, whether they be thrones, or dominions, or principalities, or powers: all things were created by him, and for him.

HEBREWS 11:3
Through faith we understand that the worlds were framed by the word of God, so that things which are seen were not made of things which do appear.

2 CORINTHIANS 4:18
While we look not at the things which are seen, but at the things which are not seen: for the things which are seen are temporal; but the things which are not seen are eternal.

MARK 11:23-24
For verily I say unto you, That whosoever shall say unto this mountain, Be thou removed, and be thou cast into the sea; and shall not doubt in his heart, but shall believe that those things which he saith shall come to pass; he shall have whatsoever he saith. [24] Therefore I say unto you, What things soever ye desire, when ye pray, believe that ye receive them, and ye shall have them.

PROVERBS 18:21
Death and life are in the power of the tongue: and they that love it shall eat the fruit thereof.

MARK 11:14
And Jesus answered and said unto it, No man eat fruit of thee hereafter for ever. And his disciples heard it.

ISAIAH 26:3
Thou wilt keep him in perfect peace, whose mind is stayed on thee: because he trusteth in thee.

COLOSSIANS 2:7
Rooted and built up in him, and stablished in the faith, as ye have been taught, abounding therein with thanksgiving.

1 JOHN 4:18

There is no fear in love; but perfect love casteth out fear: because fear hath torment. He that feareth is not made perfect in love.

MARK 8:22-26

And he cometh to Bethsaida; and they bring a blind man unto him, and besought him to touch him. [23] And he took the blind man by the hand, and led him out of the town; and when he had spit on his eyes, and put his hands upon him, he asked him if he saw ought. [24] And he looked up, and said, I see men as trees, walking. [25] After that he put his hands again upon his eyes, and made him look up: and he was restored, and saw every man clearly. [26] And he sent him away to his house, saying, Neither go into the town, nor tell it to any in the town.

MATTHEW 13:58

And he did not many mighty works there because of their unbelief.

SHOOT HIM AGAIN!

Ask & Receive

And I say unto you, Ask, and it shall be given you; seek, and ye shall find; knock, and it shall be opened unto you.

LUKE 11:9

If we would just believe Luke 11:9, then everything would be fine! However, many people can't, because at some point in their lives, they asked God for something and didn't see it come to pass. Due to that negative experience, they think, *It just can't be so simple and straightforward!*

A tremendous amount of today's "church-ianity" consists of excuses for why God's promises don't work. It's religion! It's apologetics for why Christians fail and are depressed, sick, or poor—and how God intended it for some "redemptive purpose" in their life. That's completely inaccurate!

We come up with excuses for why God's Word won't work for all people, all the time, saying, "Oh, yes, if you ask, you do receive, but sometimes God answers no. It's not for everyone." Take, for example, the baptism in the Holy Spirit. Many people who acknowledge its existence today will also turn around and dismiss it as being "not for everyone." They'll misuse 1 Corinthians 12:30 (*"Do all speak with tongues?"*) without realizing that this verse is discussing the public gift of speaking in tongues in a church service. Not everybody has that particular gift, but every born-again believer who's baptized in the Holy Spirit can and should speak in tongues.

When I first became turned on to Jesus and started out in ministry, there were entire denominations that believed miracles had passed away with the early church. Anyone who taught anything about any kind of supernatural manifestations happening today was "of the devil." However, the charismatic movement so disproved and debunked this false assumption that all there are today are little fringe groups of hardcore people who hold on to that unbelief. The predominant thought in the body of Christ today is "Yes, miracles can happen, but not to everyone."

GOD ALWAYS ANSWERS

God's Word declares the exact opposite!

For every one that asketh receiveth; and he that seeketh findeth; and to him that knocketh it shall be opened.

LUKE 11:10, EMPHASIS MINE

If you take Luke 11:9 to mean just what it says, then you'll receive if you ask. God doesn't say no. This isn't something that passed away a long time ago. It's not just available for some "super-saints." Everyone who asks receives!

We all have experiences when we prayed and asked for something that didn't come to pass. In the early part of my life, I was around a lot of death. My grandmother basically raised me because both of my parents were working. I prayed for her, but she died when I was eight years old. When I was twelve, I prayed every day for six months for my dad to be healed. Even though he was very ill and in the hospital, I fully expected him to recover, but he died. At eighteen, a girl that Jamie and I were very close to died. I've stood in faith and prayed for two hours over deceased individuals whom I believed God would raise from the dead. It didn't happen. I prayed for four different people who died before I saw my first person rise from the dead. You have your own experiences too.

Most Christians don't believe Luke 11:9-10 really is this simple, because of experiences like these. Another way of saying this is that experience carries more weight in most people's lives than the Word of God does. If you can grasp what I'm about to share with you, it'll totally transform the way you relate to God!

> Ye ask, and receive not, because ye ask amiss, that ye may consume it upon
> your lusts.
>
> JAMES 4:3

Of course, you must ask according to God's Word. If something isn't part of Christ's atonement, then God hasn't provided it for you. That's why if you ask for someone else's spouse, God won't give that person to you. Fornication, adultery, and polygamy are not provided through Jesus' death, burial, and resurrection. God is life! He's not going to kill someone because you prayed and asked Him to. In His atonement, the Lord provided all kinds of good things: joy, peace, restored relationships, healing, prosperity, and much, much more. These are the things you should ask for.

"But I did and it didn't come to pass!" If you asked for something promised in God's Word, then He gave it to you. "No, He didn't!" How do you know? "Because I didn't see it!" Really!

DID YOU RECEIVE?

The problem is, you think you can perceive with your five senses what God does or doesn't do. If you can't see, taste, hear, smell, or feel it, then that's "proof" that God didn't do it. The answer to this dilemma lies in understanding the existence of the spiritual realm.

God is a Spirit (John 4:24). When He moves, He moves in the spiritual world. The very moment you ask for something, God commands and it is given. Although it's a done deal in the spirit, whether or not you see it manifest in the physical realm depends much more on if you know how to receive than if God answered your prayer. That's an oversimplification because other people are involved sometimes, but it mainly comes down to your receiving in the natural realm what God has already given you in the spirit.

God answers every prayer that's according to His Word. However, we don't always see it manifest, because we don't know how to receive. It's not because God didn't answer.

"Are you saying it's my fault?" Yes, I am. Some people become very upset with me and think, *You're condemning me!* No, I'm not. I'm just letting you know that if somebody missed it, it wasn't God!

Knowing that God is always faithful blesses me! He's not choosing to heal this one and leave another sick, prosper that one and ignore someone else, or give joy to that one and not another. This thought that *God just wanted to bless that person and make this other one miserable* isn't true. God's not like that! In His faithfulness, the Lord has a perfect plan for each and every one of us that includes health, prosperity, joy, blessing, peace, and happiness. It's just that not everybody receives from Him. It's not because God's not faithful to give; rather, it's because not everyone knows how to receive. It's really that simple!

ANDREW'S RECOMMENDATIONS FOR FURTHER STUDY

For additional information on the baptism in the Holy Spirit and praying in tongues, please refer to my teaching entitled *The New You & The Holy Spirit.*

Outline

I. God's Word will work for everyone, but we come up with excuses for why it won't work for all people, all the time.

    A. Luke 11:9-10 tells us that we will receive if we ask and that everyone who asks does receive.

    B. But experience carries more weight in most people's lives than the Word of God does.

    C. We must believe that God means what He says—if we ask, we will receive.

II. We must ask according to God's Word (James 4:3).

    A. We have to make sure that what we ask for is part of Christ's atonement.

        i. If we asked for something promised in God's Word, then He has already given it to us.

        ii. But if something isn't part of Christ's atonement, then God hasn't provided it for us.

        iii. In His atonement, the Lord provided all kinds of good things: joy, peace, restored relationships, healing, prosperity, and much, much more.

    B. Just because we don't see what we ask for doesn't mean God hasn't provided them.

    C. We can't perceive with our five senses what God does or doesn't do, because He moves in the spiritual world (John 4:24).

    D. Whether or not we see it manifest in the physical realm depends much more on if we know how to receive than if God answered our prayers.

III. God answers every prayer that's according to His Word.

    A. If our prayers don't get answered, it's not God who missed it.

i. God is always faithful.

ii. Knowing that God is faithful should bless us.

iii. In His faithfulness, the Lord has a perfect plan for each and every one of us that includes health, prosperity, joy, blessing, peace, and happiness.

B. It's just that not everybody receives from Him.

C. This isn't because God is not faithful to give but because not everyone knows how to receive.

ANDREW'S RECOMMENDATIONS FOR FURTHER STUDY

For additional information on the baptism in the Holy Spirit and praying in tongues, please refer to my teaching entitled *The New You & The Holy Spirit*.

Teacher's Guide

1.   God's Word will work for everyone, but we come up with excuses for why it won't work for all people, all the time. Luke 11:9-10 tells us that we will receive if we ask and that everyone who asks does receive. But experience carries more weight in most people's lives than the Word of God does. We must believe that God means what He says—if we ask, we will receive.

1a.   Read Luke 11:9-10. Although God tells you that you will receive when you ask, what carries more weight in most people's lives?
Their experiences

1b.   What must you believe about God more than your experiences?
That He means what He says

2.   We must ask according to God's Word (James 4:3). We have to make sure that what we ask for is part of Christ's atonement. If we asked for something promised in God's Word, then He has already given it to us. But if something isn't part of Christ's atonement, then God hasn't provided it for us. In His atonement, the Lord provided all kinds of good things: joy, peace, restored relationships, healing, prosperity, and much, much more. Just because we don't see what we ask for doesn't mean God hasn't provided them. We can't perceive with our five senses what God does or doesn't do, because He moves in the spiritual world (John 4:24). Whether or not we see it manifest in the physical realm depends much more on if we know how to receive than if God answered our prayers.

2a.   If you ask for something promised in God's Word, what can you be sure of?
That God has already given it to you

2b.   What does the manifestation of your answer in the spiritual realm depend on?
Whether or not you know how to receive it

3.   God answers every prayer that's according to His Word. If our prayers don't get answered, it's not God who missed it. God is always faithful. Knowing that God is faithful should bless us. In His faithfulness, the Lord has a perfect plan for each and every one of us that includes health, prosperity, joy, blessing, peace, and happiness. It's just that not everybody receives from Him. This isn't because God is not faithful to give but because not everyone knows how to receive.

3a.   If your prayers don't get answered, how can you know that it's not God who missed it?
Because God is always faithful

3b.   Why doesn't everyone receive from God?
Because not everyone knows how to receive

Discipleship Questions

1. Read Luke 11:9-10. Although God tells you that you will receive when you ask, what carries more weight in most people's lives?

2. What must you believe about God more than your experiences?

3. If you ask for something promised in God's Word, what can you be sure of?

4. What does the manifestation of your answer in the spiritual realm depend on?

5. If your prayers don't get answered, how can you know that it's not God who missed it?

6. Why doesn't everyone receive from God?

Answer Key

1.   Their experiences

2.   That He means what He says

3.   That God has already given it to you

4.   Whether or not you know how to receive it

5.   Because God is always faithful

6.   Because not everyone knows how to receive

Scriptures

LUKE 11:9-10

And I say unto you, Ask, and it shall be given you; seek, and ye shall find; knock, and it shall be opened unto you. [**10**] For every one that asketh receiveth; and he that seeketh findeth; and to him that knocketh it shall be opened.

1 CORINTHIANS 12:30

Have all the gifts of healing? do all speak with tongues? do all interpret?

JAMES 4:3

Ye ask, and receive not, because ye ask amiss, that ye may consume it upon your lusts.

JOHN 4:24

God is a Spirit: and they that worship him must worship him in spirit and in truth.

The Variable

Daniel's example clearly illustrates God's faithfulness to always answer prayer. Daniel prayed and asked the Lord about Jeremiah's prophecy that the children of Israel would be in captivity for seventy years (Dan. 9:1-3 and Jer. 25:11-12). More than seventy years had already come and gone, so it appeared as if God's promise had failed to come to pass.

Just like in our day, their theologians probably tried to explain it away, saying maybe it was this or that or all these other things. But Daniel prayed and asked the Lord what this prophecy meant, since it had already been more than 70 years of captivity. God answered his prayer and showed him that it was 70 weeks of years, which is actually 490 years of captivity (Dan. 9:24). He also gave Daniel an important prophecy concerning the coming Messiah (Dan. 9:25-27). This is a major revelation in God's Word!

> *And I* [Daniel] *set my face unto the Lord God, to seek by prayer and supplications, with fasting, and sackcloth, and ashes: [4] And I prayed unto the* Lord *my God, and made my confession, and said, O Lord, the great and dreadful God…. [9] O Lord, hear; O Lord, forgive; O Lord, hearken and do; defer not, for thine own sake, O my God: for thy city and thy people are called by thy name.*
>
> DANIEL 9:3-4 AND 19, BRACKETS MINE

> *And whiles I was speaking, and praying, and confessing my sin and the sin of my people Israel, and presenting my supplication before the* Lord *my God for the holy mountain of my God; [21] Yea, whiles I was speaking in prayer, even the man Gabriel* [This was an angel—the same one who later spoke to Zacharias and Mary (Luke 1:19 and 26-27)], *whom I had seen in the vision at the beginning, being caused to fly swiftly, touched me about the time of the evening oblation. [22] And he informed me, and talked with me, and said, O Daniel, I am now come forth to give thee skill and understanding.*
>
> DANIEL 9:20-22, BRACKETS MINE

THREE MINUTES

While Daniel was still praying, the angel Gabriel showed up and gave him God's answer. Daniel's whole prayer couldn't have taken more than three minutes, yet the Lord answered while he was still in the midst of praying it. That's powerful!

> *At the beginning of thy supplications the commandment came forth, and I am come to shew thee; for thou art greatly beloved: therefore understand the matter, and consider the vision.*
>
> DANIEL 9:23, EMPHASIS MINE

Notice what the angel said concerning when God had answered: "At the very beginning of your supplication, God gave the command, and I'm here with your answer."

Many people contend that there is no such thing as time, space, or distance with God, but this assumption can't be proved in Scripture. They think that if God wanted to heal, prosper, deliver, give joy, etc., to someone, all He has to do is just will it and—BOOM—it's instantly there. They believe if God wants it done, then—BANG—it's done, that nothing can stop or delay God from doing what He wants to do. This leads to the wrong assumption that when we don't see anything, God hasn't done anything. However, Daniel 9 gives us an example where God spoke, and it took approximately three minutes for it to manifest.

I'm not sure why, but there was a period of time between when God moved and when it manifested. Perhaps Gabriel was a hundred million light-years away, and it took him three minutes to cover that distance. Maybe he had to pack his bags or brush his teeth. Who knows what he was doing? But it took three minutes before what God had commanded manifested.

CONSIDER THE SPIRIT REALM

Three minutes isn't so bad! You can handle it if you go forward in a meeting for prayer, and everything's just fine by the time you hit the floor at the altar. But what if it takes three weeks instead of three minutes? That's when most people lose their faith. If they can't see or feel their answer very soon, then they conclude, "I asked, but God didn't answer." How do you know? How can you be sure that the Lord hasn't already commanded your answer and that it's in the process of coming out of the spirit realm into the physical realm? Can you see all the activity taking place in the spirit realm on your behalf?

Most of the time, people don't even consider this. They just believe that if God wanted to, He could instantly do anything. Then, if something isn't immediately manifest, He hasn't moved. This is really just an exaltation of our own abilities.

If you think you can perceive everything that's going on around you in the spirit realm, you're thinking too highly of yourself! In the natural, there are microscopic bugs and specks of dust floating in the air. Even though you can't perceive them with your physical senses, you know they exist. In the spiritual world, there are all kinds of things happening that you don't realize. It's the height of arrogance to pray and think that absolutely nothing happened if you can't immediately see, taste, hear, smell, or feel your answer. There's simply more to it than what you can figure out with your brain!

It would be easy for you to assume that I'm different from you if I were to share an illustration from my life. You'd say, "Well, that's just how it happens for you, Andrew. Somehow or another, things work better for you than for me. Besides, you aren't facing the problems I have in my life right now!" If I gave you an example from Jesus' life, you could blow it off, too, with "But that's Jesus! He could do it back then, but this is me, here and now." Jesus was God, but He didn't operate out of His divinity. He acted by faith as a man under the Covenant. It's the same with the disciples. There's really no difference between them and you as a born-again believer, except in your own mind!

THREE WEEKS

Daniel makes a great example. The same man prayed two different times and received two different results. If anything, he should have had more faith after his miraculous encounter in chapter 9. He should have been so pumped that the results of his prayer life could only improve. Instead, they became worse! The next time, it took three whole weeks to receive his answer.

> *In those days I Daniel was mourning three full weeks. [3] I ate no pleasant bread, neither came flesh nor wine in my mouth, neither did I anoint myself at all, till three whole weeks were fulfilled.*
>
> DANIEL 10:2-3

Daniel afflicted himself and focused totally on God, but it still took three full weeks to receive his answer, instead of just three minutes like before.

Have you ever had that happen? Has something you prayed for instantly come to pass, but then something else took a long period of time? Why does God answer one prayer in three minutes and another in three weeks? That's an invalid question. God didn't answer one in three minutes and the other in three weeks. He answered both of them immediately!

"At the beginning of thy supplications the commandment came forth" (Dan. 9:23) and *"from the first day that thou didst set thine heart to understand, and to chasten thyself before thy God, thy words were heard"* (Dan. 10:12).

God answered both prayers instantly; however, one time took three minutes before the person could perceive it, and the other took three weeks. Luke 11:9-10 says that if you ask, you receive. God instantly answers every prayer that's based on a promise in His Word. He's answered every prayer that every believer has ever prayed this way. God has never failed to answer any such prayer, ever!

However, things happen in the spiritual realm that determine how fast the answers come, or not, into the physical realm. The manifestation of your answer is affected when you become discouraged or depressed, or if you give up. There could have been tremendous activity in the spiritual realm. You could have been very close to seeing the physical manifestation, but you gave up and quit!

What if Daniel had given up on day twenty in chapter 10? The Scripture shows that God had already spoken, and the answer was coming. If Daniel would have said, "Man, last time it only took three minutes. This time tomorrow makes three weeks. I quit!" Even though all of these things were happening in the spirit realm, his answer wouldn't have manifested. God's Word reveals that it's according to the power that works in us (Eph. 3:20). From the human perspective, it would have appeared as if God didn't answer Daniel's second prayer.

DEMONIC HINDRANCE

But the prince of the kingdom of Persia withstood me [the angelic messenger] *one and twenty days: but, lo, Michael, one of the chief princes, came to help me; and I remained there with the kings of Persia.*

DANIEL 10:13, BRACKETS MINE

The angelic messenger told Daniel what the holdup had been: demonic opposition. Jude 9 and Revelation 12:7 reveal Michael to be an archangel. Notice how the messenger had been withstood since the first day Daniel prayed. God had instantly responded, but for Daniel to receive his answer, the messenger needed Michael's help to break through the demonic opposition.

Many people don't understand that we're living in a world that has demonic opposition. They think that if God wants something done, He can just do it. God is greater than the devil, but Satan can hinder Him if a physical person cooperates and gives the Enemy authority to do so. Things don't work automatically just because they're God's will or because we prayed for it.

That's why I met all kinds of opposition when I went to empty out the hospital. I'd just become excited about healing and thought, *This is awesome! It's God's will for everyone to be healed!* Although that's true and I was in faith, the sick people there didn't receive it very well.

A man confined to a wheelchair actually grabbed his crutch and rolled himself down the hall, chasing me. Angrily swinging that crutch at me, he kept yelling, "God made me this way! It's His will that I be sick. You are blaspheming God!"

Another time, an African man lay before me, dying. The relatives had been called in, and the doctors were diligently working. One of the family members had invited me in to pray for him. While there, I watched the medical professionals revive him from death through shock treatment. Gently, I told him, "I'm going to pray for you. It's God's will for you to be healed right now."

He answered, "Well, if it's God's will."

"It is God's will! You are going to be well."

Then this guy, who had been revived once before right there on his deathbed, became angry and screamed at me, "No! You can't say it's God's will to heal me!" Rising up out of his bed, he continued at the top of his lungs, "God's going to kill me!" The doctors physically picked me up and threw me out on the sidewalk, simply for telling him it was God's will for him to be well. He died. It was God's will for him to be healed, but his unbelief kept it from happening.

IT'S THEIR DECISION

A woman who had been praying for a certain family member to be healed was struggling and confused due to the lack of manifestation. When she asked what she was doing wrong, I told her that it might be nothing. The issue could very well be the way this family member truly believed in his or her heart. Just because people sound and look like they're in faith to receive healing doesn't mean they really are.

My friend Don Krow and I went to a certain man's house nearly every day for months. We ministered to him constantly. One day, he was so weak, he could barely pick up the phone. His wife had to hold the receiver up to his ear while I told him, "Don't you dare die until I get there!" Don and I went over and started ministering to him. He improved so much that he was up walking, eating, driving a car, and doing pretty good for a while.

Then he became discouraged. Even though he wasn't letting on about it to others, the Lord spoke to my heart one day while I was with him: "He's quit. He just decided that he's coming home to be with Me." This fellow was older and struggling. Although it wasn't God's best for him to just check out, it wasn't sin either.

I told his wife, "The Lord spoke to me and said that your husband has quit and decided to go home. I believe it's God's will for him to be well, but do you know what? If he wants to go home, there's nothing wrong with that." I continued, "You have a choice. Either you can keep believing against his will that he'll recover, which won't work, or you can enjoy your last days together. You can make these days a mess, or you can praise God that you know where he's going and love him on his way."

Angrily, she rebuked me, accusing, "You're not in faith!"

I went ahead and kept visiting, praying for his healing and going through the motions, but I knew in my heart what God had spoken. This man died. At his funeral, people were asking, "Why didn't it work? I just don't understand!"

After his death, his wife found his journal. On the exact day I had spoken to her, he'd written, "I have just decided to go home but will continue to act like I'm believing so that the people around me won't be disappointed." He went through the motions, and we wondered, *Why?*

GOD IS ALWAYS CONSTANT!

You don't always know what's going on inside someone else's heart. For you to take responsibility and say "I prayed and believed, but God didn't answer. If it was truly His will to heal, then they would've been healed!" is to claim knowledge and ability you don't have. You don't always know what's truly going on.

However, God is always constant! According to His Word—which is all we can base our lives on—God declares, "By His stripes, we were healed" (1 Pet. 2:24). He would have all to be healed of their sicknesses and diseases. That's what the Bible teaches. You must go by what the Word says!

The variable isn't God; it's the devil! God answered both of Daniel's prayers instantly, but Satan opposed and delayed the answer from manifesting the second time.

Many people erroneously believe that the devil is infallible and always faithful to strike at the right time. They think he never misses a beat! Although they might not admit it, that's truly what they believe. People often tell me how they've done everything they know to do but still aren't sure if God will come through for them. However, if they do the slightest thing wrong, they have no doubt whatsoever that Satan will get them every time. These Christians have more faith in the devil than they do in God!

You need to know that Satan blows it lots of times. Why didn't he fight the prayer in Daniel 9? He probably missed it!

THE DEVIL IS THE DIFFERENCE!

Demons don't procreate and have "baby demons." There aren't new ones coming all the time. There may have been many evil spirits per person back in Adam and Eve's time, but since then, they've probably been getting spread pretty thin.

Therefore, not everyone has a personal devil. So many people believe they do, but Satan can't speak to everyone every day. He's short-handed! He has to pick and choose whom he personally afflicts. Just like a predator preys on a herd of animals, he chooses the weak ones and those who separate themselves from the pack. There are things that draw evil spirits to us, but the truth is that not everyone has a demon attacking them every single day!

The devil was busy doing everything he could against the kingdom of God when Daniel prayed. He probably thought Daniel's prayer didn't stand a chance of getting through, so he let it squeak by in Daniel 9. However, after that tremendous answer and revelation came, Satan assigned a major demonic power to make sure Daniel didn't get any other prayers through.

There's a big difference between the way they prayed in the Old Covenant and the way we pray in the New Covenant. They had to get a prayer through, but as believers in Christ, we have God Himself already living in us. However, the principle I want you to see is that the devil assigned a demon to hinder Daniel's prayer. This caused the difference between three minutes and three weeks. God isn't the variable; Satan is.

Outline

I. While Daniel was still praying about Jeremiah's prophecy, the angel Gabriel showed up and gave him God's answer.

   A. Daniel 9:23 says that as soon as Daniel started praying, God's commandment to answer the prayer came forth.

   B. Daniel 9 gives us an example of God's faithfulness to always answer prayer.

II. God will do the same with us, but our answer may take some time to get from the spirit realm to the physical realm.

   A. Most people assume God did not answer their prayer if they can't see or feel anything right away, but things are always happening in the spirit realm.

   B. It's arrogance to think that nothing happened if we can't immediately see, taste, hear, smell, or feel our answers.

III. Later, Daniel prayed again, and it took him three weeks to receive an answer.

   A. The same man prayed two different times and received two different results.

   B. It didn't take God longer to answer one prayer over another; He answered both prayers instantly.

   C. God always instantly answers every prayer that's based on a promise in His Word.

   D. But things happen in the spiritual world that determine how fast the answers make it into the physical realm.

   E. For instance, the manifestation of our answers is affected when we become discouraged or depressed, or if we give up.

   F. God's Word reveals that it's according to the power that works in us (Eph. 3:20).

IV. In Daniel 10, God had instantly responded to Daniel's prayer, but demonic opposition held up the answer (Dan. 10:13).

A. God's messenger needed Michael the archangel's help to break through the demonic opposition.

B. God is greater than the devil, but Satan can hinder Him if a physical person cooperates and gives the Enemy authority to do so.

C. Things don't work automatically just because they're God's will and we prayed for it.

D. Unbelief can keep our answers from coming to pass.

V. Just because people sound and look like they're in faith to receive healing doesn't mean they really are.

A. We don't always know what's going on inside someone else's heart.

B. We can't blame God for not answering our prayer for someone when it is up to that person.

C. God is always constant!

D. According to His Word—which is all we can base our lives on—God declares, "By His stripes, we were healed" (1 Pet. 2:24).

E. We must go by what the Word says!

VI. God answered both of Daniel's prayers instantly, but Satan opposed and delayed the answer from manifesting the second time.

A. Many people erroneously believe that the devil is infallible and always faithful to strike at the right time.

B. Satan blows it lots of times, yet Christians sometimes have more faith in the devil than in God.

C. Satan can't attack everyone at once.

D. Not everyone has a personal devil; Satan has to pick and choose whom he personally afflicts.

Teacher's Guide

1.   While Daniel was still praying about Jeremiah's prophecy, the angel Gabriel showed up and gave him God's answer. Daniel 9:23 says that as soon as Daniel started praying, God's commandment to answer the prayer came forth. Daniel 9 gives us an example of God's faithfulness to always answer prayer.

1a.   Read Daniel 9:23. What happened to Daniel while he was still praying?
The angel Gabriel showed up and answered his prayer

1b.   What is Daniel 9 an example of?
God's faithfulness to answer prayer

2.   God will do the same with us, but our answer may take some time to get from the spirit realm to the physical realm. Most people assume God did not answer their prayer if they can't see or feel anything right away, but things are always happening in the spirit realm. It's arrogance to think that nothing happened if we can't immediately see, taste, hear, smell, or feel our answers.

2a.   Just because you don't always see an answer to your prayers immediately, what can you know for sure?
That things are always happening in the spirit realm

2b.   When people don't see or feel an answer to their prayers, what do they usually assume?
That God didn't answer their prayer

3.   Later, Daniel prayed again, and it took him three weeks to receive an answer. The same man prayed two different times and received two different results. It didn't take God longer to answer one prayer over another; He answered both prayers instantly. God always instantly answers every prayer that's based on a promise in His Word. But things happen in the spiritual world that determine how fast the answers make it into the physical realm. For instance, the manifestation of our answers is affected when we become discouraged or depressed, or if we give up. God's Word reveals that it's according to the power that works in us (Eph. 3:20).

3a.   If you pray according to a promise in God's Word, what does He always do?
Instantly answer it

3b.   How can you affect the manifestation of your prayers being answered?
By getting discouraged, depressed, or giving up

4.   In Daniel 10, God had instantly responded to Daniel's prayer, but demonic opposition held up the answer (Dan. 10:13). God's messenger needed Michael the archangel's help to break through the demonic opposition. God is greater than the devil, but Satan can hinder Him if a physical person cooperates and gives the Enemy authority to do so. Things don't work automatically just because they're God's will and we prayed for it. Unbelief can keep our answers from coming to pass.

4a.   Read Daniel 10:13. Why did it take Daniel three weeks to receive the answer to his prayer?
       It was held up by demonic opposition
4b.   How can Satan hinder God?
       When a physical person cooperates and gives him authority to do so

5.   Just because people sound and look like they're in faith to receive healing doesn't mean they really are. We don't always know what's going on inside someone else's heart. We can't blame God for not answering our prayer for someone when it is up to that person. God is always constant! According to His Word—which is all we can base our lives on—God declares, "By His stripes, we were healed" (1 Pet. 2:24). We must go by what the Word says!

5a.   Why can't you go by how people look and sound to determine whether or not they're in faith?
       Because you don't know what's in their hearts
5b.   Why can't you blame God when your prayers for someone else don't get answered?
       Because answered prayer can depend on the faith and will of the other person

6.   God answered both of Daniel's prayers instantly, but Satan opposed and delayed the answer from manifesting the second time. Many people erroneously believe that the devil is infallible and always faithful to strike at the right time. Satan blows it lots of times, yet Christians sometimes have more faith in the devil than in God. Satan can't attack everyone at once. Not everyone has a personal devil; Satan has to pick and choose whom he personally afflicts.

6a.   What was the variable in Daniel's prayers getting answered?
       The devil
6b.   What do many people erroneously believe about Satan?
       That he is infallible and always faithful to strike at the right time

Discipleship Questions

1. Read Daniel 9:23. What happened to Daniel while he was still praying?

2. What is Daniel 9 an example of?

3. Just because you don't always see an answer to your prayers immediately, what can you know for sure?

4. When people don't see or feel an answer to their prayers, what do they usually assume?

5. If you pray according to a promise in God's Word, what does He always do?

6. How can you affect the manifestation of your prayers being answered?

7. Read Daniel 10:13. Why did it take Daniel three weeks to receive the answer to his prayer?

8. How can Satan hinder God?

9. Why can't you go by how people look and sound to determine whether or not they're in faith?

10. Why can't you blame God when your prayers for someone else don't get answered?

11. What was the variable in Daniel's prayers getting answered?

12. What do many people erroneously believe about Satan?

Answer Key

1. The angel Gabriel showed up and answered his prayer

2. God's faithfulness to answer prayer

3. That things are always happening in the spirit realm

4. That God didn't answer their prayer

5. Instantly answer it

6. By getting discouraged, depressed, or giving up

7. It was held up by demonic opposition

8. When a physical person cooperates and gives him authority to do so

9. Because you don't know what's in their hearts

10. Because answered prayer can depend on the faith and will of the other person

11. The devil

12. That he is infallible and always faithful to strike at the right time

Scriptures

DANIEL 9:1-4

In the first year of Darius the son of Ahasuerus, of the seed of the Medes, which was made king over the realm of the Chaldeans; [2] In the first year of his reign I Daniel understood by books the number of the years, whereof the word of the LORD came to Jeremiah the prophet, that he would accomplish seventy years in the desolations of Jerusalem. [3] And I set my face unto the Lord God, to seek by prayer and supplications, with fasting, and sackcloth, and ashes: [4] And I prayed unto the LORD my God, and made my confession, and said, O Lord, the great and dreadful God, keeping the covenant and mercy to them that love him, and to them that keep his commandments.

JEREMIAH 25:11-12

And this whole land shall be a desolation, and an astonishment; and these nations shall serve the king of Babylon seventy years. [12] And it shall come to pass, when seventy years are accomplished, that I will punish the king of Babylon, and that nation, saith the LORD, for their iniquity, and the land of the Chaldeans, and will make it perpetual desolations.

DANIEL 9:19-27

O Lord, hear; O Lord, forgive; O Lord, hearken and do; defer not, for thine own sake, O my God: for thy city and thy people are called by thy name. [20] And whiles I was speaking, and praying, and confessing my sin and the sin of my people Israel, and presenting my supplication before the LORD my God for the holy mountain of my God; [21] Yea, whiles I was speaking in prayer, even the man Gabriel, whom I had seen in the vision at the beginning, being caused to fly swiftly, touched me about the time of the evening oblation. [22] And he informed me, and talked with me, and said, O Daniel, I am now come forth to give thee skill and understanding. [23] At the beginning of thy supplications the commandment came forth, and I am come to shew thee; for thou art greatly beloved: therefore understand the matter, and consider the vision. [24] Seventy weeks are determined upon thy people and upon thy holy city, to finish the transgression, and to make an end of sins, and to make reconciliation for iniquity, and to bring in everlasting righteousness, and to seal up the vision and prophecy, and to anoint the most Holy. [25] Know therefore and understand, that from the going forth of the commandment to restore and to build Jerusalem unto the Messiah the Prince shall be seven weeks, and threescore and two weeks: the street shall be built again, and the wall, even in troublous times. [26] And after threescore and two weeks shall Messiah be cut off, but not for himself: and the people of the prince that shall come shall destroy the city and the sanctuary; and the end thereof shall be with a flood, and unto the end of the war desolations are determined. [27] And he shall confirm the covenant with many for one week: and in the midst of the week he shall cause the sacrifice and the oblation to cease, and for the overspreading of abominations he shall make it desolate, even until the consummation, and that determined shall be poured upon the desolate.

LUKE 1:19
And the angel answering said unto him, I am Gabriel, that stand in the presence of God; and am sent to speak unto thee, and to shew thee these glad tidings.

LUKE 1:26-27
And in the sixth month the angel Gabriel was sent from God unto a city of Galilee, named Nazareth, [27] To a virgin espoused to a man whose name was Joseph, of the house of David; and the virgin's name was Mary.

DANIEL 10:2-3
In those days I Daniel was mourning three full weeks. [3] I ate no pleasant bread, neither came flesh nor wine in my mouth, neither did I anoint myself at all, till three whole weeks were fulfilled.

DANIEL 10:12-13
Then said he unto me, Fear not, Daniel: for from the first day that thou didst set thine heart to understand, and to chasten thyself before thy God, thy words were heard, and I am come for thy words. [13] But the prince of the kingdom of Persia withstood me one and twenty days: but, lo, Michael, one of the chief princes, came to help me; and I remained there with the kings of Persia.

LUKE 11:9-10
And I say unto you, Ask, and it shall be given you; seek, and ye shall find; knock, and it shall be opened unto you. [10] For every one that asketh receiveth; and he that seeketh findeth; and to him that knocketh it shall be opened.

EPHESIANS 3:20
Now unto him that is able to do exceeding abundantly above all that we ask or think, according to the power that worketh in us.

JUDE 9
Yet Michael the archangel, when contending with the devil he disputed about the body of Moses, durst not bring against him a railing accusation, but said, The Lord rebuke thee.

REVELATION 12:7
And there was war in heaven: Michael and his angels fought against the dragon; and the dragon fought and his angels.

1 PETER 2:24
Who his own self bare our sins in his own body on the tree, that we, being dead to sins, should live unto righteousness: by whose stripes ye were healed.

THE VARIABLE

Hindrances Removed

Most Christians doubt God when they pray and don't instantly see their answers. They whine, "Lord, what are You doing? Why haven't You answered my prayer?" These believers fail to consider that maybe the devil is hindering them, or maybe their answers are simply taking some time to manifest.

This false idea that God *can do anything instantly* serves as a huge inroad for all kinds of unbelief. The Lord established this world with things such as time and space. If you remember that it can take time for things to happen and that demons can hinder your answer, it'll help when you pray and don't see the manifestation instantly. Instead of immediately doubting God, you'll either doubt yourself or the devil. A multitude of factors can enter in and hinder, or slow down, the manifestation of God's power.

My friend heard me teach this more than fifteen years ago. At the time, he'd been trying to sell his house for over two years. Since he didn't want to pay a realtor's commission, he'd put a sign up in his front yard: *For Sale by Owner.* Almost every day for those two years, he had faithfully prayed, "God, I'm asking You to sell my house." However, very few people had looked at it, and virtually nothing had happened.

Then he heard me preach this message and applied it to his situation. The Lord told him, "Bob, I spoke to someone to buy your house the very first day you put that sign in your yard. I have moved to sell your house, but there are demonic hindrances against it."

Most people pray, "God, please sell my house." Then, if it doesn't sell, they wonder, *Lord, why haven't You done it?* God isn't personally going to buy your house. He'll send someone else to do it. You need to realize that other people are often involved in the manifestation of your answer to prayer.

GOD SENDS PROVISION THROUGH PEOPLE

When you ask God for money, He sends it through people.

> *Give, and it shall be given unto you; good measure, pressed down, and shaken together, and running over,* shall men give into your bosom.
> LUKE 6:38, EMPHASIS MINE

God supplies your requested provision through people. He doesn't have U.S. currency of His own, and He definitely won't counterfeit or steal any. God doesn't just create money and stick it in your wallet either. He speaks to individuals and meets your needs through them. That's why all Satan has to do to hinder your finances is hinder people.

A while ago, the Lord led our ministry to expand the television outreach and purchase a new building. Since I understand that He manifests provision through people, I've been very open with our increasing financial needs. Due to this, I've received numerous rebukes from individuals, saying, "If you were a man of faith, you'd never have to ask people for anything. God would take care of you!" They are under this concept that if you have a need, God just supernaturally meets it.

One fellow used George Mueller as an example. George ran a large orphanage in England and supported many missionaries around the world. He was famous for believing God for provision. Mueller would sit down at the table to eat with hundreds of kids and begin to pray over the food, all the while knowing there wasn't any to serve yet! Right then, people would show up with all kinds of food. This man wrote, "George Mueller never spoke to anyone of his need, except God. You aren't a man of faith if you have to tell people what you need!"

While it's true those things happened, my friend missed the fact that George Mueller also put out a monthly newsletter that included a detailed list of all their current needs. It just so happened that as he prayed over the meal in faith, someone who had read the newsletter arrived with their contribution. Of course, that's supernatural, but God uses people!

BREAK THE OPPOSITION

Our ministry's finances were hindered in the late 1980s when two famous televangelists got in trouble. I hadn't started broadcasting on television yet but was preaching God's Word all around the country on radio. Why did our income drop tens of thousands of dollars those months? God uses people to supply our needs!

Even though we didn't have anything to do with either one of those men, people lost faith in media ministers. Fear, doubt, and criticism came, and people stopped giving to media ministries. I suffered for it for a while, but not because of my unbelief. Satan hindered our finances through the fear and mistrust that other people felt. I didn't become angry with God and demand, "Why did You decrease my offerings?" It wasn't the Lord; the devil was hindering people.

When folks go on vacation in the summer, many don't take their commitment to support our ministry seriously. Instead, they use the money they normally give to God for their trip. Our ministry suffers for it, but I'm not mad at God. He uses people.

My friend who had been asking God to sell his house repented and prayed, "Father, thank You that the very first day I put my house on the market, You spoke to somebody to buy it. It's not You who hasn't answered but Satan who's hindered." Then he bound the devil. Since my friend didn't know how the Enemy was doing it, he prayed in tongues over the situation and believed that God would take care of it.

Two days later, a man came with cash in hand to buy his house. As they were closing, the buyer told my friend, "The very first day you put that sign in your yard two years ago, I told my wife, 'That's our house!' Since then, I've been trying to get my finances in order." Even though he wasn't a Christian, he remarked, "It's supernatural what's happened! The guy who wanted to buy my house had to sell his first. He'd been hindered for two years, but then the strangest thing happened. Two days ago, he came to me, he had the money, we closed, and here I am, buying your house!"

Satan had been hindering my friend's answer through other people. God broke the devil's opposition, and the answer manifested when my friend changed his prayer. Instead of asking the Lord every day to sell his house and then wondering why He hadn't done it yet, my friend started praying, "Father, I believe You've answered my prayer. You have already spoken, but there must be some way the Enemy has been hindering it. Please give me Your wisdom on how to pray." What a difference!

SHORTEN THE TIME

As an Old Testament saint, Daniel didn't have authority over the devil. Therefore, he couldn't rebuke the demonic entity called *"the prince of the kingdom of Persia"* (Dan. 10:13). Even if Daniel had known that the problem was demonic, he wouldn't have been able to do anything about it. However, as New Covenant believers, we do have authority over the devil (Luke 9:1).

God always answers prayer instantly. If you understand this principle, you'll know that when your answer delays in manifestation, it's either your faith wavering or the devil hindering—or both.

> *Therefore I say unto you, What things soever ye desire, when ye pray, believe that ye receive them, and ye shall* [future tense] *have them.*
>
> MARK 11:24, BRACKETS MINE

Also, you need to recognize that some things take a period of time to manifest. Healing should be instant, but you can't microwave a ministry! That's dependent on your maturity and character. Some things must grow and develop before you can see them come to pass. But God is always faithful to answer every prayer.

I had a ganglion cyst on my arm back in 1976. It didn't hurt, but it stood up so high that I kept my watchband over it so people wouldn't see. Even though I had one of those expandable watchbands, the cyst finally grew to where it bulged out from underneath my watch. After praying over it each day and saying "Father, I receive my healing," I'd stick that hand behind my back so I wouldn't have to look at it. I'd ignore that ganglion cyst, thinking it was faith. I didn't want to look at anything contrary to what I was believing for. Hey, that's better than praying, looking at it, and then saying, "It didn't work!" But there's a better way to pray.

Since then, I've learned that it's better to look right at the problem and declare, "I know God has already answered my prayer, because His Word says so!" If His answer isn't manifest, I know now that it's not the Lord who hasn't given, but it's me or the devil or something else in the way. I take my spiritual weapons and use them to shorten the amount of time between "amen" and "there it is" (manifestation).

When you know in your heart that God has already given it to you in the spirit realm, you don't have to hold on for three weeks, like Daniel did, for the answer to manifest in the physical realm. As a believer in Jesus Christ, take your authority and command the devil to leave. Instead of telling God about it, speak directly to the problem, and then act on God's Word. Don't just sit idly by, waiting—do something!

IT'S UP TO YOU!

A woman testified to me of her toothache. She'd been praying and doing everything she knew to do. After speaking to the tooth, she started praising God and thanking Him that her healing was already done. When she asked the Lord for wisdom, He led her to exercise her authority and say, "Satan, in the name of Jesus, I command you to leave me alone!" As soon as she spoke those words, the pain immediately and completely left. Apparently, her toothache wasn't just physical; it was a spiritual, demonic thing.

God always answers your prayers instantly, but you don't always immediately know what the hindrance might be. Sometimes it takes a period of time for you to discover how to work through it. Use wisdom and pray in the Spirit until God leads you in a certain direction. Then, take your authority and deal with it. This will shorten the amount of time between "amen" and "there it is." It's basically up to you as to how quickly your answers to prayer manifest.

Jesus used this same strategy while praying for a blind man (Mark 8:22-26). He took the man out of town, prayed for him, and then asked what he saw. Some would say, "Well, that's unbelief!" No, Jesus wasn't asking "Did it work?" He knew God had given. The reason He took the man out of town in the first place was because Bethsaida was so full of unbelief.

Jesus said, *"Woe unto thee, Bethsaida! for if the mighty works had been done in Tyre and Sidon, which have been done in you, they had a great while ago repented"* (Luke 10:13).

Bethsaida was one of the most unbelieving cities Jesus ever visited. He had to take this man by the hand and lead him away from the unbelief of the people in town.

Even though Jesus had the man out of the town, He knew He hadn't gotten all of the town out of the man! The Lord perceived that there were still some hindrances of unbelief in him. Jesus prayed, knowing His Father had released the power. Therefore, He wasn't asking "Did it work?" but rather "Have you received? Are you still having problems?" The Lord confronted the physical problem head-on and looked squarely at it.

When the man manifested only a partial healing, Jesus prayed for him again. That would get Him kicked out of most Bible colleges today because "it's not faith to ask for something twice." The Lord didn't ask for anything twice; He believed and received it the first time. The second time, He used His spiritual power and authority. The devil may have withstood one dose, but surely he wouldn't withstand two! So, Jesus prayed again, and the man saw clearly.

That's how our prayer ministers pray in our meetings. We don't just ask God for healing and then smile at the person, saying, "Depart in peace. Be warmed and filled!" No, we ask if you've received the full manifestation. "Is your pain gone? Are you able to move?" If you don't have full manifestation, we begin taking authority, speaking to the affected parts of your body, and commanding them to work. Although we don't see every single individual healed, most people do receive their full manifestation of healing. Glory to God!

Outline

I. Most Christians doubt God when they pray and don't instantly see their answers.

    A. But sometimes, answers to prayer may take time to manifest.

    B. One reason is that the devil may be hindering them.

    C. If we remember that it can take time for things to happen and that demons can hinder our answers, it'll help when we pray and don't see the manifestation instantly.

    D. Instead of immediately doubting God, we'll either doubt ourselves or the devil.

    E. A multitude of factors can enter in and hinder, or slow down, the manifestation of God's power.

II. Sometimes other people are involved in the manifestation of our answers to prayer.

    A. God will speak to individuals and meet our needs through them.

    B. That's why all Satan has to do to hinder our finances is hinder those people God wants to use to help us.

    C. Sometimes people wrongly assume that God just supernaturally provides for us without using others.

III. Daniel, an Old Testament saint, didn't have authority over the devil, so even if he had known that his problem was demonic, he wouldn't have been able to do anything about it.

    A. However, as New Covenant believers, we do have authority over the devil (Luke 9:1) and can keep him from hindering us.

    B. When our answer delays in manifesting, it's our faith wavering and/or the devil hindering.

IV. When we know in our hearts that God has already given us our answer in the spirit realm, we don't have to hold on for three weeks, like Daniel did, for the manifestation in the physical realm.

   A. As believers in Jesus Christ, we can take our authority and command the devil to leave.

   B. Instead of telling God about it, we can speak directly to the problem.

   C. We can use our spiritual weapons to shorten the time until our answers manifest—the time between "amen" and "there it is."

   D. Instead of just sitting idly by, waiting, let's do something!

V. Even though God always answers prayers instantly, we don't always immediately know what the hindrance might be.

   A. We should use wisdom and pray in the Spirit until God leads us in a certain direction.

   B. Then, we can take our authority and deal with it.

   C. It's basically up to us how quickly our answers to prayer manifest.

VI. When Jesus prayed for a blind man (Mark 8:22-26), the man only manifested a partial healing.

   A. Jesus perceived that the man still had unbelief so He asked him what he saw, then He prayed for him again.

   B. The Lord didn't ask for anything twice—He believed and received it the first time.

   C. The second time, He took His spiritual power and authority and used it to overcome the hindrance.

Teacher's Guide

1.   Most Christians doubt God when they pray and don't instantly see their answers. But sometimes, answers to prayer may take time to manifest. One reason is that the devil may be hindering them. If we remember that it can take time for things to happen and that demons can hinder our answers, it'll help when we pray and don't see the manifestation instantly. Instead of immediately doubting God, we'll either doubt ourselves or the devil. A multitude of factors can enter in and hinder, or slow down, the manifestation of God's power.

1a.   What happens when Christians pray then don't immediately see answers to their prayers?
They doubt God

1b.   What can hinder, or slow down, the manifestation of God's power?
A multitude of factors

2.   Sometimes other people are involved in the manifestation of our answers to prayer. God will speak to individuals and meet our needs through them. That's why all Satan has to do to hinder our finances is hinder those people God wants to use to help us. Sometimes people wrongly assume that God just supernaturally provides for us without using others.

2a.   By what means does God typically provide for you?
Other people

2b.   All Satan has to do to hinder your finances is what?
Hinder those people God wants to use to help you

3.   Daniel, an Old Testament saint, didn't have authority over the devil, so even if he had known that his problem was demonic, he wouldn't have been able to do anything about it. However, as New Covenant believers, we do have authority over the devil (Luke 9:1) and can keep him from hindering us. When our answer delays in manifesting, it's our faith wavering and/or the devil hindering.

3a.   Read Luke 9:1. If Daniel realized that his problem was demonic, what could he have done about it?
Nothing

3b.   As a New Covenant believer, what do you have that Daniel didn't?
Authority over the devil

4.   When we know in our hearts that God has already given us our answer in the spirit realm, we don't have to hold on for three weeks, like Daniel did, for the manifestation in the physical realm. As believers in Jesus Christ, we can take our authority and command the devil to leave. Instead of telling God about it, we can speak directly to the problem. We can use our spiritual weapons to shorten the time until our answers manifest—the time between "amen" and "there it is." Instead of just sitting idly by, waiting, let's do something!

4a.   As a believer in Jesus Christ, what can you do to shorten the time it takes for your answers to prayer to manifest?
Take your authority and command the devil to leave

4b.   What should you do instead of telling God about it?
Speak directly to your problem

5.   Even though God always answers prayers instantly, we don't always immediately know what the hindrance might be. We should use wisdom and pray in the Spirit until God leads us in a certain direction. Then, we can take our authority and deal with it. It's basically up to us how quickly our answers to prayer manifest.

5a.   What should you do until God leads you in a certain direction concerning what the hindrance to your prayers may be?
Use wisdom and pray in the Spirit

5b.   Who is it up to as to how quickly your answers to prayers manifest?
You

6.   When Jesus prayed for a blind man (Mark 8:22-26), the man only manifested a partial healing. Jesus perceived that the man still had unbelief so He asked him what he saw, then He prayed for him again. The Lord didn't ask for anything twice—He believed and received it the first time. The second time, He took His spiritual power and authority and used it to overcome the hindrance.

6a.   Read Mark 8:22-26. What did Jesus do when the man manifested only a partial healing?
Jesus prayed for him again

6b.   What did Jesus do the second time He prayed for him?
Jesus took His spiritual power and authority and used it to overcome the hindrance

Discipleship Questions

1.   What happens when Christians pray then don't immediately see answers to their prayers?

2.   What can hinder, or slow down, the manifestation of God's power?

3.   By what means does God typically provide for you?

4.   All Satan has to do to hinder your finances is what?

5.   Read Luke 9:1. If Daniel realized that his problem was demonic, what could he have done about it?

6.   As a New Covenant believer, what do you have that Daniel didn't?

7.   As a believer in Jesus Christ, what can you do to shorten the time it takes for your answers to prayer to manifest?

8.   What should you do instead of telling God about it?

9.   What should you do until God leads you in a certain direction concerning what the hindrance to your prayers may be?

10.   Who is it up to as to how quickly your answers to prayers manifest?

11.   Read Mark 8:22-26. What did Jesus do when the man manifested only a partial healing?

12.   What did Jesus do the second time He prayed for him?

Answer Key

1. They doubt God

2. A multitude of factors

3. Other people

4. Hinder those people God wants to use to help you

5. Nothing

6. Authority over the devil

7. Take your authority and command the devil to leave

8. Speak directly to your problem

9. Use wisdom and pray in the Spirit

10. You

11. Jesus prayed for him again

12. Jesus took His spiritual power and authority and used it to overcome the hindrance

Scriptures

LUKE 6:38

Give, and it shall be given unto you; good measure, pressed down, and shaken together, and running over, shall men give into your bosom. For with the same measure that ye mete withal it shall be measured to you again.

DANIEL 10:13

But the prince of the kingdom of Persia withstood me one and twenty days: but, lo, Michael, one of the chief princes, came to help me; and I remained there with the kings of Persia.

LUKE 9:1

Then he called his twelve disciples together, and gave them power and authority over all devils, and to cure diseases.

MARK 11:24

Therefore I say unto you, What things soever ye desire, when ye pray, believe that ye receive them, and ye shall have them.

MARK 8:22-26

And he cometh to Bethsaida; and they bring a blind man unto him, and besought him to touch him. [23] And he took the blind man by the hand, and led him out of the town; and when he had spit on his eyes, and put his hands upon him, he asked him if he saw ought. [24] And he looked up, and said, I see men as trees, walking. [25] After that he put his hands again upon his eyes, and made him look up: and he was restored, and saw every man clearly. [26] And he sent him away to his house, saying, Neither go into the town, nor tell it to any in the town.

LUKE 10:13

Woe unto thee, Chorazin! woe unto thee, Bethsaida! for if the mighty works had been done in Tyre and Sidon, which have been done in you, they had a great while ago repented, sitting in sackcloth and ashes.

You Can Receive from God!

So then faith cometh by hearing, and hearing by the word of God.

ROMANS 10:17

When you hear teaching from God's Word concerning healing, deliverance, prosperity, or anything else Jesus provided in His atonement, your faith is strengthened to receive. Once you know you've already got it (in the spiritual realm), manifestation (in the physical realm) comes swiftly. As your knowledge and understanding of something increases from the Word, you can release your faith and see it manifest more quickly.

When ministering healing, you need to realize that the people you're praying for play a large role in whether or not they receive. You can't take responsibility for them, but you can be a positive part of the process. Even Jesus couldn't override someone else's unbelief (Mark 6:5-6).

GOD IS FAITHFUL!

I've ministered my way down prayer lines in services many times. I've prayed for one person who didn't get it, but the next was instantly healed. Going on to the next individual, he or she didn't receive, but the following person did. There's no way I can be that inconsistent in a single service!

I've prayed for an entire row of ten people. Nine received and one didn't. That doesn't mean that one person was evil or didn't love God. You can love God with your whole heart and still not understand how faith works.

Leonardo da Vinci was a genius. He designed helicopters several hundred years ago that people have now built and flown. He was brilliant in his day, but he was ignorant of electricity. Just because Leonardo didn't know something you do doesn't make him stupid; it just means he was ignorant of something you know.

Faith works by knowledge of the Word. God has already healed every person. When you ask and believe, the power is instantly released. If you don't see it manifest, it's not that God hasn't given. Either you haven't received yet, or there's a demonic obstacle preventing the manifestation. God is faithful! Believe it and never move off it.

You'll never see God's miraculous power on a consistent basis if you give up and start saying, "Well, there are exceptions. Maybe God makes some sick to teach them something. Perhaps He wants some to suffer. They probably haven't been good enough, fasted enough, and so forth." God's Word is absolutely true. It never fluctuates or varies. Never compromise on the truth of God's unwavering faithfulness. If you don't see something come to pass, it's not God's fault—it's your fault! I'm not trying to condemn you but to bless, inform, and instruct you. If God's faithfulness is in question, then all of us are in trouble!

"CAN YOU SEE MY FINGER?"

I ministered this message in 1976 in Childress, Texas. We advertised it as a healing service: "Bring the blind, the deaf, and the lame!" After giving the Word, I invited people to come forward to receive ministry. A seventeen-year-old boy who was blind in one eye responded. I prayed over him and commanded his eye to see. Then I had him cover up his good eye and look through the bad one. I asked, "Can you see my finger?" He couldn't even perceive light. I had to turn his head and say, "No, it's over that way." Immediately, I felt the unbelief of the people. To them, if they didn't see something, that meant God didn't do it.

So, I dismissed the crowd, saying, "Those of you who don't understand and don't agree, leave. But those of you who believe that God has done it whether you can see it or not and that it's up to us to manifest it, stay." About twenty of us were left.

We just kept on praying over him. Every five minutes or so, I'd stop and ask, "Can you see my hand?" He couldn't see a thing!

In my heart, I said, "God, I know this is true. Give me a word of wisdom so we can overcome this and demonstrate to these people the truth of Your Word!" As I kept praying, I asked, "God, what's the problem?" This thought came into my heart: *He doesn't need a healing; he needs a miracle!* When the Lord told me that, I hadn't ever thought about the difference between a healing and a miracle. So, I just kept meditating on this and praying in tongues, wondering, *God, what's this: he doesn't need a healing—he needs a miracle?*

MIRACLE RECEIVED & MANIFEST

While I was thinking, Don Krow announced, "God just spoke to me and said that he doesn't need a healing; he needs a miracle!" I thought, *This has to be God!* So, we stopped and I asked the young man, "What's wrong with you?"

He answered, "When I was a baby, I had an infection in my eye, and they had to surgically remove the lens and retina. I don't even have the necessary parts to be able to see."

I said, "You don't need a healing; you need a miracle!" Then I cupped my hands over his eye and spoke, "Lens and retina, I command you to come into this eye now, in the name of Jesus." Then I had him cover his good eye and asked, "How many fingers do I have up?" He answered, "One!" He could see!

Some people think, Well, when you did that, then God moved. No! God moved 2,000 years ago in the death, burial, and resurrection of His Son. He instantly answered my prayer thirty minutes earlier, and His power had already been working. We just hadn't directed it right. We hadn't yet spoken to the mountain!

If we hadn't persevered in prayer, that boy might still be blind in that eye and wondering, *God, what happened?* It was our unbelief as much as it was his, but we decided to just stand there and pray. Even though it took us thirty minutes to get a word from God to do what it took, we received and the miracle manifested! To us, it was well worth it.

ADOPT THIS ATTITUDE

You let doctors do procedures, treatments, and operations to you that last hours, days, and weeks, and cost hundreds and thousands of dollars, but if you ask God for healing and it doesn't happen by the time you hit the floor at the altar, then He failed? Come on!

You may not be Jesus, but you're the best God has to work through at the moment! Your perseverance in prayer could mean the difference between others receiving their miracles or not. It might take you a while, but I encourage you to adopt this attitude: *If I can move the devil an inch, I can move him a mile—an inch at a time if I have to!*

You can receive from God!

Outline

I.   When we hear teaching from God's Word concerning healing, deliverance, prosperity, or anything else Jesus provided in His atonement, our faith is strengthened to receive:

So then faith cometh by hearing, and hearing by the word of God.

ROMANS 10:17

A.   Once we know we've already got it (in the spiritual realm), manifestation (in the physical realm) comes swiftly.

B.   As our knowledge and understanding of something increases from the Word, we can release our faith and see it manifest more quickly.

C.   Those we pray for play a large role in whether or not they receive.

D.   Sometimes people are just ignorant of how faith works—even though they love God—and that will keep them from receiving.

II.   Faith works by knowledge of the Word.

A.   God has already healed every person.

B.   When we ask and believe, the power is instantly released.

C.   If we don't see it manifest, it's not that God hasn't given—either we haven't yet received, or there's a demonic obstacle preventing the manifestation.

D.   It's not God's fault, but ours, if we don't see something come to pass.

E.   God is always faithful.

F.   If God's faithfulness ever comes into question, then all of us are in trouble.

III.   God moved 2,000 years ago in the death, burial, and resurrection of His Son.

    A.   He instantly answers our prayers as soon as we pray, but sometimes those prayers need to be properly directed.

    B.   We may not be Jesus, but we're the best God has to work through at the moment!

    C.   Our perseverance in prayer could mean the difference between others receiving their miracles or not.

    D.   It might take us a while, but let's adopt this attitude: If we can move the devil an inch, we can move him a mile—an inch at a time if we have to!

    E.   We can receive from God!

Teacher's Guide

1.   When we hear teaching from God's Word concerning healing, deliverance, prosperity, or anything else Jesus provided in His atonement, our faith is strengthened to receive:

> *So then faith cometh by hearing, and hearing by the word of God.*
>
> ROMANS 10:17

Once we know we've already got it (in the spiritual realm), manifestation (in the physical realm) comes swiftly. As our knowledge and understanding of something increases from the Word, we can release our faith and see it manifest more quickly. Those we pray for play a large role in whether or not they receive. Sometimes people are just ignorant of how faith works—even though they love God—and that will keep them from receiving.

1a.   Read Romans 10:17. How is your faith strengthened to receive?
When you hear teaching from God's Word concerning healing, deliverance, prosperity, or anything else Jesus provided in His atonement

1b.   When will manifestation come in the physical realm?
Once you know you've already got it in the spiritual realm

2.   Faith works by knowledge of the Word. God has already healed every person. When we ask and believe, the power is instantly released. If we don't see it manifest, it's not that God hasn't given—either we haven't yet received, or there's a demonic obstacle preventing the manifestation. It's not God's fault, but ours, if we don't see something come to pass. God is always faithful. If God's faithfulness ever comes into question, then all of us are in trouble.

2a.   How does faith work?
By knowledge of the Word

2b.   When is God's power released?
When you ask and believe

3.   God moved 2,000 years ago in the death, burial, and resurrection of His Son. He instantly answers our prayers as soon as we pray, but sometimes those prayers need to be properly directed. We may not be Jesus, but we're the best God has to work through at the moment! Our perseverance in prayer could mean the difference between others receiving their miracles or not.

It might take us a while, but let's adopt this attitude: If we can move the devil an inch, we can move him a mile—an inch at a time if we have to! We can receive from God!

3a.   Why do you need to persevere at prayer?
       Because it could mean the difference between others receiving their miracles or not
3b.   What attitude should you adopt concerning prayer?
       If you can move the devil an inch, you can move him a mile—an inch at a time if you have to!

Discipleship Questions

1. Read Romans 10:17. How is your faith strengthened to receive?

2. When will manifestation come in the physical realm?

3. How does faith work?

4. When is God's power released?

5. Why do you need to persevere at prayer?

6. What attitude should you adopt concerning prayer?

Answer Key

1. When you hear teaching from God's Word concerning healing, deliverance, prosperity, or anything else Jesus provided in His atonement

2. Once you know you've already got it in the spiritual realm

3. By knowledge of the Word

4. When you ask and believe

5. Because it could mean the difference between others receiving their miracles or not

6. If you can move the devil an inch, you can move him a mile—an inch at a time if you have to!

Scriptures

ROMANS 10:17

So then faith cometh by hearing, and hearing by the word of God.

MARK 6:5-6

And he could there do no mighty work, save that he laid his hands upon a few sick folk, and healed them. [6] And he marvelled because of their unbelief. And he went round about the villages, teaching.

Receive Jesus as Your Savior

Choosing to receive Jesus Christ as your Lord and Savior is the most important decision you'll ever make!

God's Word promises, *"That if thou shalt confess with thy mouth the Lord Jesus, and shalt believe in thine heart that God hath raised him from the dead, thou shalt be saved. [10] For with the heart man believeth unto righteousness; and with the mouth confession is made unto salvation"* (Rom. 10:9-10). *"For whosoever shall call upon the name of the Lord shall be saved"* (Rom. 10:13).

By His grace, God has already done everything to provide salvation. Your part is simply to believe and receive.

Pray out loud, "Jesus, I confess that You are my Lord and Savior. I believe in my heart that God raised You from the dead. By faith in Your Word, I receive salvation now. Thank You for saving me!"

The very moment you commit your life to Jesus Christ, the truth of His Word instantly comes to pass in your spirit. Now that you're born again, there's a brand-new you!

Please contact me and let me know that you've prayed to receive Jesus as your Savior or to be filled with the Holy Spirit. I would like to rejoice with you and help you understand more fully what has taken place in your life. I'll send you a free gift that will help you understand and grow in your new relationship with the Lord. *Welcome to your new life!*

Receive the Holy Spirit

As His child, your loving heavenly Father wants to give you the supernatural power you need to live this new life.

"For every one that asketh receiveth; and he that seeketh findeth; and to him that knocketh it shall be opened.... [13] How much more shall your heavenly Father give the Holy Spirit to them that ask him?" (Luke 11:10 and 13b).

All you have to do is ask, believe, and receive!

Pray, "Father, I recognize my need for Your power to live this new life. Please fill me with Your Holy Spirit. By faith, I receive it right now! Thank You for baptizing me. Holy Spirit, You are welcome in my life!"

Congratulations—now you're filled with God's supernatural power!

Some syllables from a language you don't recognize will rise up from your heart to your mouth (1 Cor. 14:14). As you speak them out loud by faith, you're releasing God's power from within and building yourself up in your spirit (1 Cor. 14:4). You can do this whenever and wherever you like.

It doesn't really matter whether you felt anything or not when you prayed to receive the Lord and His Spirit. If you believed in your heart that you received, then God's Word promises that you did. *"Therefore I say unto you, What things soever ye desire, when ye pray, believe that ye receive them, and ye shall have them"* (Mark 11:24). God always honors His Word—believe it!

Please contact me and let me know that you've prayed to receive Jesus as your Savior or to be filled with the Holy Spirit. I would like to rejoice with you and help you understand more fully what has taken place in your life. I'll send you a free gift that will help you understand and grow in your new relationship with the Lord. *Welcome to your new life!*

About the Author

For over four decades, Andrew Wommack has traveled America and the world teaching the truth of the Gospel. His profound revelation of the Word of God is taught with clarity and simplicity, emphasizing God's unconditional love and the balance between grace and faith. He reaches millions of people through the daily *Gospel Truth* radio and television programs, broadcast both domestically and internationally. He founded Charis Bible College in 1994 and has since established Charis Bible College extension schools in other major cities of America and around the world. Andrew has produced a library of teaching materials, available in print, audio, and visual formats. And, as it has been from the beginning, his ministry continues to distribute free audio materials to those who cannot afford them.

Andrew's Teaching Recommendations in This Study Guide

Lesson 7
THE WAR IS OVER

Many wars have been fought throughout history, and more are yet to come. However, the most important one—the one between God and man—is over, and most Christians don't even know it.

Item Code: 1053-C 5-CD series
Item Code: 1053-D DVD series
Item Code: 326 Paperback book
Item Code: 426 Spiral-bound study guide
Item Code: 733 Spanish book

Lesson 8
REDEMPTION

It's more than theology; it's practical. Your understanding of redemption will determine what you are able to receive from God—not just in eternity, but here and now.

Item Code: 1056-C 5-CD series
Item Code: 1056-D DVD series
Item Code: 3201-D Live DVD series

THE GOSPEL, THE POWER OF GOD

The book of Romans is Paul's greatest masterpiece on the doctrine of grace. These truths have literally changed the world, and they will change your world as well.

Item Code: 1014-C 4-CD series
Item Code: 1014-D DVD series
Item Code: 322 Paperback book
Item Code: 422 Spiral-bound study guide
Item Code: 731 Spanish book

WHOSE RIGHTEOUSNESS?

Every Christian's relationship with God is based on his or her understanding of righteousness. What is righteousness? What makes a person righteous? Discover the answers to these questions and more!

Item Code: 1022-C 3-CD series

Lesson 15
WHAT TO DO WHEN YOUR PRAYERS SEEM UNANSWERED

You've prayed but nothing happened—now what? What's hindering your prayer? In this teaching from the *Christian Survival Kit*, find out how to shorten the time between "amen" and "there it is."

Item Code: SK16-C Single CD

Lesson 16
NIKI OCHENSKI: THE STORY OF A MIRACLE!

When she finally understood, her miracle manifested. It may be the same thing that's holding you back from receiving your miracle too! Watch this moving story and testimony.

Item Code: 3002-D DVD

Lesson 18
THE NEW YOU & THE HOLY SPIRIT

You need to understand what happened when you received Jesus as your Lord and Savior. When you do, you're ready for what's next: the baptism of the Holy Spirit! Learn what the Bible has to say about the Holy Spirit's role in your life. This is crucial to a successful walk with God.

Item Code: 1078-C 4-CD series
Item Code: 1078-D DVD series
Item Code: 323 Paperback book
Item Code: 423 Spiral-bound study guide
Item Code: 734 Spanish book